A Vision for Universal Preschool Education

Decades of research point to the need for a universal preschool education system in the United States to help give our nation's children a sound cognitive and social-emotional foundation on which to build future educational and life successes. In addition to enhanced school readiness and improved academic performance, participation in high-quality preschool programs has been linked to reduction in grade retentions and school dropout rates and cost savings associated with a diminished need for remedial education and criminal justice services. This book brings together nationally renowned experts from the fields of psychology, education, economics, and political science to present a compelling case for expanded access to preschool services. They describe the social, educational, and economic benefits for the nation as a whole that may result from the implementation of universal preschool in America, and they provide guiding principles on which such a system can best be founded.

Edward Zigler is Sterling Professor of Psychology Emeritus at Yale University and Director Emeritus of the Edward Zigler Center in Child Development and Social Policy. He helped to plan Head Start and Early Head Start and founded the School of the 21st Century. He served in government as the first director of what is now the Administration on Children, Youth and Families and as Chief of the U.S. Children's Bureau. His research on the cognitive and social aspects of child development and early intervention helped to advance the field of applied developmental psychology and to shape national social policies.

Walter S. Gilliam is Assistant Professor of Child Psychiatry and Psychology at the Yale University Child Study Center and Director of the Edward Zigler Center in Child Development and Social Policy. Dr. Gilliam's research focuses on early childhood education, ways to improve the quality of prekindergarten and child care services, the impact of early childhood education programs on children's school readiness, and developmental evaluation of young children.

Stephanie M. Jones is Assistant Professor of Psychology at Fordham University. Her research is focused on tracking the longitudinal impact of broad ecological risks, such as poverty and exposure to community violence, and on social-emotional problems and competencies in early childhood and adolescence. In addition, Dr. Jones is currently involved in a number of policy-relevant evaluation studies of preschool and school-based programs targeting emotional and behavioral problems of children at risk.

A Vision for Universal Preschool Education

EDWARD ZIGLER
Yale University

WALTER S. GILLIAM
Yale University

STEPHANIE M. JONES
Fordham University

CAMBRIDGE
UNIVERSITY PRESS

CAMBRIDGE UNIVERSITY PRESS
Cambridge, New York, Melbourne, Madrid, Cape Town, Singapore, São Paulo

Cambridge University Press
32 Avenue of the Americas, New York, NY 10013-2473, USA

www.cambridge.org
Information on this title: www.cambridge.org/9780521848541

First published 2006

Printed in the United States of America

A catalog record for this publication is available from the British Library.

Library of Congress Cataloging in Publication data

Zigler, Edward, 1930–
A vision for universal preschool education / Edward Zigler, Walter S. Gilliam,
Stephanie M. Jones. – 1st ed.
    p.   cm.
ISBN 0-521-84854-7 (hardcover) – ISBN 0-521-61299-3 (pbk.)
1. Education, Preschool – United States.   I. Gilliam, Walter S.
II. Jones, Stephanie M.   III. Title.
LB1140.23.Z54   2006
372.21'0973 – dc22   2005023913

ISBN-13   978-0-521-84854-1 hardback
ISBN-10   0-521-84854-7 hardback

ISBN-13   978-0-521-61299-9 paperback
ISBN-10   0-521-61299-3 paperback

This book is dedicated to a wise journalist, the late Fred Hechinger, who placed preschool on the nation's policy agenda, and to Susan Urahn of The Pew Charitable Trusts, an insightful thinker who is leading preschool into the 21st century and toward its logical conclusion – universal access to high-quality preschool for all families who want to enroll their young children.

Contents

Contributors

Ramona Blackman-Jones is a School Psychologist Trainee at Winthrop University, Rock Hill, South Carolina.

Richard M. Clifford is a Senior Scientist at the Frank Porter Graham Child Development Institute at the University of North Carolina at Chapel Hill and a Research Associate Professor in the School of Education. He is Co-Director of both the National Prekindergarten Center and the National Center for Early Development and Learning.

Matia Finn-Stevenson is a Research Scientist at Yale University, Associate Director of the Edward Zigler Center in Child Development and Social Policy, and Director of the School of the 21st Century program.

Christopher C. Henrich is Assistant Professor in the Department of Psychology at Georgia State University in Atlanta.

Marguerite Malakoff is a researcher in Pasadena, California. She was formerly Associate Professor of Psychology at Randolph-Macon College in Ashland, Virginia, and Assistant Professor of Psychology at Harvey Mudd College in Claremont, California.

Kelly L. Maxwell is a Scientist at the Frank Porter Graham Child Development Institute at the University of North Carolina at Chapel Hill and a Clinical Assistant Professor in the School of Education. She is also Co-Director of the National Prekindergarten Center.

Arthur J. Reynolds is Professor of Child Development at the Institute of Child Development at the University of Minnesota.

Sally J. Styfco is Associate Director of the Head Start Section at the Edward Zigler Center in Child Development and Social Policy at Yale University and Research Associate at the Yale Child Study Center.

Judy A. Temple is Associate Professor of Public Affairs and Applied Economics at the University of Minnesota.

Acknowledgments

The financial support that made this book possible was provided by the Smith Richardson Foundation, the National Institute for Early Education Research, and the Mailman Foundation. Nancy Hall had responsibility for the initial editing directed toward making the content accessible to the educated layperson and putting all of the chapters into a single voice. Leigh Esparo and Jill Powers handled the complicated logistics of the book and were responsible for keeping it on track. Sara Watson of The Pew Charitable Trusts provided help at various critical points. The authors owe their greatest debt to Sally Styfco, who has been a close collaborator of Edward Zigler for more than four decades. In addition to taking the lead on the Head Start chapter, her diligence and impressive scholarship are woven throughout the book. The authors express their gratitude to these wonderful colleagues.

Introduction

Over the past 40 years, the field of applied developmental psychology has come into prominence. Scholars in this field work to deploy the store of knowledge about human development to help decision makers construct effective social policies and build evidence-based social action programs that improve the lives of children and their families. This book is an exemplar of this type of undertaking.

The first author has studied children's growth and development for half a century and has been closely involved with a number of early intervention initiatives for more than 40 years. He helped design several national programs, including Head Start, Early Head Start, the School of the 21st Century, and the Child Development Associate training credential for early childhood workers. On the policy front, he was the federal official responsible for administering Head Start during the Nixon administration, chaired a panel that produced the first draft of what became the Family and Medical Leave Act, and has advised Republican and Democrat federal and state leaders since the time of the Kennedy administration. Coauthors Walter Gilliam and Stephanie Jones trained at the Zigler Center in Child Development and Social Policy at Yale University. They have become outstanding young scholars in developmental science and its application to informed social policy.

This book is an effort to translate our knowledge into practice. We review the accumulated evidence about children's development and helpful interventions and show how to apply it to create a voluntary preschool system with universal access. We are convinced that if every child in America is to enter school ready to succeed, it is necessary to move beyond our current categorical programs directed toward poor and at-risk children and adopt a universal approach to preschool education.

The Business Roundtable has called for a federal role in establishing universal prekindergarten, but that role remains uncertain. In the presidential campaign in 2000, a plank in Vice President Gore's platform was the creation of a universal preschool program. Although the White House is indeed a "bully pulpit" for the advocacy of national initiatives, we do not believe that universal prekindergarten will come about through the federal government. The history of education in America, as well as the current political climate, signal that preschool for all will be developed state by state, district by district, and school by school.

In many other countries, education ministries control a national school system. The leadership can simply order that a program be instituted, and that program will appear in due time in every school. Education in America is primarily the province of state, county, and local governments. There are 50 state boards of education and state superintendents, and more than 15,000 school districts, each with its own board and superintendent, containing more than 80,000 individual schools. Such a complex system will never move in lockstep. But it is abundantly clear that in most of our 50 state capitals, pivotal action on universal preschool is taking place.

Today, the states are extremely heterogeneous in regard to how far along they are in developing prekindergartens. Some states have no preschool programs at all, four states have legislated universal programs, and many states run limited programs targeted to certain groups of children. Of note are Georgia and Oklahoma, which both have well-established prekindergarten systems with universal access. The development of the programs in these two states is informative in regard to how we should proceed. Both states began with programs for high-risk children. State leaders quickly learned that they must be more inclusive to attract the widespread constituency and support necessary to maintain funding. Therefore they moved toward universality. As this is being written, a number of other states are demonstrating this same evolution from at-risk to open programs.

While many experts in educational policy are convinced that universal preschool will eventually come about state by state, there is no consensus about how long this will take. Estimates range from 15 to 25 years. Many see the evolution of universal preschool as similar to the addition of kindergartens to school systems throughout the nation. Of course, it took kindergarten much longer than two or three decades to become commonplace. As we show in Chapter 1, however, the impetus for universal preschool is far greater than was the impetus for kindergartens early in their history.

The important question for the authors was not exactly when, but exactly what? What are the specific requirements of a preschool program that will fulfill the promise of school readiness for all children? From the time Head Start was begun 40 years ago, decision makers at both the federal and state levels have been remiss in their lack of sufficient concern with the importance of quality in both program design and implementation. Yet the benefits of preschool that accrue to children, their families, and society will be determined in large part by the quality of the programs that are mounted. We drew on the wisdom of the field, scientific evidence, and experience to compose a vision of an optimal preschool program for all children. Quality controls and evolutionary plans for evaluation and improvement are added to ensure that quality does not slacken as the program matures.

Our model is offered as a goal to which each state should aspire. Having a vision, or distant goal, is helpful for states beginning the journey toward universal preschool education so they have a plan for moving in the right direction toward the end they want to achieve. The various features of the model do not all have to be put into place simultaneously. For example, for states that currently run a program for four-year-olds, a next step should be to expand access to three-year-olds. The importance of program intensity is discussed in Chapter 6. The evidence is clear that attendance for two years has greater benefits than the typical nine-month session.

Although the optimal program advanced in this book is admittedly a vision, it is not a "pie-in-the-sky," unrealistic proposal. The authors have worked with real decision makers at both the federal and state levels, so we know the constraints they face. Some features of our program are operative in Chicago's Child-Parent Centers in that city's public school system and in the Connecticut School Readiness Initiative. The viability of components of the model has also been proved in 1,300 Schools of the 21st Century operating in 20 states and in 3,000 Parents as Teachers sites. As we write, Arkansas is expending considerable resources and effort to implement statewide the universal preschool system presented in this book. These efforts stand as proof that, although ambitious, our model is doable if states find the resources and muster the will.

CONTENTS OF THE BOOK

Each of the authors took primary responsibility for various chapters but collaborated on the final product. As we developed our outline and discussed who would cover each topic, we realized that none of us had the expertise to fully research and present certain issues. We therefore asked respected colleagues to prepare chapters in relevant areas where their knowledge would be valuable to readers.

The teacher is the most important factor in determining the quality of a preschool program. The core of educational progress at the preschool level resides in the relationship between the teacher and the child. To deal with the teacher issue, we turned to longtime colleagues Kelly Maxwell, a recognized authority on the preschool movement, and Richard Clifford, who is a former president of the National Association for the Education of Young Children. Both authors are at the Frank Porter Graham Center at the University of North Carolina, which has been at the heart of preschool research and policy for many years.

Much of the momentum propelling the preschool movement stems from two well-known experimental models and a mainstream early intervention program: the Perry Preschool, the Abecedarian Project, and the Chicago Child-Parent Centers. All three programs included a cost-benefit analysis in their outcome evidence. They convincingly demonstrated that preschool interventions should not be approached as a simple matter of cost and affordability, but as sound social investments that generate exceptional return on the money spent. Because policy makers are very interested in these numbers, we invited Arthur Reynolds, a former Zigler student, and his colleague Judy Temple to write a chapter about the cost-effectiveness data. In addition to being the primary investigator for the Chicago Child-Parent Centers, Reynolds is a nationally visible worker in the field of early intervention. In their chapter, Reynolds and Temple not only mine data from studies of early intervention for low-income children but extrapolate from data collected in child care and state prekindergarten settings that serve broader populations. They present quantitative evidence that children from middle-class families also profit from preschool experience, returning cost savings to society.

There is ample evidence proving the benefits that children in at-risk groups derive from school readiness programming. This raises the question as to why society should provide the service to middle-class children, who do not appear to have as much to gain and whose parents are likely already paying for early education. We asked another Zigler student and longtime collaborator, Marguerite Malakoff, to review the literature on the effects of preschool and early intervention on child outcomes across the socioeconomic spectrum. We used her synthesis in two chapters documenting the need for universal preschool for children from poor families as well as those from wealthier homes. The evidence that nonpoor children also benefit from quality preschool experiences bolsters our argument that prekindergarten should be universal.

The preschool system we advance in this book is open all day and all year to accommodate the needs of working parents who are already paying for child care, often in settings of questionable quality that do little to promote children's school readiness. Our plan contains a fee calibrated to family income to support the cost of the extended day program, deflating the argument that public preschool will give greater economic savings to wealthy families than to those with lower incomes.

Educators have learned that successful schooling at any level involves a partnership between the school and parents. This partnership is particularly salient at the preschool level. Indeed, a major reason for the success of our nation's Head Start program has been a deep commitment to parent involvement. Head Start is actually a two-generation program, providing services to children and their parents, and parent participation is encouraged in both the classroom and program governance. To cover the issue of parent involvement, we turned to another Zigler student, Christopher Henrich, who has become an authority on the role of parents in children's education, and his collaborator Ramona Blackman-Jones.

Head Start is the nation's largest early intervention program, currently serving more than 900,000 young children and their families throughout the nation and U.S. territories. Zigler has been involved with Head Start since its inception, and he continues to advise policy makers on its future direction. As public prekindergarten becomes more widely available, Head Start's role in the early education delivery system will necessarily change. To help plot its future course, Zigler turned to his longtime collaborator Sally Styfco, who for decades has headed the Head Start unit of the Zigler Center in Child Development and Social Policy at Yale.

The preschool model advanced in this book shares many similarities with the School of the 21st Century, a constellation of early care and education services administered by public schools in more than 1,300 sites. We thought an explanation of the operations of these schools would be particularly helpful to prekindergarten planners. To describe the program, Zigler asked another longtime collaborator, Matia Finn-Stevenson. Matia is the scholar who, with her group at Yale, directs the large network of 21C Schools, helping them implement and improve the quality of their programs.

Zigler, Gilliam, and Jones prepared the remaining chapters, several with the invaluable assistance of our colleague Sally Styfco. The first chapter describes the national momentum that has developed for universal preschool education. The number of champions of preschool programs has grown exponentially over the past decade and a half. Supporters in the fields of child development and early education have been joined by philanthropists in the foundation world as well as by economists and business leaders. State policy makers are now at the forefront of the momentum, capturing its energy and implementing a rapidly growing number of prekindergarten systems. The ultimate purpose of our book is to guide their efforts.

Chapter 2 deals with what we all agree is the primary goal of preschool education, school readiness. Although school readiness is the legislated goal of Head Start and was Goal 1 of the Educate America Act (initiated by the nation's governors and the first President Bush), much controversy exists about how to define and measure a child's preparedness for school. We discuss this dilemma and advance a resolution that encompasses a child's physical, academic, and social-emotional readiness to tackle the challenges of school.

A point of clarification is necessary here. Parents, educators, decision makers, and economists all agree that school readiness is the goal of preschool programming. The term "education" is clear, and everyone is knowledgeable about it. Education is perceived to be important for the good of individuals and of society, and polls consistently show that it is at or near the top of issues that concern voters and elected officials. Our view of preschool education, however, is more expansive. Children, of course, need exposure to academic content like preliteracy and early math skills to prepare for school. But they also need to be physically healthy, to develop a solid foundation in verbal language, and to have some degree of socialization and emotional self-regulation.

In the critical early years, there are four major social systems that affect the child's development and eventual school readiness. The first and most important is the child's family. (Parents are indeed the child's first teachers.) The others are the health care system, the education system, and the child care system (a caregiving environment the majority of our children experience before entering school). While our plan for universal preschool is based in the education system, it extends beyond the school building to touch the other systems that influence child development.

Following the Reynolds and Temple chapter on the economic returns of investing in preschool, Chapters 4 and 5 highlight the benefits accruing to both poor and nonpoor children from preschool attendance.

The importance of program quality, intensity, and duration is discussed in Chapter 6. This chapter is must reading for those responsible for actually mounting preschool programs. The evidence presented in this book makes clear that preschool possesses great potential for improving the overall development and school readiness of children. However, this potential will be realized only if the programs they attend are of high quality. This means that states must spend the money necessary to mount quality programs and assure that they are fully and completely implemented. Otherwise they will end up with tokenistic programs that do not produce much in the way of results. The authors embrace the principle of accountability in all programs that consume taxpayer dollars. Thus, programs must not only be good enough to justify the expense, but continuing quality must be assured by close monitoring and periodic assessments. Sound assessments can facilitate program improvements and provide objective evidence that the program is meeting its goals.

Developmental psychologists and early childhood educators have long emphasized the importance of social-emotional development to a child's school readiness and later academic success. This topic is covered in Chapter 7. We wrote it as a counterweight to the current overemphasis on the importance of cognitive achievements, particularly literacy and "numeracy." We do not deny that these skills are invaluable to children's academic careers. However, we view cognitive development as only one of several important subsystems of human growth that together affect schooling. The cognitive system interacts with biological factors such as health and psychological factors such as motivation and socialization to impact competence in school. We decided against a parallel chapter on cognitive development because every school of thought agrees on its importance in the learning process.

Chapters 8 and 9 cover the issues of parent involvement and the professional development of teachers. Chapters 10 and 11 deal with the School of the 21st Century and the role of Head Start in the landscape of state universal preschool programs. All of these chapters build a case for the model program presented in our vision chapter – Chapter 12.

We found it necessary to permit some overlap among the chapters. We wanted each chapter to be a complete statement of its particular topic so a reader interested, for example, in the evidence that quality preschool experiences benefit children from middle-class families or what impact teacher training has on classroom quality could learn about the issue in one place. Another reason for a certain degree of repetition is that quality indicators are highly correlated with one another, and the evidence supporting them – and, for that matter, the value of universal preschool education itself – is derived from the same bodies of empirical and theoretical literature.

LOGISTICS OF PREPARATION

Universal preschool education will come about because parents and business leaders appreciate the value of preschool, and they will elect state decision makers who champion these programs. Thus we did not write this book for other scholars but for the educated public, elected officials and their staff members, and others who work to shape and implement state policies. We therefore wanted to write at a level accessible to this broad audience. Because different authors took the lead on various chapters, their individual writing styles were edited to present a consistent tone of voice. A colleague who has written for the popular media for many years and who has considerable knowledge of the issues did the initial editing of each chapter so the book as a whole was written at a nontechnical level and in a single voice. Then all of the chapters underwent content and stylistic editing and a final reading by the first author and a colleague who is a professional writer and scholar in the field of child development and social policy.

Throughout his career, Zigler has advised students interested in entering the real world's policy arena to take the long view on social policy development. That long view is certainly represented by this book. The federal Head Start program, the polyglot child care nonsystem, and the many versions of state preschool programs will all be with us for the foreseeable future. Further, universal preschool education will continue to have potent foes among well-financed groups that advocate highly conservative views of the role of women and the place for young children. Yet, as we write, the momentum toward a universal preschool system continues to build, one state at a time.

As the evidence mounts, and new programs appear to run successfully, even onetime foes of universal preschool are becoming advocates. For example, for many years the K–12 educational establishment was ambivalent about becoming involved in preschool. Historically, there was a wide chasm between preschool and elementary school educators, as evidenced by huge differences in pay and prestige. Further, mandates imposed on K–12 educators made more and more demands on their time, so they understandably shunned adding preschool education to their responsibilities.

Over time, a shift in this attitude has occurred. Today there is a growing awareness among public school educators that the early years are critical in laying the foundation for later development in general and for school performance in particular. An important catalyst for this awareness is parent and media fascination with early brain development research, a subject that has been widely covered in the popular media. In addition, an increasing number of working parents are struggling with child care needs. Much of the available care is not of very good quality, and educators are noticing the result – children are arriving in kindergarten lacking in school readiness skills. All of this information has converged into the recognition that starting school at age five misses too much of important periods of development and learning. Evidence of this shift in thought is obvious in a recent statement by the National Association of Elementary School Principals, which is now advocating for universal preschool education programs that optimally begin at birth. Under the auspices of the Foundation for Child Development, the former education editor of the *New York Times*, Gene Maeroff, wrote a widely distributed overview also making a strong case for the value of universal preschool services for families and infants. The ages zero to three, after all, constitute half of the preschool stage.

Our blueprint for a comprehensive system of universal preschool starts at birth and lasts through the transition to kindergarten. Our model is designed around a whole child approach to early education and includes parents and teachers as close partners. Quality standards are imposed on every component so the system achieves what it is supposed to – school readiness for every child. Decades of research in child development provide a compelling rationale for universal preschool, and state policy makers are becoming more willing and eager to act upon this knowledge. The vision is worth attaining for the future of the nation and the coming generations of children who deserve the best the American education system can offer.

Edward Zigler
June 2005

1

The Universal Preschool Movement

The term "school age" carries significant meaning in American society. The day a child walks through the schoolhouse doors marks an unforgettable benchmark for the young student and his or her family. Of course, the first day of kindergarten is not the first "teachable moment" the child has experienced. A vast amount of learning has preceded that eventful day. Knowledge, skills, and abilities have been acquired and practiced at home, in the playground, and – for the majority of children born in the 21st century – in child care settings. The difference between "preschool" and "school age," then, is not really about teaching and learning but about where and how these activities take place, and who assumes responsibility for them.

In the United States today, formal schooling is largely the responsibility of state and local governments. In most communities, children are eligible to enroll in the public education system when they are about five years old. Historically, it was not unusual for children to be admitted at younger ages. The first kindergartens in America commonly served children younger than five – for example, New York City schools admitted four-year-olds, and Boston's public schools enrolled toddlers as young as 22 months (Mitchell, Seligson, & Marx, 1989). Wisconsin's state constitution has contained "a commitment to free education for four-year-olds" since the middle of the 19th century (Barnett, Hustedt, Robin, & Schulman, 2004, p. 170). Until about that time, Massachusetts three- and four-year-olds were allowed to tag along with their older siblings to school (Beatty, 2004). But as age-graded classrooms became the norm, and as public schools became more institutionalized, very young children were no longer welcomed.

It is not clear why the ages five to seven were set as the entrance requirement to public education. A likely explanation is that long before psychologists plotted the stages of development, teachers and parents were aware of the "developmental shift" that takes place during these years. (Child development's premier thinker on this shift was Sheldon White; see e.g., White, 1965.) The cognitive system advances to new thought processes that enable symbolic representation – for groups of letters to *mean* something, for instance, or for math problems to be done with paper and pencil instead of with fingers and other manipulatives. Children of this age also have more physical and social control. They no longer need frequent naps, can usually sit in one place for more than a few minutes, and can at least try to accommodate the needs of others. Of course, to get to this point, a great deal of cognitive, physical, and social-emotional development has already occurred. "School age," therefore, is a somewhat arbitrary designation. In this book we argue that the learning that takes place *before* the magical age of school entrance has a powerful influence on the learning that takes place afterward, so more attention must be paid to the type and quality of learning experiences provided during the preschool years.

In the chapters that follow we build a case for a nationwide, universal system of preschool education that is of high quality, is developmentally appropriate, and is comprehensive in scope, targeting the cognitive, social-emotional, and physical domains of development. The preschool system will be available to all three- and four-year-old children whose parents want them to attend. (We also propose that an optimal program will eventually address all the foundational years from the prenatal period to school entry.) The mission of public prekindergarten will be to enable every single child to begin school with the skills needed to succeed. This goal dovetails with that of the K–12 system, which is to enable every single student to succeed throughout schooling and in adult life.

STEPS TOWARD PUBLIC EDUCATION FOR PRESCHOOLERS

The development of America's public education system began within the private, generally nonprofit sector. Over time, local governments became involved, and eventually the K–12 system became an obligation of the states. The federal government issued some rules and policies, but it generally took a hands-off approach to schooling, deferring control to local authorities and state overseers. In the past 30 years, there have been only two major exceptions to this laissez-faire stance. The Individuals with Disabilities Education Act (originally passed in 1975) gives all children with disabilities the right to a free public education in the least restrictive environment. The No Child Left Behind Act of 2001 mandates achievement testing and strict consequences for schools where student scores do not show adequate yearly progress. Even with these major federal policies, however, local and state governments pay nearly all of the costs of public schooling and theoretically make most of the decisions.

Unlike the history of the K–12 system, the initial impetus for public preschool came from the federal level. The federal government sponsored preschools during the Great Depression, as a way to provide work for unemployed teachers, and child care centers during World War II, so mothers could work to produce war materials while men were serving in the military. For the most part, these efforts ceased once the crises passed. Sustained federal involvement in preschool education began during the 1960s War on Poverty. One weapon in that war was Project Head Start, launched to help poor children begin school on an equal footing with those from wealthier homes. Now in its fifth decade, Head Start has served more than 22 million young children and their families. The program and its future are the topic of Chapter 11.

Relevant to the topic of this chapter is that Head Start was an instant success with the American people (see Zigler & Muenchow, 1992). Previously a private matter, the education of preschoolers suddenly emerged as a popular undertaking that citizens enthusiastically supported. This was true even though Head Start targets children from extremely poor families and those with disabilities. One would expect the program to be popular among its constituents, and it is. In 1999 a survey by the President's Management Council found that Head Start received the highest customer satisfaction rating of any government agency or private company, even Mercedes-Benz and BMW (Administration for Children and Families, 1999). Yet Head Start remains popular among the general population as well. A national survey by Opinion Research Corporation reported that four out of five respondents favored expanding the program to serve more eligible children (PaxWorld/NHSA Survey, 2003).

Public support for preschool is not limited to services for poor children. Today there is widespread enthusiasm for universal access to high-quality early education for all preschoolers. For example, a national poll conducted by the National Institute for Early Education Research in 2001 revealed that nearly 90 percent of people who responded agreed there should be state-funded, universally accessible preschool (Barnett, Robin, Hustedt, & Schulman, 2003). In public opinion polling of voters and leaders from the business, organized labor, government, religious, media, education, and child care communities in Massachusetts, Blood (2000) reported that 100 percent of those asked believe that education should begin before kindergarten. It would be difficult to find any other social policy poll that resulted in a perfect score.

Building the Case for Preschool

How did so many Americans move from the position that young children are best taught by their mothers at home to overwhelming endorsement of public prekindergarten? The answer is that a confluence of events sparked interest in preschool, and that interest was magnified by a variety of powerful players. An important factor has been the increasing participation of women in the work force. For women between the ages of 25 and 54, three out of four, or 75 percent, were in the labor force in 1999 (U.S. Department of Labor, 2000). Refining these data further, 28 percent of all children, and 57 percent of black children, were living with a single parent – the majority of whom have no choice but to work because they are the main support of their households.

This demographic picture explains why the need for child care has grown rampantly. Yet most parents want more than a safe place to leave their children while they go off to work. They want a place where their children will learn new words, manners, how to get along with others, and more academic items like letters and numbers. Preschool fills part of this bill. Of course, to meet child care needs preschool programs would have to be open for the length of the workday all year long. Such a model exists in more than 1,300 Schools of the 21st Century discussed in Chapter 10, and other schools are rapidly moving to meet the needs of the parents they serve by extending sessions. Currently, however, the majority of preschool programs are part-day, part-year. Nonetheless, most working parents are big supporters of preschool as a venue for learning and as a partial solution to what to do with their children while no one is home.

Events in the research community also fed the growing acceptance of preschool education. One landmark report was released by the Consortium for Longitudinal Studies (1983), a group of researchers who had evaluated 11 different early intervention programs during the 1960s and early 1970s. The scientists attempted to locate as many of the original program participants as they could and collected the same types of information about their progress. Data from the individual programs were combined and subjected to rigorous statistical analyses. The results showed that children who attended quality preschool programs gained an initial boost in IQ scores that lasted for a few years but eventually disappeared. The same was basically true for reading and math achievement. Lasting benefits were found in other areas of particular interest to educators and taxpayers. Preschool graduates were much less likely to be assigned to special education classes than peers without preschool, and they were somewhat less likely to be held back a grade in school. The findings of immediate benefits and some still in evidence when program participants were 12 to 22 years old did much to focus public attention on the value of early intervention.

Positive reaction to the Consortium studies was quickly fanned by publication of the long-term results of the Perry Preschool Program (Berrueta-Clement, Schweinhart, Barnett, Epstein, & Weikart, 1984). One of the Consortium studies, the Perry Preschool was created in 1962 and provided poor, black children with quality preschool for one to two years, and their parents with weekly home visits to encourage their participation in the educational process. By the time program graduates were 19 years old, they were considerably more competent than a comparison group. They were more likely to be high school graduates and self-supporting rather than on welfare, they were less likely to have a history of juvenile delinquency or criminal arrest, and female participants reported fewer pregnancies. (All but the pregnancy outcomes still held at age 27 [Schweinhart, Barnes, & Weikart, 1993], and at age 40 the former preschoolers still had higher earnings and had committed fewer crimes [Schweinhart et al., 2005].)

The finding that created the most excitement came from a cost-benefit analysis. Economists projected savings to society from the lower rates of grade retention, special education, and usage of the welfare and criminal justice systems, as well as from the increased earnings and tax contributions of program graduates. They concluded that every $1 spent on the preschool program returned between $3 and $6 to taxpayers. (This amount increased to $7 by age 27, and to $17 by age 40 [Schweinhart et al., 2005].) This analysis urged a new way of thinking about preschool programs as sound investments that eventually would pay for themselves many times over. The investment theme caught the attention of the economic community; for example, beginning in the 1980s the Committee for Economic Development issued a series of reports calling for quality preschool education for all children (see CED, 2002). Many business and economic leaders have now become staunch advocates of universal preschool, a point we return to later in this chapter.

Policy Makers Respond

More evidence about the effectiveness of preschool intervention began to accumulate. For example, participants of the Abecedarian Project and the federally funded Chicago Child-Parent Centers (both discussed in more detail later in this book) displayed better school adaptation and social competence and less special education placement than comparison groups years after the interventions ended. Policy makers began to take note. They rediscovered Head Start, which had been operating with minimal budget increases and little attention to research and development or quality issues. After the first President Bush proposed a massive increase in Head Start funding, half the nation's senators cosponsored a bill to make the program an entitlement to all eligible children. The Human Services Reauthorization Act of 1990 gave Head Start the largest budgetary increase in its history and authorized money for expansion until there was room for every eligible child. Although those funds never materialized, the program did grow rapidly during the 1990s and received substantial funds for quality improvements.

While federal officials might have started the ball rolling with expansion of the national Head Start program, state policy makers picked up the ball and ran with it. In 1990, President George H. Bush and the governors of all 50 states held a summit where they adopted six national education goals. These and two additional goals received legislative and financial backing in the Goals 2000: Educate America Act, signed into law by President Clinton in 1994. The first objective was that by the year 2000, all children would arrive at school ready to learn. Details of the act are covered in Chapter 2. Of significance to the present discussion is that the governors agreed that all children should have access to high-quality preschool education. They returned to their home states and began planning how to make the vision a reality.

Unlike the states, federal support for early education was short-lived for a variety of reasons (see Zigler & Styfco, 1996). As mentioned, the moneys authorized to fully fund Head Start were never appropriated. Annual budget increases slowed dramatically, and because quality improvement funds were tied to these increases, so did efforts to raise quality. The election of President George W. Bush brought in the first administration that was openly unfriendly toward Head Start. This president thought the program was not doing a good enough job teaching children literacy and other academic skills. He made two proposals that would effectively end Head Start. One was to move it to the Department of Education, where it would be block-granted to the states like the huge Title I education program for at-risk students (which includes a small preschool component). When that idea failed to win enough support, the president tried to turn Head Start's administration over to eight states as an experiment. The program's budget stagnated, halting quality improvement efforts altogether and, for the first time in decades, reducing the number of children and families who could be served. Bush's focus was on reforming the K–12 system through the mandates of the No Child Left Behind Act. He did launch the Good Start, Grow Smart initiative to strengthen early learning, but the thrust was almost entirely on fundamental literacy and language skills in line with his narrow education goals. Head Start, and all preschool programs accredited by the National Association for the Education of Young Children, have always been about more than academic training. While they certainly include early education, they also address physical and mental health and social skills because these are such strong contributors to school readiness.

STATE INITIATIVES

As federal officials began to withdraw their support of early education, state policy makers increased theirs. In 1989, 27 states funded 33 preschool programs and 12 contributed to their Head Start programs (Mitchell et al., 1989). By the 2001–2002 school year, 40 states funded 45 preschool programs (Barnett et al., 2003), and additional pre-K planning is taking place at various levels of government all across the nation.

There is tremendous variation in the state-funded prekindergarten programs. Some are half day, others full day. Most of the programs are for four-year-olds, but some permit enrollment of three-year-olds. Many of the programs are operated through local school districts, while many others offer services through private and public centers, including Head Start. The majority of the programs target children who have identified risk factors such as poverty, low parental education, and English as a second language, but some state and city programs are open to all children. Here we discuss some of these initiatives that currently provide universal access or are on the road to doing so.

Two states, Georgia and Oklahoma, are, at least in intent, universal for all four-year-olds whose parents want them to attend. The Georgia Voluntary Pre-Kindergarten Program began in 1993 with the passage of the Georgia lottery for education. Initially the program was open to children judged to be at-risk of beginning school without the necessary readiness skills. In 1995 the program was opened to all four-year-olds without regard to family income. In the 2002–2003 school year, approximately 55 percent of Georgia's four-year-olds were enrolled (Barnett et al., 2004). The program is delivered at several thousand sites by providers in the for-profit and nonprofit sectors, including schools and Head Start. According to a quality standards checklist developed by Barnett and colleagues (2004), the program meets 7 of 10 quality benchmarks.

Oklahoma's Early Childhood Four-Year-Old Program began in 1980 as a pilot project. In 1990 it was opened to all four-year-olds eligible for Head Start, and in 1998 it became universally available. Enrollment in the 2002–2003 year was at 60 percent, the highest preschool attendance rate in the nation. According to Barnett et al. (2004), Oklahoma's program meets 8 of 10 quality benchmarks. As described in detail in later chapters, this program has been subject to an intensive and rigorous evaluation. Initial findings indicate that there is a positive impact on children's language and cognitive test scores (e.g., Gormley, Gayer, Phillips, & Dawson, 2005).

Other states are following suit. Around the same time that Georgia's and Oklahoma's programs were becoming universal, New York's state legislature voted to make prekindergarten universally accessible to four-year-olds. Primarily because of budget shortfalls, universality has not been attained. The Experimental Prekindergarten program has been established, but priority enrollment goes to low-income children. In the 2002–2003 year, the state was serving only 26 percent of four-year-olds (Barnett et al., 2004). Florida has likewise had problems launching its universal preschool. In 2002 Florida voters approved an amendment to their state constitution requiring that the state begin implementing universal prekindergarten for four-year-olds by 2005. However, officials struggled to find the funds to pay for the program, and arguments arose in the state legislature over quality standards (Caputo, 2004; Kjos, 2004). Experts argued that the standards contained in the preschool bill that passed the legislature guaranteed a program of poor quality that would not achieve school readiness goals. At this writing, these issues remain unresolved, and Florida's universal prekindergarten is off to a rocky start.

West Virginia's Public School Early Childhood Education program began by serving both three- and four-year-olds, with admission criteria such as age and at-risk status left to local control. Legislation now mandates that universal preschool for four-year-olds be available by the 2012–2013 school year, but only three-year-olds with special needs are included (Barnett et al., 2004). The District of Columbia has offered preschool to all four-year-olds for decades, but enrollment remains limited by space and funding (Barnett et al., 2004).

Although not statewide, another large effort is underway in New Jersey. In 1998 a landmark State Supreme Court decision, *Abbott vs. Burke,* mandated 30 of New Jersey's highest poverty school districts to offer prekindergarten classes to all three- and four-year-olds in their locales. The goal of these programs is to provide children with the skills and resources necessary to achieve at the same level as their middle-class peers at school entry. As described later in this book, the Abbott programs have very high structural quality standards. Early indications suggest that the provision of universal preschool, adequate K–12 funding for standards-based education, small class sizes, tutors, and other supplemental programs in these districts are beginning to make a substantial difference at least with regard to fourth-grade reading and math scores (Mooney, 2004).

California has for some time been moving toward universal preschool education. Several years ago a group of experts recommended that the state mount a prekindergarten program available to all children. Another group of experts then developed guidelines for curriculum and quality. In 1998 the First 5 initiative was passed to provide funds for child development services from the prenatal period through school age. Many counties are using these moneys to expand access to preschool. Los Angeles, for example, has created a plan to provide high-quality universal preschool and will quickly expand capacity as more money becomes available. Such initiatives will surely gain momentum following a report by the Rand Corporation that concluded state taxpayers would eventually save billions of dollars in remedial education and social service expenses by providing access to quality preschool for all of California's young children (Karoly & Bigelow, 2005).

Other states, including Arkansas, Connecticut, Illinois, and Massachusetts, are also actively working to develop comprehensive state plans for universal preschool, but so far their programs target the highest-risk children. Efforts to provide prekindergarten to all area children are also underway in cities and counties across the nation, ranging in size from New Haven, Connecticut, to San Mateo County in California.

Clearly, a national movement toward universal preschool education is well underway. Like the establishment of kindergartens, and for that matter the free public education system itself, the momentum is being carried by individual states. When advocates for universal kindergarten failed to achieve a federal policy, they redirected their efforts and energy to the state level (Beatty, 2004). Likewise, the federal Comprehensive Child Development Act of 1971, which would have made early care and education available to all children in the United States whose parents wanted to enroll, passed both the House and Senate but was vetoed by President Richard Nixon. Sometime later, the idea was resurrected by the National Governors Association at its education summit, and the National Conference of State Legislatures has come onboard. The result has been a flurry of state legislation expanding access to preschool. "Indeed, the field of early care and education is at a crossroads, where the hoped-for remedy is not a national framework of care but the evolution of 50 unique state solutions" (Washington, 2004, p. A22).

FRIENDS IN THE RIGHT PLACES

The push for high-quality, universally available preschool education has been helped along by a number of influential supporters. Some are expected advocates such as the National Association for the Education of Young Children, the National Head Start Association (2005), and the National Council of Chief State School Officers. Another ally is the National Conference of State Legislatures, which featured early childhood education and school readiness at its 2004 meeting. The Education Commission of the States, a national organization of state and education leaders, proposed a P–16 model for a student-focused, comprehensive, and integrated system that links all education levels from preschool (P) through the senior year of college (Krueger, 2002). Obviously, those involved in early education or in education policy are convinced of the value of universal preschool and are working hard to attain it.

These groups have been joined by a chorus of voices from outside of the educational and policy establishments. John Merrow and Gene Maeroff, two experienced and well-regarded journalists and commentators, have both written extensively on the pressing need for high-quality, universal preschool education (e.g., Maeroff, 2003; Merrow, 2002). A national group of law enforcement officials has called for increased funding for universal prekindergarten, basing its position on research findings that high-quality preschool can help children's academic performance and reduce later crime and violence (Fight Crime: Invest in Kids, 2000). The group has become an organized force in the nation's capital and has been assisted by noted legal professionals such as former U.S. attorney general Elliot Richardson and child development experts including T. Berry Brazelton.

Foundations Adopt the Mission

A strong thrust to achieve universal early childhood education has occurred within the world of private philanthropic foundations. Recognizing their common goal and the strength in unity, a group of them has now joined together in a loose coalition with a solitary purpose: moving America, state by state, toward the adoption of preschool education for all three- and four-year-old children regardless of risk status or family income. This effort is determined to change the face of American education, giving preschoolers the same entitlement to free public schooling now granted to students in kindergarten through 12th grade. Taking a leadership role in the coalition is The Pew Charitable Trusts, which has committed approximately $75 million to this effort over five years. The trusts' president, Rebecca Rimel, stated publicly at a conference in Washington, D.C., that Pew will remain committed until this goal has been achieved. Heading the effort at Pew is Susan Urahn (2001), who prepared a scholarly and convincing paper on the demonstrated value of preschool education to gain the support of the trusts' board.

The trust has developed an impressive strategy to make universal preschool education a reality. In addition to important work being done internally at the organization, two national programs have been put into place. One is an analytical-research arm, the National Institute for Early Education Research, headed by nationally acclaimed economist W. Steven Barnett. The institute has released a number of important reports on preschool education including the State Preschool Yearbook (Barnett et al., 2004). The other is an advocacy arm, Pre-K Now, headed by Libby Doggett. This division acts as a catalyst in helping advocates in individual states achieve universal preschool education through policy and grass-roots initiatives.

Other foundations joining Pew to achieve universal preschool have been pursuing related agendas. For example, the Foundation for Child Development's MAP initiative is focused on developing a model of

early education that spans prekindergarten to grade three and emphasizes strategies necessary to "align" educational experiences in the early
years (Bogard, 2004). Alignment in this context means developing a system that provides seamless educational experiences for children three
to eight years old. The PNC Foundation has committed tens of millions of dollars to move universal preschool forward. The W. K. Kellogg
Foundation's SPARK initiative, the Ewing Marion Kauffman Foundation's Set for Success program, and projects of the Packard, Joyce, and
McCormick Tribune foundations and the Schuman Fund are just some
of many other national nonprofit efforts that focus on preparing children for success in school. Foundations at the state level are also playing
active roles. A good exemplar of this is the William Graustein Memorial
Fund in Connecticut, which is developing the infrastructure within the
state to make universal prekindergarten possible.

Although private foundations have long been involved in issues
relating to children and families, their support has been limited to specific, defined projects like a conference, publication, or demonstration
program. Never before have they attempted a major national effort to
achieve a specific, circumscribed goal. They have separately funded a
wealth of research over the decades and are now deploying the amassed
findings to influence not only broad policy but important details. We
are particularly impressed that the consortium's members have been
adamant in asserting that to achieve the benefits that are possible, states
must not mount weak or diluted programs that are offered for one year
only. The group is insisting on high-quality programs, taught by trained
professionals, for both three- and four-year-olds.

The Business Community Signs On

Strong support for universal preschool education also comes from
economists and business leaders. Although not generally linked with
advocacy for young children, these groups will unquestionably have a
great deal of influence, particularly among policy makers. The arguments made by these typically practical, hard-headed professionals
are quite different from those of developmentalists and early childhood educators. Rather than the better development of children, the
economists' case is based on the huge economic returns to society as a
result of preschool education. To them, funding preschool is viewed not
so much as a societal cost but as a very efficient investment in human
capital that will pay for itself many times over in the future. In essence,

these business and number-crunching leaders see universal preschool education as a way to improve the quality of our nation's work force, which will make the United States more competitive in world markets and business more profitable, and thus increase national prosperity.

One of the earliest major economists to emphasize the value of preschool programs to society was Isabel Sawhill (1999) at the Brookings Institution, who wrote a very convincing paper making the case for a national investment in preschool education. Another is Nobel laureate and University of Chicago economics professor James Heckman, who conducted a broad evaluation of job training programs, tax policies, school reform efforts, and financial incentives. He concluded that the most promising of these efforts is high-quality early education: "The best evidence supports the policy prescription: invest in the very young and improve basic learning and socialization skills" (2000, p. 8).

Another influential voice came from the Research and Policy Committee of the Committee for Economic Development, which is composed of some 250 business and education leaders. The group released a report entitled, *Preschool for All: Investing in a Productive and Just Society*. The opening summary explicitly "calls on the federal and state governments to undertake a new national compact to make early education available to all children age 3 and over" (2002, p. 1).

A surprising entrant joining supporters of expanded access to preschool came from the Federal Reserve Bank of Minneapolis. In collaboration with the McKnight Foundation and the University of Minnesota, the bank hosted a conference on the topic, "The Economics of Early Childhood Development: Lessons for Economic Policy." Art Rolnick and Rob Grunewald (2003, p. 11), both of the Minneapolis Fed, stated "the return on investment from early childhood development is extraordinary, resulting in better working public schools, more educated workers, and less crime."

Some economic groups advocate preschool for targeted groups. For example, the Economic Policy Institute (Lynch, 2004) issued a report, *Exceptional Returns: Economic, Fiscal, and Social Benefits of Investment in Early Childhood Development*, focusing on the economic benefits of high-quality early childhood development programs for low-income children. Specifically, the report concludes that high-quality programs generate a $3 return in the long term for every $1 invested. This return is considerably lower than that calculated by most economists and child development researchers. Yet even using this more conservative number, the report concludes that the institute's study "demonstrates . . . that

providing all 20% of the nation's three- and four-year-old children who
live in poverty with a high-quality [early childhood development] program would have a substantial payoff for governments and taxpayers in
the future" (Lynch, 2004, p. 1). Other reports from the business community have come to similar conclusions (e.g., Business Roundtable, 2003;
Oppenheim & MacGregor, undated). The only disagreement among this
segment appears to be whether preschool programs should be universal or targeted to high-risk groups. We discuss this debate in the final
chapter of this book.

The Opposition

It would be unrealistic to assume that the move toward universal
preschool education will be nothing but smooth sailing. Some people fear that young children are being pushed too hard, too soon, to
excel academically, and that institutionalized preschool will further this
attack on childhood. Many conservative, right-wing groups are against
the idea because they believe children are best taught by their mothers
at home, and/or because they fear that government will overstep its
areas of responsibility by usurping traditional family roles. Conservative think tanks such as the Cato Institute, the Goldwater Institute, and
the Heritage Foundation have taken issue with the professional community's interpretation of decades of research, arguing that the evidence is
not convincing that preschool has a lasting impact on children's educational success. Another criticism is that children acquire the most important skills for kindergarten readiness "best by experiencing the first years
of their life in a loving home environment where they receive individual attention and nurturing from a parent rather than in a preschool
classroom with other children and strangers" (Salisbury, 2002). Other
conservative critiques of universal preschool are that it will result in a
"nanny state," where the government and other individuals have more
control over children than their own parents (Olsen, 1999).

A common thread in these right-wing views is a strong and persistent
belief that mothers should stay home and raise their families instead of
joining the work force. These groups judge the fact that the majority of
American mothers now work outside the home as an indicator of the
wrongheadedness of our society. We respect the power of this segment
to raise a significant barrier to universal preschool education. The first
author witnessed firsthand the ability of these conservatives to defeat
a congressionally approved plan to create a national high-quality child

care system (the Comprehensive Child Development Act of 1971). They failed to see then and they fail to see now that Head Start, all the current state preschool programs, and the universal pre-K system recommended in this book are totally voluntary. A family can choose to enroll a child in preschool and can choose not to participate as well.

Some education leaders are also opposed to universal preschool because they fear another unfunded mandate, with the government requiring them to provide preschool for all without the resources to do so. Further, many professionals in the K–12 system have been reluctant to support preschool education, a remnant of the long-standing chasm between early and later childhood educators. There are some signs that opponents within the education establishment are beginning to change their minds. In a shift of opinion, for example, the National Association of Elementary School Principals issued a statement endorsing universal preschool beginning either at birth or at age three. These leaders have apparently been swayed by the evidence that educational performance in the K–12 period will be enhanced by school readiness programming.

WHERE TO GO FROM HERE

In this chapter, we have described the building movement to give all children in America the opportunity to attend preschool. A large body of scientific literature has proved the value of high-quality early education to children's development. Economic theorists have concluded that investments in preschool programming are well worth the cost, creating large returns to society in the form of a higher-skilled work force, a stronger tax base, and lower social service costs. Business leaders agree and are using their corporate muscle and resources to advance the case of universal preschool. Private foundations have adopted this goal as a mission and are working diligently to achieve it. The states are rapidly moving to expand access to preschool. In 2005, 20 state governors proposed increased funding for their state pre-K programs, nearly twice the number who did so just a year earlier (Pre-K Now, 2005). Although opponents exist and have some valid concerns, it appears that universal preschool education is on its way to becoming established.

When we began planning this book, our tentative title was "The Case for Universal Preschool." We wanted to present the evidence of the value of quality early care and education to convince policy makers of the wisdom of moving in this direction. When we began to gather materials and resources for the book, however, we realized the movement was well underway. The question was not whether we should have universal preschool but what the preschool system should look like. We therefore changed our title to "A Vision for Universal Preschool Education." We present that vision, and the evidence that formed it, in the following chapters.

References

Administration for Children and Families. (1999, December 13). *Head Start bests Mercedes and BMW in customer satisfaction.* Washington, DC: U.S. Department of Health and Human Services. http://www.acf.hhs.gov/news/press/1999/hssatisfies.htm. Accessed March 2005.

Barnett, W. S., Hustedt, J. T., Robin, K. B., & Schulman, K. L. (2004). *The state of preschool: 2004 state preschool yearbook.* New Brunswick, NJ: National Institute for Early Education Research.

Barnett, W. S., Robin, K., Hustedt, J., & Schulman, K. (2003). *The state of preschool: 2003 state preschool yearbook.* New Brunswick, NJ: National Institute for Early Education Research.

Beatty, B. (2004, November). Past, present, and future: What we can learn from the history of preschool education. *American Prospect*, pp. A3–A5.

Berrueta-Clement, J. R., Schweinhart, L. J., Barnett, W. S., Epstein, A. S., & Weikart, D. P. (1984). *Changed lives: The effects of the Perry Preschool program on youths through age 19.* Monographs of the High/Scope Educational Research Foundation (No. 8). Ypsilanti, MI: High/Scope Press.

Blood, M. (2000). *Our youngest children: Massachusetts voters and opinion leaders speak out on their care and education.* Boston: Stride Rite Foundation.

Bogard, K. (2004). *Mapping a P–3 continuum (MAP): P–3 as the foundation of education reform.* New York: Foundation for Child Development. http://www.fcd-us.org/uploadDocs/4.30.04.bogard.MAPrelease.final.pdf. Accessed June 2005.

Business Roundtable & Corporate Voices for Working Families. (2003, May). *Early childhood education: A call to action from the business community.* http://www.businessroundtable.org/pdf/901.pdf. Accessed April 2005.

Caputo, M. (2004, April 21). Factions airing ads on preschool plans. *Miami Sun Herald.*

Committee for Economic Development. (2002). *Preschool for all: Investing in a productive and just society.* Washington, DC: Author.

Consortium for Longitudinal Studies. (1983). *As the twig is bent: Lasting effects of preschool programs.* Hillsdale, NJ: Erlbaum.

Fight Crime: Invest in Kids. (2000). *America's child care crisis: A crime prevention tragedy.* Washington, DC: Author.

Gormley, W. T., Gayer, T., Phillips, D., & Dawson, B. (2005). The effects of universal pre-K on cognitive development. *Developmental Psychology, 41,* 872–884.

Heckman, J. (2000). Policies to foster human capital. *Research in Economics, 54,* 3–56.

Karoly, L. A., & Bigelow, J. H. (2005). *The economics of investing in universal preschool education in California*. Santa Monica, CA: Rand.

Kjos, L. (2004, February 19). Study: Preschool woefully lacking. *United Press International*. http://www.commondreams.org/headlines04/ 0219–06.htm.

Krueger, C. (2002). *The case for P–16: Designing an integrated learning system, preschool through postsecondary education*. Denver, CO: Education Commission of the States. (No. P16-02-01).

Lynch, R. G. (2004). *Exceptional returns: Economic, fiscal, and social benefits of investment in early childhood development*. Washington, DC: Economic Policy Institute.

Maeroff, G. (2003). Universal preschool: State of play. In *First things first: Prekindergarten as the starting point for education reform* (pp. 4–12). New York: Foundation for Child Development.

Merrow, J. (2002, September 25). The "failure" of Head Start. *Education Week*, p. 52.

Mitchell, A., Seligson, M., & Marx, F. (1989). *Early childhood programs and the public schools*. Dover, MA: Auburn House.

Mooney, J. (2004, November 19). A model in early learning. *New Jersey Star Ledger*.

National Head Start Association. (2005). *Position paper: Our vision for universal pre-kindergarten and Head Start programs, investments in America's future*. Discussion draft. Alexandria, VA: Author.

Olsen, D. A. (1999). *Universal preschool is no golden ticket: Why government should not enter the preschool business*. Cato Policy Analysis No. 333. Washington, DC: Cato Institute.

Oppenheim, J., & MacGregor, T. (Undated). *The economics of education: Public benefits of high-quality preschool education for low-income children*. Entergy, New Orleans.

Pax World/NHSA Survey. (2003, September 4). *More than 9 out of 10 Americans support existing Head Start program*. Washington, DC: Pax World Funds. http://www.paxworld.com/newsmcenter03/nr090403.htm. Accessed March 2005.

Pre-K Now. (2005). *Leadership matters: Governors' pre-k proposals Fiscal Year 2006*. Washington, DC: Author. http://www.preknow.org/documents/ LeadershipReport.pdf. Accessed April 2005.

Rolnick, A., & Grunewald, R. (2003, October). Early childhood development: Economic development with a high public return. *The Region* (supplement). Minneapolis, MN: Federal Reserve Bank of Minneapolis. http://minneapolisfed.org/research/studies/ earlychild/abc-part2.pdf.

Salisbury, D. (2002, January 10). Preschool is no answer. *USA Today*.

Sawhill, I. V. (1999). Early education: A national priority. *Brookings Children's Roundtable Report. Policy Brief # 1*. Washington, DC: Brookings Institution. www.brookings.edu.

Schweinhart, L. J., Barnes, H. V., & Weikart, D. P. (1993). *Significant benefits: The High/Scope Perry Preschool study through age 27*. Monographs of the High/Scope Educational Research Foundation (No. 10). Ypsilanti, MI: High/Scope Press.

Schweinhart, L. J., Montie, J., Xiang, Z., Barnett, W. S., Belfield, C. R., & Nores, M. (2005). *Lifetime effects: The High/Scope Perry Preschool study through age 40*. Monographs of the High/Scope Educational Research Foundation (No. 14). Ypsilanti, MI: High/Scope Press.

Urahn, S. K. (2001). *Promoting universal access to high quality early education for three and four year olds: The Pew Charitable Trusts and the Starting Early, Starting Strong Initiative*. Philadelphia: Pew Charitable Trusts.

U.S. Department of Labor. (2000). *Employment and earnings. January 2000*. Washington, DC: Bureau of Labor Statistics.

Washington, V. (2004, November). Where do we go from here? Building a movement on behalf of young children. *American Prospect*, pp. A22–A23.

White, S. H. (1965). Evidence for a hierarchical arrangement of learning processes. In L. P. Lipsitt & C. C. Spiker (Eds.), *Advances in child development and behavior* (Vol. 2). New York: Academic Press.

Zigler, E., & Muenchow, S. (1992). *Head Start: The inside story of America's most successful educational experiment*. New York: Basic Books.

Zigler, E., & Styfco, S. J. (1996). Head Start and early childhood intervention: The changing course of social science and social policy. In E. Zigler, S. L. Kagan, & N. Hall (Eds.), *Children, families, and government: Preparing for the twenty-first century* (pp. 132–155). Cambridge: Cambridge University Press.

2

School Readiness

Defining the Goal for Universal Preschool

The purpose of universal prekindergarten (UPK) is to help all children get ready for the learning opportunities that will be presented when they begin formal schooling. How school readiness is defined has important implications for how UPK should be organized, the types and quality of services that should be provided, and the length and intensity of programming needed to have the best chance of achieving this goal. To paraphrase an old adage, it's impossible to know what direction to head if we don't know where we want to go. The definition of school readiness influences more than policy statements and mandates about curricula, class sizes, teacher training, and other details regarding how UPK is to be delivered. The definition spells out the desired results and therefore gives program designers a master plan for determining whether their efforts are successful.

The immediate goal for any system of universal preschool is of course to increase the school readiness of all students. By implication, the ultimate goal is to increase their chances of succeeding in school and later in life. In this chapter, we discuss why school readiness is so critical for later educational success. We also look at various approaches to dealing with "unready" students, approaches that are shaped by how one defines being ready for school. We examine current debates about what it means to be prepared for school and offer a comprehensive model of school readiness to be used by state policy makers for strategic planning for a universal UPK system.

PRESCHOOL OBJECTIVES

During the 1990s education reform in the United States was guided by a set of six education goals drafted at a national summit attended by President George H. Bush and the governors of all 50 states. The goals were later expanded to eight and codified in the Goals 2000: Educate America Act, signed by President Clinton in 1994. The act focused our nation's attention on education and lifelong learning, led to consensus about the aspects of our educational systems that needed revision, and emphasized the value of early care and education in preventing later school failure. The very first goal stated:

1. SCHOOL READINESS
(A) By the year 2000, all children in America will start school ready to learn.
(B) The objectives for this goal are that –
   (i) all children will have access to high-quality and developmentally appropriate preschool programs that help prepare children for school;
   (ii) every parent in the United States will be a child's first teacher and devote time each day to helping such parent's preschool child learn, and parents will have access to the training and support parents need; and
   (iii) children will receive the nutrition, physical activity experiences, and health care needed to arrive at school with healthy minds and bodies, and to maintain the mental alertness necessary to be prepared to learn, and the number of low-birthweight babies will be significantly reduced through enhanced prenatal health systems. (Pub.L. 103–227)

In other words, the goal of universal school readiness was to be achieved by universal preschool of sufficiently high quality to prepare all children for school (see Chapter 6), parent involvement (see Chapter 8) facilitated through parent support and education, and health and mental health promotion beginning prenatally. Throughout the 1990s, state officials used these objectives as a guide to reform their educational and social service systems. Although the consensus of educators, researchers, and decision makers was that there was still work to do, the Educate America Act was not reauthorized by President George W. Bush. Yet definite progress was made (National Education Goals Panel, 1999), and the goal of universal school readiness remains the thrust of early education policy development at the federal, state, and local levels.

Examples abound of how various levels of government are trying to promote school readiness. When Head Start was reauthorized in 1998, Congress specified school readiness as the mandated goal of this largest and oldest public-funded early intervention program. (This was always Head Start's goal, but the wording had been rather nebulous.) School readiness is also the mission of educators in the 40 states that fund prekindergarten services. Although everyone seems to agree that school readiness is the desired outcome, there appears to be little consensus on how best to achieve it. With the exception of those states that have chosen to follow Head Start's performance standards, the components of school readiness are conceptualized in very different ways across the state systems (Gilliam & Ripple, 2004).

Why Is School Readiness a Pillar of Education Reform?

As discussed in Chapters 4 and 5, many children enter American schools with significant deficits in the skills they need to profit from the educational experiences of kindergarten and first grade. Unready children lag behind their school-ready peers from the first day of school. Starting out behind, many never catch up. Although the risk is greatest for children from low-income families and communities (especially children of color, those of recent immigration, and those living in poor inner-city and rural areas), school failure is not completely dictated by demography. Just as there are many examples of children from high-risk groups who show remarkable resilience and succeed in school and adult life despite the odds against them, there are many children who do not appear to be at risk but fall through the educational cracks and experience great difficulty in school.

For students who start school significantly behind their peers, the readiness gap is never closed but tends to widen as they move through school (Lee & Burkam, 2002). That is, children who are not prepared for kindergarten may have a hard time mastering the curriculum, so they won't be ready for what will be taught in first grade, and on and on. Indeed, school readiness has been shown to be predictive of virtually every educational benchmark (e.g., achievement test scores, grade retention, special education placement, dropout, etc.). Thus, it is not an exaggeration to fear that lack of school readiness sets the stage for dismal educational trajectories and diminished lifelong outcomes (Lewitt & Baker, 1995).

The implications of early educational failure are broad and profound. School difficulties are associated with significantly higher expenses for extra help, special education, and grade retention (Alexander & Entwisle, 1988; Shepard & Smith, 1988). The added costs are not limited to those incurred at the school level. Children who experience school failure are more likely to be truant, and when they are not in school they may engage in unhealthy or delinquent behaviors. These students are more likely to drop out of school or to be pushed out through expulsion. This obviously makes them less likely to receive the postsecondary education that is increasingly required for gainful employment in an American work environment that demands specialized skills. When they reach adulthood, the societal costs continue to mount because of higher reliance on welfare and other social supports, increased crime and incarceration, and underemployment with the resultant loss of tax revenue. (Low-wage earners contribute less through income, payroll, sales, and property taxes.) Due to the intergenerational nature of poverty, the costs of school failure at the individual child level tend to compound over successive generations.

The problems presented by school failure are clearly serious. Decision makers and educators have long attempted to address the issue through various school-based interventions aimed at improving school climates, supporting underachieving students, increasing educational standards and accountability, and ending social promotion. Many of these attempts have shown limited success largely because, in our opinion, they offer too little too late.

As research accumulates on the causes of school failure and the circumstances that place children at increased risk, it has become evident that for many children the trajectory for school failure is set well before kindergarten registration. Many children who will struggle in school can be identified very early in their school careers. When they enter kindergarten, these children are often targeted for special services, retained, or suspended or expelled from school. As many as one-third of teachers in schools in high-poverty areas report that their students do not have the abilities to transition successfully to kindergarten, although for some communities the proportion may be much higher (Love, Logue, Trudeau, & Thayer, 1992). Citing results from a survey of more than 7,000 kindergarten teachers across the nation, Boyer (1991) reported that 35 percent of all kindergarteners start school without the skills they need to succeed, and 42 percent of kindergarten teachers feel the problem is getting worse. Additionally, as many as 8 percent of children enter kindergarten with behavioral and/or emotional problems so severe as to warrant a psychiatric diagnosis (Keenan & Wakschlag, 2004), and many more exhibit less serious behavioral problems and social delays that impede their educational progress (Howes, Calkin, Anastopoulos, Keane, & Shelton, 2003).

Our reading of the literature and experience in the field lead us to conclude that 30 to as high as 40 percent of American children are not ready for school when they enter kindergarten. School readiness programming is therefore imperative to strengthen their chances of educational success and, ultimately, secure the nation's future.

How Have Schools Accommodated "Unready" Students?

As a result of concern about children's general readiness to begin their public education, a variety of educational responses grew in popularity and utility during the 1970s and subsequent decades (Graue, 1993). During the last quarter of the 20th century, the developmental sciences were embracing a transactional understanding of child development that acknowledges the interacting contributions of physical maturation and environmental forces. Approaches to school readiness, however, were generally based on a maturational view of the process by which children "become ready" for school. The problem of school "unreadiness" was generally blamed on developmental immaturity that would resolve spontaneously over time as the child grew older.

Historically, school administrators have tried to ensure that more children are ready for kindergarten by raising the entry age requirements. This created an older cohort of beginning kindergarteners. School readiness testing also became popular, with test scores used to identify developmentally immature students who were judged not quite ready for school. The results of these measures were that children were held out of formal schooling for an extra year, with the belief that the added time for maturation would help them be more ready for formal classroom education. As this institutionalized practice became more prevalent, some parents – seeking to give their children a better start to school – voluntarily began to delay their children's entry into kindergarten. Studies of the effects of delayed entry, due to either formal entry criteria or parental choice, have not supported this strictly maturational approach to school readiness (Cameron & Wilson, 1990). Schools later began to offer "transitional kindergarten" classes for younger or less mature children. These classes essentially provide an extra year of kindergarten, since children typically enroll in regular kindergarten after they complete the transitional year. Studies of the effects of these "extra-year" practices on improving children's educational achievement in elementary school suggest these efforts have limited success (Grendler, 1984; Shepard & Smith, 1988). Despite evidence indicating that both delayed entry and transitional classes are ineffective, both practices continue in American schools.

In contrast to these maturational approaches to school readiness, high-quality early education has been found to be an effective way of preparing young children for school. Model preschool programs have been shown to help children acquire more skills by kindergarten entry and to benefit their later educational achievement (see Chapters 3, 4, and 5). Why is preschool education more successful than transitional kindergarten programs?

At first consideration, it seems that preschool programs should have the same impact as transitional kindergarten classes. Both offer extra classroom time to children before they start kindergarten, and both have the same goal of helping children get ready for school. Because there have been no studies comparing preschool and transitional kindergarten programs, the answer is not clear. One plausible explanation is that inherent philosophical differences in the two interventions result in different pedagogical approaches by teachers. In transitional kindergarten programs, the curriculum is likely the same as regular kindergarten but with somewhat relaxed expectations. Preschool curricula, on the other hand, may be more child-directed and focused on a holistic approach to facilitating child development across a variety of domains of functioning. This means that attention is given to academics, social and emotional skills, and physical and mental health, as well as involving parents as partners in their child's education. Indeed, research has shown that children who attend early education programs that have a child-focused approach to instruction that nurtures their innate curiosities and facilitates their social development tend to do better academically during their elementary school years than peers who attend more teacher-directed and academically focused preschool programs (Marcon, 1999).

The methods used in child-focused pedagogical approaches are designed to promote an active approach to learning. The value placed on developing independent learners was recognized by the Goal 1 Technical Planning Group that fleshed out a working definition of school readiness for the National Education Goals (Kagan, Moore, & Bredekamp, 1995). Rather than conceptualizing school readiness as consisting simply of a set of skills that could be learned, children were viewed as active partners in the educational process. This view suggests why the maturational approach to school readiness is misguided. Holding children out of school for an extra year may not be effective because they miss the carefully guided, active learning geared to their level of development and inspiring the next level of development.

WHAT IS SCHOOL READINESS?

Currently, there is a major controversy within the scholarly, practice, and policy arenas about how best to define school readiness. At the two poles of this controversy are those who champion a very broad, ecological perspective of school readiness versus those who advocate a narrow, academically oriented view. These two positions, and their shortcomings for developing effective preschool policy, are discussed next, followed by the school readiness model we recommend – the *whole child model*.

The Broad Ecological View

This wide-angle perspective on school readiness is grounded in Bronfenbrenner's (2004) bioecological perspective that stresses the importance of the environment in shaping human development. This framework encompasses nearly every possible environmental context that might impact a child's development and readiness for school (National Governors Association Task Force on School Readiness, 2005; Pianta & Cox, 1999; Piotrkowski, 2004). The major areas of influence are typically categorized by the resources of the child, family, school, and larger community.

Child resources involve being physically healthy and having age-appropriate motor skills and abilities to care for oneself, emotional and behavioral regulation, appropriate adult and peer interaction skills, secure attachments, ability to communicate needs and feelings, being interested and engaged in the world around and motivated to learn, mastery of certain cognitive and academic skills, and the ability to adjust to the social and independence demands of the kindergarten classroom. Family resources include financial security, nurturing parenting, good mental health, adequate social supports for caregiving, and a highly verbal and print-rich environment. School resources include strong and accountable leadership, transition programming, parent involvement, professional development and support for teachers, and high-quality curricula and instruction (Shore, 1998). Finally, community resources may include affordable and high-quality child care and early education, good employment opportunities, well-stocked libraries, and safe playgrounds and streets.

With such a broad host of supports, school readiness itself becomes a multidirectional condition. Not only should children be ready for school, but schools should be ready to accommodate all children, parents and other caregivers should be ready to support children's education, and communities should be ready to support children and families and the educational mission of the schools. This broad conceptualization of school readiness is undoubtedly correct. Children need strong families, high-quality child care, good schools and teachers, and communities that provide everything they need to help them grow and learn. However, this definition is of limited value when it comes to designing a system of universal prekindergarten because it holds so much more than preschools can reasonably be expected to address.

The fact is that not all families and classrooms and neighborhoods are in a position to support child development optimally. Poverty, for example, is a deep-rooted social problem that undermines school readiness. When Head Start was launched as part of the ambitious War on Poverty, many people actually believed that a few weeks of summer preschool would end the cycle of poverty and set children on a course of lifelong success. When it became evident that a brief early education program could not change community and social structures, or undo the profound deleterious effects of growing up in poverty, Head Start came close to being shut down. The point is that definitions of what it means to be ready for school must provide a reasonable set of expectations for preschool programs in order to focus their mission and provide a fair basis for public accountability. At issue is not whether the ecological definition of school readiness is correct – it certainly is. Rather, what matters most is that a definition is useful (Zigler, Balla, & Hodapp, 1984). The broad definition promoted by many respected scholars and the National Governors Association is simply too expansive to lead to effective policy development. As much as we would like, preschool alone cannot change the world.

The Academic Skills View

On the opposite end of the spectrum is the strictly academic view of school readiness favored by the George W. Bush administration and some members of Congress. This approach focuses on the importance of literacy and math skills in getting prepared for school. As an example of the premium placed on academics, during the 1998 reauthorization of Head Start Congress mandated that all children exiting this comprehensive program of child development and family support be able to identify 10 letters of the alphabet. Later, the Head Start National Reporting System (NRS) was created and required that all four-year-olds in the program be tested on literacy and other cognitive abilities. The NRS and the scholastic approach to school readiness have been criticized vigorously by early childhood experts for excluding other domains of child development and well-being. Their arguments do not deny that early literacy and math skills are important, but emphasize that their mastery is dependent upon physical and mental health, social and emotional development, and motivation and eagerness to learn.

Although the breadth of K–12 public school curricula is a matter of continual debate – with some favoring an emphasis on reading, writing, and arithmetic, while others espouse more comprehensive coursework – it is clear that being successful in school requires more than the ability to acquire factual information and rules. Teaching and learning are inherently social processes, in which children learn skills and behaviors through listening, observing, and interacting with adults, peers, and educational materials. Some skills may be acquired through self-motivated efforts or for the feeling of accomplishment that comes from meeting a challenge. For the most part, however, young students learn academic content and complete school tasks out of a desire to please the adults in their lives, conform to social demands, and reap the social rewards of praise and attention (Salovey & Pizarro, 2003).

As later discussed in Chapter 2, kindergartners who fail to master the social competence skills necessary to understand classroom routines and to engage positively with teachers and peers achieve lower scores on educational achievement tests (Howes et al., 2003). Difficulties in acquiring the social, emotional, and behavioral skill sets necessary to function adequately in a classroom setting are often evident before kindergarten entry (Keenan & Wakschlag, 2004). For example, in a sample of child care programs in Massachusetts, nearly 3 percent of the preschoolers exhibited behavioral difficulties so great that they were permanently expelled from their program (Gilliam & Shahar, in press). Their inability to negotiate the social and behavioral demands of their early care and education settings meant they could not take full advantage of the learning opportunities available to them. Once they were expelled, of course, those opportunities were no longer available. The best curriculum and literacy training in the world offer nothing to the child who is not there to absorb them, or is physically there but is disengaged from the lesson. This is why the purely academic approach to school readiness is an oversimplification of what children need to prepare for school.

Teacher and Parent Views of School Readiness

While theoretical views have value, it is also important to consider parents' and teachers' perspectives of school readiness. Parents know their own children better than anyone else, and their views can influence school policies. Kindergarten teachers are the professionals responsible for educating all children and see the differences between children who enter school with varying levels of readiness. Moreover, their impressions carry unique weight because they can influence educational expectations and opportunities for individual students. When a teacher feels that a child has a better chance for educational success, that child may get more attention and encouragement, creating a self-fulfilling prophecy (Rosenthal & Jacobson, 1992). Further, a kindergarten teacher's beliefs about what types of skills are most needed for success in her classroom may give the child who possesses these skills some initial advantages.

When asked about the skills that make a child ready for school, parents tend to emphasize academic skills more than kindergarten teachers do (Knudson-Lindauer & Harris, 1989; West, Hauskens, & Collins, 1993). That is, parents tend to equate school readiness with attributes such as academic knowledge, language skills, counting, and letter and number recognition. Kindergarten teachers, on the other hand, are more likely to focus on social-emotional skills that help the child to be a more independent and active learner and to refrain from behaviors that might be disruptive (Harradine & Clifford, 1996). Although kindergarten teachers as a group tend to place a higher premium on social-emotional skills, differences exist among them depending on the demographics of their students. Relative to kindergarten teachers in more affluent communities, those in predominately minority and low-income communities expect children to enter kindergarten with a higher level of academic preparation (Heaviside & Farris, 1993).

In a study of school readiness beliefs in a high-need urban school district serving predominantly African American and Latino children (Piotrkowski, Botsko, & Matthews, 2000), some consensus was found. Parents, preschool teachers, and kindergarten teachers were asked to rate the importance of 45 indicators of school readiness. Children being rested, well-nourished, and healthy rated first among both preschool and kindergarten teachers and tied for second among parents. Self-control and paying attention to the teacher were also rated highly by all three groups. Where the groups differed in their opinions concerned the importance of general knowledge and emerging literacy in determining whether a child was ready for school. Parents rated basic knowledge (counting; knowing letters, colors, body parts, etc.) as significantly more important for school readiness than did preschool teachers. Kindergarten teachers in general placed the least importance on basic knowledge, but those in highly disadvantaged communities placed a higher premium on basic skills.

School readiness obviously means different things to different people. Theorists differ among themselves, as do those in the trenches. Developing a consensus is important to designing a universal preschool system everyone will support. The variety of opinions are all represented in the whole child approach to preparing children for school.

THE WHOLE CHILD PERSPECTIVE

The views of school readiness just described fall short of providing a useful framework for developing universal preschool policy and effective systems of public accountability. Focusing on literacy and numeracy misses too much of what it means to be equipped for school. Focusing on everything that might possibly impact a child's ability to succeed in school and life, while theoretically sound and helpful for thinking about the contexts within which preschool must operate, does not lead to realistic expectations of what preschool programs can accomplish. Teachers' and parents' opinions vary too much to create what everyone can agree is the best program.

A basic definition is the first step to bringing clarity to the area. Simply stated, school readiness is the set of skills and attributes that a child needs at school entry in order "to profit from the kindergarten experience and meet societal expectations of competence" in the classroom (Piotrkowski et al., 2000, p. 540). Rather than *learning readiness, educational readiness,* or *academic readiness,* which are more abstract in focus, *school readiness* implies being ready for adequate functioning in a tangible location – school. To understand what it takes to be ready to function in a school setting, one must consider all the demands of that setting. It would be overly simplistic to say all that children need to learn at school comes from their teachers and textbooks. Rather, schools are complex social settings, where children learn how to interact with adults who are in positions of authority, to make and sustain friendships with peers, to become increasingly independent, and to take a more active role in their own learning and completion of academic projects.

Of course, the exact skills necessary to succeed in a given classroom depend heavily on the expectations and supports present in that setting. The 80,000 schools in America vary significantly from one another in terms of student population, curricular approaches, grading and promotion standards, and supportive services. What may be sufficient skills to succeed in one kindergarten class may not be sufficient in another. Likewise, some schools may have more student supports available than others, such as behavioral consultants, health services, and compensatory or remedial education services. Finally, parent involvement may be encouraged in some districts more than others. In this respect, school readiness reflects the fit between the school's characteristics and the personal resources that the child brings to school.

It is noteworthy that Goals 2000 did not imply that children would start school knowing any of the content matter typically associated with kindergarten. Rather, the aspiration was that children would enter school ready to participate actively in the learning environment of the kindergarten classroom. The difference is quite significant: the goal was for children to have the skills needed to succeed as learners in kindergarten, not to have already mastered a portion of the academic skills that kindergarten teachers feel is their job to teach. Although some of the skills needed to take advantage of kindergarten may include precursor abilities in literacy and numeracy, being "ready to learn" in a kindergarten classroom involves much more.

The National Education Goals Panel asked a group of stellar developmental scientists to delineate what skills school readiness involves. That technical planning group identified five component domains (Kagan et al., 1995):

1. Physical well-being and motor development
2. Social and emotional development
3. Approaches to learning (learning motivation, independence, etc.)
4. Language use
5. Cognition and general knowledge

Note that of these domains, only the last and part of the fourth address the more traditional academic skills measured by achievement tests. The

TABLE 2.1. *Head Start Child Outcomes Framework: Domains and Elements*

1. Language Development a. Listening and understanding b. Speaking and communicating	**5. Creative Arts** a. Music b. Art c. Movement d. Dramatic play
2. Literacy a. Phonological awareness b. Book knowledge and appreciation c. Print awareness and concepts d. Early writing e. Alphabet knowledge	**6. Social and Emotional Development** a. Self-concept b. Self-control c. Cooperation d. Social relationships e. Knowledge of families and communities
3. Mathematics a. Number and operations b. Geometry and spatial sense c. Patterns and measurement	**7. Approaches to Learning** a. Initiative and curiosity b. Engagement and persistence c. Reasoning and problem solving
4. Science a. Scientific skills and methods b. Scientific knowledge	**8. Physical Health and Development** a. Gross motor skills b. Fine motor skills c. Health status and practices

other domains involve nonacademic requirements for success in school. The keyword here is *requirements*. To learn what they are supposed to, children need to be healthy and well nourished, and be able to follow adult directions, tolerate being away from their families during the school day, get along with classmates, direct their attention, participate appropriately in classroom activities, and use language to make their needs known and to navigate social and academic challenges.

Head Start administrators further articulated these domains of school readiness in the *Head Start Child Outcomes Framework* (*HSCOF*; Head Start Bureau, 2003). The *HSCOF* provides a description of what Head Start students are to learn during preschool. These outcomes are organized into 8 general domains, 27 domain elements, and 100 specific outcome indicators (see Table 2.1). The *HSCOF* draws heavily on the wealth of scientific research and conceptualization during the course of Head Start's four decades of experience promoting children's development, well-being, and school readiness. The framework builds on the Head

Start Program Performance Measures, developed for use in longitudinal research on children's and families' experiences in the program (see Administration on Children, Youth and Families, 1998). It also incorporates the work of the Goal 1 Technical Planning Group of the National Education Goals Panel, described earlier. The "whole child" approach to early education and learning is evident in the *HSCOF*, which covers Head Start's mission of addressing children's physical and mental health and developing their social and emotional skills and the language and academic abilities necessary to succeed in school (Raver & Zigler, 1997).

Beyond being more complete and detailed, the *HSCOF* differs from the Goal 1 Technical Planning Group conceptualization of school readiness in two important ways. First, many of the domains more closely align to traditional academic subject areas (e.g., literacy, mathematics, science, etc.). Learning standards for state-funded prekindergarten systems also tend to define school readiness in terms that are recognizable within a K–12 curricular framework. Some degree of alignment with school learning expectations is necessary to create a shared vision of what educational preparation is needed for the next grade or level of schooling.

Second, the HSCOF learning outcomes are conceptually tied to the program's structure and goals. This is necessary so the program is not held accountable for outcomes outside of its mission or services. The group that developed the Head Start Program Performance Measures made this point clear: "The measures should focus on results for which Head Start would be willing to accept ownership and hold itself responsible. Relevant considerations include both the types of results to be achieved and the likelihood that they *can* be achieved during the time that children and families are in the program" (Head Start Bureau, 1995, p. vii; emphasis added). Alignment of program goals and outcome measures not only informs areas where services need improvement but allows a fair and effective system of public accountability.

Outside of Head Start, a national project to identify what it means to be ready for school is being completed across 17 states with prekindergarten systems (Bryant & Walsh, 2004). School readiness indicators will include both child outcomes across a variety of domains of functioning (e.g., physical, cognitive, social, and emotional) and systems indicators that provide a measure of community resources available for providing services that might promote school readiness (e.g., availability of accredited child care programs). The purpose is to develop a common core of school readiness indicators that are shared across these 17 states.

These efforts to measure school readiness in Head Start and state preschools share the whole child perspective. Unlike the NRS that tests literacy and cognitive skills, the assessments described here represent what appears to be an emerging agreement that children do not need to know how to recite the alphabet and count to 10 the day they start kindergarten if they are to make it to first grade. Rather, they must be physically, mentally, and socially prepared to *learn* the alphabet and numbers and everything else that is offered in kindergarten to prepare for first grade.

CONCLUSION

Given what is known about how young children learn, research on school readiness, and the perspectives of kindergarten teachers, preschool teachers, and parents, the learning standards itemized in the *Head Start Child Outcomes Framework* are appropriate expectations for preschool programs. The *HSCOF* provides a well-conceptualized starting point for states to develop their own standards that capture the goals of their preschool systems and map onto their own K–12 educational expectations. The framework has solid empirical and theoretical grounding and should prove very helpful in informing a national vision of what it means to be school ready.

A uniform definition of school readiness, and a framework for measuring outcomes of school readiness programming, have value on a number of levels. They will eliminate a lot of duplication of effort among policy makers who, after all, are not experts in child development. This point was obvious during the Head Start reauthorization process in 2004. Senators attempted to draft a list of achievements to mandate for children graduating from Head Start. When experts pointed out that many of the tasks on the list were more appropriate for third-graders than entering kindergartners, and that individual differences in development in various skill areas meant that it would be impossible for most children to meet all the requirements, the list was discarded. State officials, too, could benefit from the considerable amount of work and expertise that has already been done to define and measure school readiness – work they (like the senators) may not even be aware of or have ready access to as they strive to write their own preschool standards.

The whole child approach to school readiness has many advantages, not the least of which is empirical grounding. The approach has appeal to different factions on the readiness issue. Those who take the ecological view of school readiness will be comfortable with the attention to child, family, and school factors. Those who believe preschool should be about academic training will find attention to cognitive tasks in the whole child view. Children have a lot to accomplish to prepare for school, so a useful concept of school readiness needs to encompass a lot. A solid definition can inform the design of preschool curricula; point out ways to evaluate how successful a preschool program is, which is useful for both accountability purposes and to aid individual programs in the continuous process of improving their practices; and facilitate the goal of school readiness for all children. In the end, it can tell us in what direction we want to go.

References

Administration on Children, Youth and Families. (1998). *Head Start Program Performance Measures. Second progress report.* Washington, DC: U.S. Department of Health and Human Services. (Pub. No. ACYF-IM-HS 98-19)

Alexander, K. L., & Entwisle, D. R. (1988). Achievement in the first two years: Patterns and processes. *Monographs of the Society for Research in Child Development, 53* (2, Serial No. 218).

Boyer, E. L. (1991). *Ready to learn: A mandate for the nation.* Lawrenceville, NJ: Princeton University Press.

Bronfenbrenner, U. (Ed.). (2004). *Making human beings human: Bioecological perspectives on human development.* Thousand Oaks, CA: Sage Press.

Bryant, E. B., & Walsh, C. (2004). Identifying school readiness indicators to stimulate policy action. Harvard Family Research Project – *The Evaluation Exchange, 2,* 26.

Cameron, M. B., & Wilson, B. J. (1990). The effects of chronological age, gender and delay of entry on academic achievement and retention: Implications for academic redshirting. *Psychology in the Schools, 27,* 260–263.

Gilliam, W. S., & Ripple, C. H. (2004). What can be learned from state-funded prekindergarten initiatives? A data-based approach to the Head Start devolution debate. In E. Zigler & S. J. Styfco (Eds.), *The Head Start debates* (pp. 477–497). Baltimore: Paul H. Brookes.

Gilliam, W. S., & Shahar, G. (in press). Prekindergarten expulsion and suspension: Rates and predictors in one state. *Infants and Young Children.*

Graue, M. E. (1993). *Ready for what? Constructing meanings of readiness for kindergarten.* Albany: State University Press of New York.

Grendler, G. R. (1984). Transitional classes: A viable alternative for the at-risk child? *Psychology in the Schools, 21,* 463–470.

Harradine, C. C., & Clifford, R. M. (1996). *When are children ready for kindergarten? Views of families, kindergarten teachers, and child care providers.* Paper presented at the annual meeting of the American Educational Research Association, New York. (ERIC Document Reproduction Service No. ED 399 044)

Head Start Bureau. (1995). *Charting our progress: Development of the Head Start Program Performance Measures.* Washington, DC: U.S. Department of Health and Human Services.

Head Start Bureau. (2003). *The Head Start path to positive child outcomes: The Head Start child outcomes framework.* Washington, DC: U.S. Department of Health and Human Services.

Heaviside, S., & Farris, E. (1993). *Public school kindergarten teachers' views on children's readiness for school* (NCES No. 93-410). Washington, DC: U.S. Department of Education.

Howes, R. B., Calkin, S. D., Anastopoulos, A. D., Keane, S. P., & Shelton, T. L. (2003). Regulatory contributions to children's kindergarten achievement. *Early Education and Development, 14,* 101–119.

Kagan, S. L., Moore, E., & Bredekamp, S. (Eds.). (1995). *Reconsidering children's early development and learning: Toward common views and vocabulary. National Education Goals Panel, Goal 1 Technical Planning Group.* Washington, DC: U.S. Government Printing Office.

Keenan, K., & Wakschlag, L. S. (2004). Are oppositional defiant and conduct disorder symptoms normative behaviors in preschoolers? A comparison of referred and nonreferred children. *American Journal of Psychiatry, 161,* 356–358.

Knudson-Lindauer, S. L., & Harris, K. (1989). Priorities for kindergarten curricula: Views of parents and teachers. *Journal of Research and Childhood Education, 4*(1), 51–61.

Lee, V. E., & Burkam, D. T. (2002). *Inequality at the starting gate: Social background differences in achievement as children begin school.* Washington, DC: Economic Policy Institute.

Lewitt, E. M., & Baker, L. S. (1995). School readiness. *The Future of Children, 5*(2), 128–139.

Love, J. M., Logue, M. E., Trudeau, J. V., & Thayer, K. (1992). *Transitions to kindergarten in American schools.* Washington, DC: Office of Policy and Planning, U.S. Department of Education.

Marcon, R. A. (1999). Differential impact of preschool models on development and early learning of inner-city children: A three-cohort study. *Developmental Psychology, 8,* 72–79.

National Education Goals Panel. (1999). *The National Education Goals report: Building a nation of learners.* Washington, DC: U.S. Government Printing Office.

National Governors Association Task Force on School Readiness. (2005). *Building the foundation for bright futures: Final report of the NGA Task Force on School Readiness.* Washington, DC: National Governors Association. www.nga.org/cda/files/0501TASKFORCEREADINESS.pdf. Accessed January 29, 2005.

Pianta, R. C., & Cox, M. J. (Eds.). (1999). *The transition to kindergarten.* Baltimore: Paul H. Brookes.

Piotrkowski, C. S. (2004). A community-based approach to school readiness in Head Start. In E. Zigler & S. J. Styfco (Eds.), *The Head Start debates* (pp. 129–142). Baltimore: Paul H. Brookes.

Piotrkowski, C. S., Botsko, M., & Matthews, E. (2000). Parents' and teachers' beliefs about children's school readiness in a high-need community. *Early Childhood Research Quarterly, 15,* 537–558.

Raver, C. C., & Zigler, E. F. (1997). Social competence: An untapped dimension in evaluating Head Start's success. *Early Childhood Research Quarterly, 12,* 363–385.

Rosenthal, R., & Jacobson, L. (1992). *Pygmalion in the classroom: Teacher expectation and pupils' intellectual development.* New York: Irvington Publishers.

Salovey, P., & Pizarro, D. A. (2003). The value of emotional intelligence. In R. J. Sternberg & J. Lautrey (Eds.), *Models of intelligence: International perspectives* (pp. 263–278). Washington, DC: American Psychological Association.

Shepard, L. A., & Smith, M. L. (1988). Synthesis of research on school readiness and kindergarten retention. In J. P. Bauch (Ed.), *Early childhood education in the schools* (pp. 88–94). Washington, DC: National Education Association.

Shore, R. (1998). *Ready schools.* Washington, DC: National Education Goals Panel.

West, J., Hauskens, E. G., & Collins, M. (1993). *Readiness for kindergarten: Parent and teacher beliefs* (NCES No. 93-257). Washington, DC: Office of Educational Research and Improvement, U.S. Department of Education.

Zigler, E., Balla, D., & Hodapp, R. (1984). On the definition and classification of mental retardation. *American Journal of Mental Deficiency, 89,* 215–230.

3

Economic Returns of Investments in Preschool Education

Arthur J. Reynolds and Judy A. Temple

> Given our value system, we would like to argue that any demonstrated benefits of intervention are worth the cost.... Unfortunately, for policy-makers benefits must be defined in practical terms, and these are always ones of economic feasibility. Only when gains translate into economic savings is the effectiveness of intervention truly conceded.
>
> (Zigler & Berman, 1983, p. 901)

> In an era of tight government budgets, it is impractical to consider active investment programmes for all persons. The real question is how to use the available funds wisely. The best evidence supports the policy prescription: invest in the very young and improve basic learning and socialization skills... efficiency would be enhanced if human capital investment were reallocated to the young.
>
> (Heckman, 2000, p. 8)

Early childhood education is receiving widespread attention as one of the most effective ways to promote children's educational success. Preschool programs are a centerpiece of many school and social reforms; in 2002 alone, government expenditures totaled $22 billion for programs targeting children from birth to age five (White House, 2003). The main attraction of early childhood programs is their potential for prevention and cost-effectiveness, especially when compared to the well-known limits of remediation and treatment (Durlak, 1997; Heckman, 2000). In child welfare and juvenile justice, for example, most services are

Preparation of this chapter was supported in part by the National Institute of Child Health and Human Development (R01 HD34294).

provided to treat families and children after problems have occurred rather than to prevent the need for services or to provide early intervention (Cohen, 1998; MacLeod & Nelson, 2000).

In this chapter we address three major issues about the impact of preschool programs. First, we review the evidence about their economic benefits and costs. In an age of growing budget deficits and increasing fiscal uncertainties, identification of programs that provide the greatest returns to society is a high priority. There is now a critical mass of studies about the long-term economic returns of participation in preschool programs and related early interventions. We emphasize well-known findings from the High/Scope Perry Preschool Program and new findings from the Chicago Child-Parent Centers and the Abecedarian Project. We also describe the significance of cost-benefit analysis for the evaluation of preschool programs. Our primary focus is educational enrichment programs for three- and four-year-olds.

Second, we compare the economic benefits of preschool programs to other common initiatives for children and youth, including health promotion from birth to age three, reductions in class size in the early grades, grade retention policy, and youth job training. Policy decisions about the allocation of scarce human and financial resources are best made by considering the impacts of preschool programs relative to other investments that could be made with the available resources.

Finally, we discuss the implications of the findings from our review of future investments in preschool education, including the movement toward universal access to preschool. Most of the evidence of long-term effects is from studies of children in low-income families, and the extent to which the findings apply to more economically diverse populations is not fully known. To fill some of this gap, we discuss recent evidence from child care and state-funded prekindergartens. We then offer some key principles to guide investments in preschool programs.

LIMITATIONS OF PREVIOUS RESEARCH ON EARLY EDUCATION

In the past four decades hundreds of studies have documented the links between preschool participation and child development outcomes, but three limitations reduce the usefulness of the findings for social policy construction. First, most of the evidence for the positive, long-term effects of preschool on children's well-being comes from model demonstration programs rather than large-scale public programs run by human service agencies and schools. More evidence from mainstream programs is needed to assess the relative effectiveness of current state and federal programs.

A second limitation of existing research is that until recently, cost-benefit analysis had been conducted for only one program, the High/Scope Perry Preschool (Schweinhart, Barnes, & Weikart, 1993). Although policy makers commonly cite the High/Scope findings as proof that preschool has substantial economic benefits, the truth is that no large-scale public programs had been studied for cost-effectiveness. Given the breadth of outcomes potentially impacted by preschool and the policy significance of cost-effectiveness data, this limitation deserves urgent attention. Without this type of evidence, it is impossible to compare the benefits of prevention programs versus treatment programs.

Another limitation of the research is that preschool programs may have different effects on different students, and it is not well understood who benefits most from attendance. Do programs serving middle-income families have the same magnitude of effects on child outcomes as programs serving low-income families? Similarly, do children experiencing a large number of risk factors benefit more from participation than those with few risks?

Before turning to the economic benefits of preschool, we briefly detail the evidence on long-term effects because these findings are used in cost-benefit analyses. In the past two decades, many studies have shown that preschool attendance has short- and long-term positive effects on a variety of school and social competencies such as academic achievement, need for remedial education and social services, delinquency, educational attainment, and economic well-being into adulthood (Barnett, 1995; Karoly, Greenwood, & Everingham, 1998; Reynolds, 2000). Barnett's review of 36 model and public programs provides a good indication of the magnitude of effects. Across the studies, preschool participation was associated with a 31 percent reduction in grade retention, a 50 percent reduction in special education placement, and a 32 percent reduction in high school dropout rates, although this last finding is based on fewer studies. While these are educationally meaningful benefits, it is notable that the strongest evidence came from model programs. Indeed, 90 percent of the citations in reviews of early intervention research are to model programs (Reynolds, 2000).

Since the middle 1990s, evidence has been gathered on a wider array of programs. Table 3.1 shows the most frequently cited programs in 16 reviews of the effects of preschool published from 1990 to 2001. Most were interventions serving low-income children and families, including

TABLE 3.1. *Most Frequently Cited Early Childhood Programs from 16 Research Reviews (1990–2001)*

Program	Type	Entry Age	Age at Last Follow-up	Number of Citations
High/Scope Perry Preschool Program	Model	3	27	15
Carolina Abecedarian Project	Model	Birth	21	14
Houston Child-Parent Development Center	Model	Birth	11	14
Yale Child Welfare Research Program	Model	Birth	10	10
Chicago Child-Parent Centers	Public	3	20	9
Milwaukee Project	Model	Birth	14	8
Syracuse Family Development Program	Model	Birth	15	8
Early Training Project	Model	Birth	20	6
Consortium for Longitudinal Studies	Model	Birth–3	27	6
Philadelphia Project	Model	Birth	18	6
Infant and Health Development Program	Model	Birth	8	6
ETS Service Head Start Study	Public	3	8	5
New Haven Follow-Through Study	Public	3	9	5
Elmira Prenatal/Early Infancy Project	Model	Birth	15	5
Harlem Training Project	Model	Birth	12	4
Rochester Nurse Home Visiting Program	Model	Birth	4	4
Gordon Parent Education Program	Model	Birth	10	3
NY State Experimental Prekindergarten	Public	4	8	3
PSID Head Start Longitudinal Study	Public	3	25	3
High/ Scope Curriculum Comparison Study	Model	3	23	2
Louisville Experiment (Head Start)	Model	3	7	2
Menninger Infancy Project	Model	Birth	3	2
Mother-Child Home Program	Model	Birth	5	2

Note: Entry age at birth ranges from prenatal development to age 1.

some that started at birth or even prenatally. In contrast to a decade ago, more evidence now exists on the positive benefits of public programs many years after participation. Five of the most frequently cited programs in Table 3.1 are public. The length of follow-up in some of the studies, up to 23 years after the end of preschool, is unique among social programs.

COST-BENEFIT ANALYSIS

Cost-benefit analysis (CBA) offers practical advice to policy makers who must consider which alternative policies are the best use of finite public resources. Using CBA, policy options can be ranked according to their effectiveness per dollar of expenditure. Levin and McEwan define CBA as the "evaluation of alternatives according to their costs and benefits when each is measured in monetary terms" (2001, p. 11). The use of cost-benefit analysis to document the payoffs of early education and to prioritize alternative funding choices has been highlighted in several reports (Carroll, Ochshorn, Kagan, & Fuller, 2003; Committee for Economic Development, 2002; Governor's Task Force, 2002; Heckman, 2000; Karoly, 2002; Oppenheim & McGregor, 2003; Scrivner & Wolfe, 2003). In this age of accountability, these and other reports have helped to reinforce the perceived value of preschool investments and propelled them to national attention.

The ability to conduct a CBA depends on whether it is possible to state program benefits and costs in dollar terms. Typically, but not always, it is more difficult to calculate the dollar value of the program benefits rather than the program costs. When program outcomes cannot be easily converted to monetary terms, cost-effectiveness analysis is the recommended approach. In cost-effectiveness analysis, program costs are stated in dollars but benefits remain in the metric of the outcome measure, such as achievement score points. (For example, every dollar spent on the program results in a gain of X points.) While this type of analysis can be very useful, CBA has a major advantage in that benefits for multiple outcomes can be summarized into a single metric (dollars). The results are expressed either as the net return (benefits minus costs) or return per dollar invested (benefits divided by costs).

To assess the benefits of preschool education programs, there are straightforward approaches that can quantify the payoff in dollar terms. While many of the benefits are realized further out in the future, some are evident in the first few years of elementary school. A major documented benefit of preschool programs is that they may reduce the need for future remedial school services such as special education and grade retention. Using information from school budgets, cost-benefit analysts can translate these effects into dollars. For example, if attending preschool is associated with a 10 percent reduction in the probability of needing special education, information on how much the school district spends on special education per pupil per year could be used to estimate how much will be saved. Another benefit of preschool education is that it reduces the likelihood of a student staying back in later grades. Grade retention is costly in that it increases the number of years a student is enrolled in school, and retained students sometimes receive extra help that also adds costs. Again, the predicted savings can be calculated from school budgets and then used in cost-benefit equations.

The second major benefit of preschool programs is their effect on educational attainment. There is a long history among economists (e.g., Weisbrod, 1965) of calculating the economic benefit of high school graduation or the avoidance of dropping out of school. Substantial income differences have been found between high school graduates and dropouts. Waiting for that benefit to show up takes a long time, so economists are attempting to link achievement test scores in childhood to future earnings, which provides a way of monetizing the benefits of an educational intervention that increases academic achievement. This approach currently relies on prediction estimates between test scores and earnings for a very small number of studies. In CBA, it is important not to double count benefits. A researcher attempting to place dollar values on the effects of preschool on adult earnings would thus focus either on the link between preschool attendance and education attainment or the relation between preschool programs and test scores but not both, since one important way that programs affect educational attainment is through higher test scores.

Higher earners, of course, pay more taxes. Once it has been established that successful preschool programs may affect adult earnings, it is then possible to calculate the additional tax revenues the government will collect. This is an important tool in CBAs that attempt to categorize the various benefits of a program according to who actually benefits – the preschool participant or the society as a whole.

Researchers can also use longitudinal data to estimate the relation between preschool attendance and later juvenile and adult crime. For example, preschool graduates might engage in less delinquency and have fewer arrests in adulthood (Yoshikawa, 1994). This benefit reduces costs for administration and processing of crime cases, treatment, and incarceration. Potential crime victims also realize both tangible and intangible savings. Similarly, researchers may be able to show that early childhood programs lead to a reduction in child maltreatment, which would reduce expenditures for investigations, medical care, and child welfare services. Like impacts on crime, savings to potential victims of maltreatment are a further benefit.

The benefits typically included in CBA are reduced need for remedial education services, improvements in test scores and educational attainment, lowered costs directly or indirectly linked to criminal activity, and improved health and consequent reduction in medical expenses. Benefits typically *not* included are features like social and emotional outcomes, enhanced social cohesion and citizenship, increased charitable giving, better savings habits, and "trickle down" effects like improved health of participants' family members and better educational attainment of participants' children. Many of these are discussed in Haveman and Wolfe (1984), who describe them as the nonmarket benefits of education and provide some guidelines on how they could be measured.

There are two reasons why some benefits of preschool programs might be difficult to include in a cost-benefit analysis. The first is that some of the potential benefits, such as better self-esteem or citizenship, are relatively intangible and difficult to operationalize and measure. The second reason is that cost-benefit analysts typically focus on the more obvious benefits of a program and do not venture too far afield in search for other possible advantages. (An exception is Schweinhart et al., 1993, who used creative measures like second-car ownership and how often participants' children used the library.) Although an ambitious economist could assign dollar values to the effect of preschool programs on, say, the health of one's future spouse or children using estimates from the economics literature on the relation between educational attainment and these outcomes, it is likely that the measurement errors associated with such distal calculations are sizable. However, it is important for policy makers and others to be aware of these hidden benefits and to look twice at an intuitively promising program that has an unimpressive CBA ratio.

The economic benefits reported in CBA can be categorized into three types. Benefits to participants are returned to the parents and children enrolled but do not directly benefit others in society. These include increased earnings capacity in adulthood as well as the benefit to parents who receive part-day care for their children. Benefits to the general public include reduced costs of remedial education and social welfare programs, savings to crime victims as a result of lower rates of crime, and increased tax revenues to state and federal governments as a result of higher earnings. Benefits to society at large include the sum of benefits to program participants and to the general public. In the discussion that follows, we emphasize societal benefits, which represent the total economic contributions of the programs reviewed.

OVERVIEW OF THREE PROGRAMS INVESTIGATING ECONOMIC COSTS AND BENEFITS

The key features of the three programs we focus on are summarized in Table 3.2. All three programs provided high-quality educational enrichment to at-risk children in group settings characterized by small class sizes, a focus on language and cognitive skills, and well-qualified and compensated teachers. The Carolina Abecedarian Project (ABC) was the most intensive and lengthy, providing full-day, year-round care for five years (Campbell & Ramey, 1995; Ramey, Campbell, & Blair, 1998). The High/Scope Perry Preschool Program (PPP) had the most organized curriculum, which followed the Piagetian cognitive principle of child-initiated learning (Schweinhart et al., 1993). The Chicago Child-Parent Centers (CPC) provided the most comprehensive services, including an intensive parent involvement component, outreach services, and attention to health and nutrition (Reynolds, 2000; Sullivan, 1971). It also is the only one of the programs that became established in public schools and is still in operation.

The High/Scope Perry Preschool Program (Berrueta-Clement, Schweinhart, Barnett, Epstein, & Weikart, 1984; Schweinhart et al., 1993) was implemented in Perry Elementary School in Ypsilanti, Michigan, from 1962 to 1967. It served three- and four-year-old African American children from families of low socioeconomic status (SES). All children had IQ scores in the range of 70–85, which reduces the generalizability of the findings to other groups. The program used a child-initiated instructional approach based on the learning process of "plan-do-review." As public school teachers, most staff had master's degrees in education and certification in early childhood.

The study of the program included 123 children. Initially, 58 children were randomly assigned to PPP in five consecutive cohorts beginning in 1962. With the exception of the first cohort, children attended for two years. The comparison group included 65 children who were in home

TABLE 3.2. *Background and Characteristics of Three Preschool Programs*

Characteristic	Perry Preschool	Abecedarian	Child-Parent Centers
Years of operation	1962–1967	1972–1977	1983–1985
City and context	Ypsilanti: Urban	Chapel Hill: Rural	Chicago: Inner city
Location	Elementary school	University center	Elementary school or adjacent
Number of sites	1	1	24
Child attributes	Low SES, IQs of 70–85	Low SES, high risk	Low SES, reside in Title I area
Race/ethnicity	100% black	96% black	94% black, 6% Hispanic
Entry age	3 years	1–4 months	3 years
Mean duration	1.8 years	5 years	1.6 years
Length of day	Part-day	Full-day	Part-day
Other components	Weekly home visits	Medical services, nutrition	Parent program, outreach, occasional home visits, health services
Mean class size	22	12 (infancy), 12 (preschool)	17
Mean child to staff ratio	5.7 to 1	3 to 1 (infancy), 6 to 1 (preschool)	8.5 to 1
Curriculum emphasis	Cognitive and social, child-initiated	Language and social, traditional	Language and social, teacher-directed
Staff compensation	Public school	Competitive with public schools	Public school
School-age services	None	K to grade 2	K, grades 1 to 3

care. Nearly all of the participants have been followed up to age 27, which is an unusually high rate of retention. (After this chapter was written, the age 40 results were released; Schweinhart et al., 2005.)

The Abecedarian Project (Ramey et al., 1998; Ramey et al., 2000) was a model educational day-care intervention that was implemented from 1972 to 1977 at the Frank Porter Graham Child Development Center at the University of North Carolina at Chapel Hill. Participants entered the program in infancy and attended five years of full-time, year-round care. The children were almost all African American and were determined to be at high risk of school failure, primarily due to low SES. The focus of the program was to promote optimal child development, with a special emphasis on language development. Although there was no family component, medical and nutritional services were provided. Unlike most early care today, teachers received salaries that were competitive with public schools.

The impact study included 111 families. Fifty-seven children were randomly assigned to ABC soon after birth. They began the program at an average age of four months and continued until the start of kindergarten. The control group contained 54 children who received many of the same medical and nutritional services as the program group. To investigate the added impact of school-age participation, some children from the study sample were randomly assigned to receive school-age services. Participants have been tracked up to age 21, again with a very high rate of retention (see Campbell & Ramey, 1995; Ramey et al., 1998).

The Child-Parent Center Program (Reynolds, 2000; Reynolds, Temple, Robertson, & Mann, 2001, 2002; Sullivan, 1971) began in the Chicago public schools in 1967 through federal funding from the Elementary and Secondary Education Act of 1965. Title I of the act provides grants to public school districts serving high concentrations of children from low-income families. The centers are the nation's second oldest federally funded preschool program. The CPC program is a center-based early intervention that provides comprehensive educational and family-support services to economically disadvantaged children and their parents beginning at age three and continuing until third grade, providing up to six years of intervention. In addition to classroom teachers, primary staff include a parent resource teacher, school-community representative, classroom aides, nurses, speech therapists, and school psychologists. All teachers have bachelor's degrees with certification in early childhood. Parents are heavily involved in the program through many types of school participation.

The Chicago Longitudinal Study (1999; Reynolds, 1999) investigated the program's impact for the entire cohort of 989 children born in 1980 who attended the preschool program beginning at age three and completed kindergarten in the spring of 1986. The comparison group of 550 children in this quasi-experimental design did not attend the CPCs but instead participated in an all-day kindergarten program for at-risk children in five schools. Because the CPC group was from the highest poverty neighborhoods and the comparison group attended randomly selected schools outside of CPC neighborhoods and participated in alternative interventions, estimates of impact are likely to be conservative. Study participants have been followed up to age 22,

TABLE 3.3. *Adjusted Means or Percentages for Program and Comparison Groups on Key Outcomes for Cost-Benefit Analysis*

Outcome	Perry Preschool	Abecedarian	Child-Parent Centers
Original sample sizes (program, control)	58, 65	57, 54	989, 550
Sample recovery for high school completion (%)	94	95	87
Special education services by age 15/18 (%)	15 vs. 34	25 vs. 48	14 vs. 25
Grade retention by age 15 (%)	ns	31 vs. 55	23 vs. 38
Child maltreatment by age 17	n/a	n/a	7 vs. 14
Arrested by age 19	31 vs. 51	ns	17 vs. 25
Highest grade completed by age 21/27 (mean)	11.9 vs. 11.0	12.2 vs. 11.6	11.3 vs. 10.9
High school completion by age 21/27 (%)	71 vs. 54	70 vs. 67 (graduation)	66 vs. 54
Attend college by age 21/27 (%)	33 vs. 28	36 vs. 14 (4-year)	24 vs. 18
Employed at age 21/27 (%)	71 vs. 59	70 vs. 58 (teen mothers)	n/a
Monthly earnings at age 27 ($)	1219 vs. 766	n/a	n/a

Note: For Perry, special education is for "educable mental impairment" (EMI) placement by age 15. Ages for educational attainment and employment are 27 for Perry, 21 for Abecedarian, and 22 for Chicago. ns = not significant; n/a = not available.

with good retention on most measures (see Ou, 2003; Reynolds, 1999; Reynolds et al., 2002).

Preschool Participation Enhances Children's Well-Being into Adulthood

The major long-term findings of the three studies that contribute to economic benefits are shown in Table 3.3 (also see Masse & Barnett, 2002; Reynolds et al., 2002; Schweinhart et al., 1993). The group differences reported are specific to preschool participation and are adjusted for initial differences between groups such as preprogram IQ, family SES, and other factors. The different studies adjusted for different variables that might have a bearing on outcomes. For example, the CPC study did not measure IQ but included participation in school-age services (which the PPP did not offer) and site location (it was the only program with multiple sites).

Although the magnitude of estimated effects varied, participation in all three programs was associated with significantly lower rates of special education services up to and including adolescence. The impact on special education was large, as preschool participants had rates of special education that were 40–60 percent lower than the comparison group. Similar reductions in grade retention were observed for the ABC and CPC programs. The Consortium for Longitudinal Studies (1983) showed similar results for 12 programs.

Participation in each program also was linked to significantly higher rates of high school completion up to age 27 as well as more years of education. Preschool participation was associated with about a half- to full-year increase in educational attainment. Program participants also had higher rates of postsecondary and college attendance, with ABC showing large differences in attendance at four-year colleges.

On employment and earnings, only PPP reported significant group differences, but this may reflect the fact that the sample was older at follow-up (27 years versus 21 for the ABC and 22 for CPC). For ABC, differences in employment were largest for teen mothers of program participants. Employment and earnings data are not currently available for CPC.

Finally, both PPP and CPC demonstrated significant program effects on crime. Participation in PPP was associated with a 40 percent decrease in arrests by age 19. CPC graduates had a 33 percent reduction in juvenile petitions by age 18. Only PPP has collected data on adult crime, and findings are consistent with those for earlier ages. The lack of crime prevention benefits in ABC may be due to the low base rates of crime in Chapel Hill (Clarke & Campbell, 1998) and/or to the relative absence of family services in the program. Overall, these findings show that the programs led to measurable enhancements in children's general social competence over the first two decades of life.

Not shown here are the substantial effects on cognitive skills at the time of kindergarten entry and on school achievement through the elementary grades. CPC participation also was associated with higher levels of parent involvement in school.

Summary of Results of Cost-Benefit Analyses

As shown in Table 3.4, all three programs had substantial economic returns through government savings in education, justice system, and health expenditures and in increased economic well-being. The values in Table 3.4 are the average economic return per program participant,

TABLE 3.4. *Summary of Costs and Benefits per Participant in 2002 Dollars for Three Preschool Programs*

Costs and Benefits	Perry Preschool	Child-Parent Centers	Abecedarian Project
Program costs ($)			
Average program participant	15,844	7,384	35,864
For one year of participation	9,759	4,856	13,900
Program benefits ($)			
Total benefits	138,486	74,981	135,546
Net benefits (benefits-costs)	122,642	67,595	99,682
Total benefit per dollar invested	8.74	10.15	3.78
Public benefit per dollar invested (benefit-cost ratio)	7.16	6.87	2.69

Note: Costs are program expenditures and do not include estimated costs for comparison-group experiences. For comparability to Abecedarian (Masse & Barnett, 2002), values reported in Perry (Barnett, 1996; Schweinhart et al., 1993) and CPC (Reynolds et al., 2002) were converted to 2002 dollars using the consumer price index. Ages of study participants for economic analyses were 27, 21, and 22, respectively. High/Scope and CPC programs were half-day; Abecedarian Program was full-day. Doubling the costs of High/Scope and CPC would provide a good approximation for full-day equivalents while one-half of the costs of Abecedarian would provide a half-day equivalent. The Abecedarian cost is the marginal program cost, which is the actual program cost minus the cost of in- and out-of-home child care for the comparison group. The actual cost per participant was $67,225. Based on the actual costs, total and public benefits of Abecedarian Project per dollar invested are $2.02 and $1.44, respectively. Perry and Chicago program costs are actual costs.

expressed in 2002 dollars, as reported in the CBAs. Of course, the assumptions underlying each CBA are not identical (see Barnett, 1996; Masse & Barnett, 2002; Reynolds et al., 2002; Schweinhart et al., 1993).[1]

Although the costs of the programs are significantly different from each other, the economic returns of each program far exceeded the initial

[1] The procedure for estimating costs and benefits of preschool participation in the studies was as follows: (a) program costs and benefits are calculated in dollar terms; (b) the dollar values are converted to 2002 dollars to adjust for inflation; (c) the present values of future costs and benefits are computed in 2002 dollars and evaluated at the starting age of program enrollment using an annual discount rate of 3 percent; and (d) the present value of program costs is subtracted from the present value of total program benefits to obtain the net present value of the program. Because it is common to estimate future benefits for lifetime earnings, reductions in crime, and other health-comprising behaviors from observed predictors of these outcomes, future benefits in these domains were projected throughout adulthood (Barnett, 1996; Karoly et al., 1998). The annual discount rate used to take into account that future benefits are worth less than current benefits was 3 percent, which is recommended by the U.S. Public Health Service (Lipscomb, Weinstein, & Torrence, 1996) and the U.S. General Accounting Office (1992).

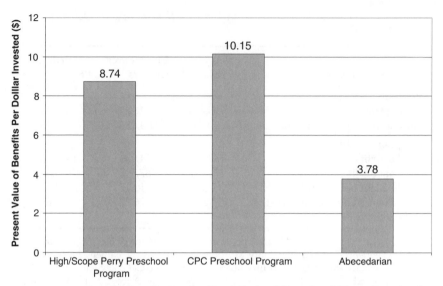

FIGURE 3.1. Benefit-Cost Ratios for Total Societal Benefit of Three Preschool Programs (in 2002 dollars)

investment. The total economic benefits per participant, both measured and projected over the life course, ranged from nearly $75,000 to more than $138,000. After subtracting the cost of each program, the net economic benefit per participant ranged from more than $67,000 to more than $122,000. The benefit for ABC is especially salient given its relatively high cost. Despite the price of full-day, year-round care for five years, the program returned nearly $100,000 per participant.

Figure 3.1 shows the economic benefits as a ratio of program costs. These ratios can be interpreted as the economic return per dollar invested, which is an indication of program efficiency. Benefit-to-cost ratios index the return on investment, whereby $2 savings per dollar invested would be a 100 percent return. All three programs showed a large return on investment, ranging from a total societal benefit of almost $4 to more than $10 per dollar invested. These are equivalent to a 278 to 915 percent return on the dollar. The CPC program showed the highest benefit-cost ratio, reflecting its relatively lower costs. Expenses were lower primarily because of a higher child-to-staff ratio (8.5 to 1 versus less than 6 to 1 for Perry and Abecedarian). That a routinely implemented school-based program demonstrates such returns holds promise for public school early education models. In terms of public benefits

TABLE 3.5. *Itemized Benefits per Participant in 2002 Dollars for Three Preschool Programs*

Costs and Benefits	Preschool Perry	Child-Parent Centers	Abecedarian Project
Child care	946	1,829	
K–12 education savings	8,812	5,377	8,836
Child welfare savings	–	850	–
Adult education savings	363	–	–
College	−1,113	−615	−8,128
Participant earnings	38,892	30,638	43,253
Smoking/health	–	–	17,781
Crime savings	90,246	36,902	–
Welfare savings	340	–	196
Maternal earnings, 26–60	–	–	73,608

Note: See the CBA reports of each program for the estimation procedures. The negative benefits of college attendance reflect the fact that taxpayers fund two-thirds of the cost of college. This cost only slightly offsets the earnings increases to participants as well as the increased tax revenues. Earnings are estimates of total compensation before taxes.

alone (i.e., government and crime victim savings), benefit-cost ratios for the three programs ranged from $2.69 to $7.16 per dollar invested.

As shown in Table 3.5, there were two main sources of economic benefits. One was increased earnings capacity over the life course, primarily by program graduates. Earnings estimates were directly measured in PPP and projected by group differences in educational attainment in CPC and ABC. The largest source of economic returns in ABC was increased maternal earnings capacity. The assumption is that, as a result of children being in full-time care, parents were able or motivated to seek employment.

The second major benefit category was crime savings associated with lower justice system expenditures and averted costs to crime victims. This category was the largest economic benefit by far for PPP and was also large for CPC. For both programs, victim costs included both averted tangible (e.g., hospitalization) and intangible (e.g., pain and suffering) expenditures.[2] ABC reported no group differences in juvenile

---

[2] The main findings in Reynolds et al. (2002) did not include intangible crime victim savings (e.g., pain and suffering, risk of death), but it was estimated as three times the amount of tangible savings. In 2002 dollars, intangible crime savings per participant was $22,270. Intangible crime victim savings per participant in the Perry preschool program was $55,585 in 2002 dollars.

TABLE 3.6. *Economic Costs and Benefits for Alternative Investments in Children and Youth in 2002 dollars*

Program and Source	Cost Per Participant ($)	Estimated Benefits ($)	Benefit-Cost Ratio
Women, Infants, and Children (WIC, Avruch & Cackley, 1995)	958	2,941	3.07
Prenatal/Early Infancy Project (Karoly et al., 1998)	6,975	35,288	5.10
Tennessee STAR class size reduction in K–3 (Krueger, 2003)	8,454	23,913	2.83
Child-Parent Center school-age program (Reynolds et al., 2002)	3,290	5,457	1.66
Grade retention (Temple et al., 2003)	7,959	−26,434	−3.32
Job Corps (Long et al., 1981)	15,141	19,958	1.32

Note: Values were converted to 2002 dollars using the consumer price index. Costs for WIC are for two years of services. In the other programs, costs are for the average length of participation.

or adult crime. Finally, all three programs were associated with K–12 education benefits, primarily through savings in special education placement.

In summary, the CBA findings show the high returns of investments in preschool education despite the differences in timing, duration, geography, time period, and content of the three programs. This consistent pattern of results strengthens the generalizability of findings to contemporary programs and contexts.

ECONOMIC RETURNS OF OTHER PROGRAMS FOR CHILDREN AND YOUTH

There is no shortage of policies and programs for investing in children and youth. In this section we review the evidence from several types of interventions and policies that have accumulated enough evidence to estimate economic benefits relative to costs. These include other early interventions, class size reductions, grade retention, and youth job training. A summary of costs and benefits is provided in Table 3.6.

The purpose of our comparisons among programs is not to identify "winners" and "losers" but to gauge the true value of investments in preschool and other programs by viewing them as a spectrum of benefits that are possible during childhood. As Heckman (2000, p. 50) noted, "in evaluating a human capital investment strategy, it is crucial to consider the entire policy portfolio of interventions together – training programs, school-based policies, school reform, and early interventions – rather than focusing on one type of policy in isolation from the others."

Prenatal and Early Infancy Programs

Since 1972 the Special Supplemental Nutrition Program for Women, Infants, and Children (WIC) has provided nutrition education, referrals to social services, and a variety of food supplements to low-income families to promote healthy growth and development from the prenatal period to preschool age. A meta-analysis of 15 cross-state studies by Avruch and Cackley (1995) found that WIC participation was associated with a 25 percent reduction in the rate of low-birth-weight births, which significantly reduced hospital costs during the first year of life. The economic return in savings to Medicaid and other payers was $3.07 per dollar invested in the program.

The Prenatal/Early Infancy Project (Olds et al., 1997) is an intensive nurse home visitation program for young mothers having their first child. For the high-risk sample, Karoly et al. (1998) found that participation from the prenatal period until the child's second birthday had long-term benefits. Participation was associated with lower rates of criminal behavior for both mothers and target children, lower rates of substantiated child maltreatment, higher earnings capacity for the mothers, and increased tax revenues projected into adulthood. The estimated economic return was $5.10 for every dollar invested.

Class Size Reductions in the Early Elementary Grades

Reducing class sizes, primarily in the early grades, is a policy that has been implemented or is being considered in many states. While some proposals are for class-size reductions in schools that draw a high proportion of students from low-income families, other proposals are for all students. Consequently, there are interesting parallels between this policy and discussions about universal access to preschool. Many of the arguments about small class sizes are based on evidence from the large-scale randomized experiment called Tennessee STAR (e.g., Krueger, 2003; Mosteller, 1995), which reduced class sizes from 22 to 15 in kindergarten through third grade. Given the high costs of reducing class sizes, there is a debate about whether significant benefits exist to make this policy a cost-effective option. Krueger (1999, 2003) presents evidence in support of reduced class sizes, reporting an economic return of $2.83 per dollar invested. The source of this benefit is an increase in test scores, which is associated with a projected increase in adult earnings.[3] Other economists, including Hanushek (1999) and Peltzman (1997), are less convinced that benefits outweigh the costs by a meaningful amount.

Additional evidence on small class sizes comes from the school-age program of the Child-Parent Centers, where class sizes were reduced from 35 to 1 to 25 to 2 (teacher and aide) during grades 1 to 3. The school-age program also included instructional resources to promote reading and math achievement and family support activities. Controlling for preschool participation and child and family attributes, school-age participation was independently associated with significantly higher levels of reading achievement, and with lower rates of grade retention and special education placement. The economic return for two years of school-age intervention was $1.66 per dollar invested (Reynolds et al., 2002). While this return is much lower than that of the CPC preschool program, it is within the range of that found for Tennessee STAR.

---

[3] In his analysis of Tennessee STAR, Krueger (2003) finds that students with an average of 2.3 years of small class sizes in years K–3 were shown to have a 0.2 standard deviation increase in test scores, and Krueger assumes that this increase in test scores is associated with a 1.6 percent increase in earnings in adulthood. The effect of small class sizes on adult earnings is estimated by using data on adult earnings in 1998 from the March 1999 Current Population Survey. Evaluated at kindergarten entry, the present value of this benefit from small class sizes is $23,913 in 2002 dollars (see p. F56). Krueger presents results for various discount rates and various assumptions about annual productivity growth. We choose his estimates for a discount rate of 3 percent. To best match the assumptions made in the CBA of the Chicago Child-Parent Centers, we choose his benefit calculations that assume an annual productivity growth rate of 1 percent.

To calculate the costs of increased class sizes, Krueger assumes that a reduction in class sizes from 22 to 15 students requires a 7/15 or 47 percent increase in school spending. The annual cost of a year of schooling per student was $7,502 in 1998, and 47 percent of that amount is $3,501. After assuming that these expenditures occur in the first 2.3 years of schooling, the present value of this increase in schooling costs is found to be $7,660 in 1998 dollars. In 2002 dollars, the present value of the per pupil cost of increased class sizes for 2.3 years is $8,454. The present value of per pupil costs of a full four years of reduced class sizes would be $14,794 in 2002 dollars. In the income calculations, adult earnings also grow over time by what appears to be an additional 1 percent annually (according to his figure 3.2 on p. F57) because of his projections of the age-earnings profile, which is generally thought to reflect experience-related earnings growth. Hence adult earnings in his study are assumed to grow by an approximately 2 percent real growth rate each year. In the Chicago study, the adult earnings also are assumed to grow by 2 percent a year.

The Educational Policy of Grade Retention

Policies that require underachieving elementary students to repeat a grade have become a popular approach in school reform. Unfortunately, most studies show that grade retention is associated with lower achievement in later grades, and an increased probability of school dropout (Heubert & Hauser, 1999). To determine the economic costs and benefits of grade retention, we multiplied the difference in high school completion rates for students ever retained or not retained in the Chicago Longitudinal Study by the projected difference in lifetime earnings per participant between high school graduates and dropouts, using estimates by the U.S. Census Bureau. The estimated economic return of grade retention was minus $3.32 for every dollar invested. Notably, our estimates of the negative link between grade retention and school completion are smaller than in other studies (see Alexander, Entwisle, & Dauber, 2003; Temple, Reynolds, & Ou, 2003).[4]

Youth Job Training

The federally funded Job Corps is an established training program for at-risk youth, most of whom have dropped out of school. Participants receive up to seven months of vocational training and education in a residential setting. Job Corps graduates typically earn more than their comparison group counterparts and may have lower rates of crime (Heckman, 2000). The estimated economic return is $1.32 per dollar invested (Long, Maller, & Thorton, 1981). Most other job training programs for young people and adult education programs show benefits relative to costs of less than $1 per dollar invested (see Heckman, 2000; Karoly, 2001).

In summary, the economic benefits of preschool education far surpass those of the other programs reviewed. Only WIC and the Prenatal/Early Infancy Project showed economic returns that were sizable relative to costs. Benefits of the Tennessee STAR class size experiment were slightly lower. This does not mean the programs have little value or do not

---

[4] In 2002 dollars, discounted at 3 percent and assuming 2 percent annual increases in productivity, high school completers would be expected to earn $202,176 more than high school dropouts by age 65. The per-participant cost of retention was $7,959, one additional year of schooling. The large negative return is exclusive of lost tax revenues due to the projected lost income and factors in the optimistic assumption that students who are retained will be less likely to receive special education services.

deliver other benefits. However, programs offered before kindergarten appear to have the highest economic returns.

Evidence from Child Care and State-Run Preschools

The consistent findings of the economic analyses of the Perry, Chicago, and Abecedarian programs, despite their major differences in social context and location, time period, and content, form strong support for policies to expand preschool access. Nevertheless, the participants of the three programs were almost exclusively low-income, African American children. While there is no comparable longitudinal evidence from studies of middle-income families or from more ethnically diverse groups, research on the short-term effects of high-quality child care has employed more heterogeneous samples. Because the Perry, Chicago, and Abecedarian programs achieved their long-term effects primarily or at least initially by enhancing children's cognitive and school readiness skills, we compared the school readiness findings from the three intensive preschool programs with those of two major studies of child care and a research synthesis of state-run preschools.

The NICHD Study of Early Child Care (Vandell & Pierce, 2003) included an original sample of 1,364 children from primarily middle-income families in nine states. The Cost, Quality, and Child Outcomes study (Peisner-Feinberg, 1999) included 579 children in four states. The synthesis of state-funded prekindergartens (Gilliam & Zigler, 2001) included impact estimates on school readiness in preschool and kindergarten up to 1998 in six states and the District of Columbia. Although the programs primarily served children at risk, participants were more heterogeneous on family income and race and ethnicity than those in the intensive preschool programs.

As can be seen in Table 3.7, the research reports cited show that both high-quality child care and preschool programs offered routinely in many states provide educationally meaningful effects on school readiness in the language-cognitive domain. They are smaller in size but within the range of effects found for the intensive preschool programs for low-income children reported previously. Overall, effect sizes for child care and state-run preschools were approximately 30–40 percent lower than those of PPP, ABC, and CPC. These differences may be due to the possibilities that the children faced fewer risks, were already close to developmental norms so had less progress to make, or any number of program or participant variables. Nevertheless, these programs did

TABLE 3.7. *Effect Sizes for Alternative Early Education Programs on School Readiness (values are standard deviation units)*

Program/Study	Urbanicity, N of Sites	SES Attributes	Language-Cognitive Skills by Age 5
Child care and state-funded preschool			
High-quality child care (Vandell & Pierce, 2003)	Mixed, 9 states	Middle income	.43
High-quality child care (Peisner-Feinberg et al., 2003)	Mixed, 4 states	Mixed income	.40
State Preschools (Gilliam & Zigler, 2001)	Mixed, 7 states and cities	Lower income	.36
Intensive preschools			
High/Scope Perry Preschool (Schweinhart et al., 1993)	Urban, 1 site	Low income	.72
Abecedarian Project (Campbell & Ramey, 1995)	Rural, 1 site	Low income	.75
Child-Parent Centers (Reynolds, 2000)	Inner city, 20 sites	Low income	.61
Consortium for Longitudinal Studies (1983)	Mixed, 13 sites	Low income	.50

Note: Language-cognitive skills were measured by one of the following: IQ tests (Perry, Abecedarian, and Consortium), the Bracken school readiness composite (Vandell & Pierce), receptive language (Peisner-Feinberg et al.), and measures of cognitive, language, or literacy development or early academic achievement. Effect sizes were measured at age 3 in Vandell & Pierce, preschool or kindergarten for Peisner-Feinberg et al., and state preschools, the beginning of kindergarten for Chicago, and the end of preschool for Perry, Abecedarian, and Consortium. Both Vandell & Pierce and Peisner-Feinberg et al. employed adjusted group differences for children in high-quality and low-quality care. The state study used the measures in either preschool or kindergarten that showed the greatest difference between groups. If effect sizes for both preschool and kindergarten were reported, the average effect size was used.

demonstrate significant impacts on school readiness, adding to the evidence in support of universal access to preschool.

Of course, there are many other benefits of expanding access to early education that cannot be easily measured in effect sizes and economic returns. For example, a universal access system would create equal opportunity to attend preschool. Today, that opportunity depends on where a family happens to live or on ability to pay. There would be increased coordination and integration of services, reducing the duplication and overlap of competing efforts. Moreover, this system would increase the demand for qualified teachers and trained staff, adding much-needed professionalism to the early childhood field.

PATHS OF INFLUENCE THAT PROMOTE LONG-TERM OUTCOMES

To promote generalization of findings from previous research to contemporary state and local programs, better understanding of the processes that contribute to learning gains is needed. Identifying the processes through which early education impacts long-term educational and social outcomes can inform the design of all types of early childhood programs, for children across the socioeconomic spectrum.

Figure 3.2 shows five hypotheses by which early childhood programs can affect long-term outcomes that lead to significant economic returns. In the cognitive advantage hypothesis, for example, the long-term effects of intervention are accounted for primarily by the initial improvement in children's cognitive development, which enables them to do better when they start school and provides cumulative advantages over time. In the family support hypothesis, enduring intervention effects are due to changes at home. Equivalent processes occur for the social adjustment, motivational advantage, and school support hypotheses. Empirical support for the cognitive advantage, family support, and school support hypotheses in explaining the long-term effects of intervention has been demonstrated (Campbell, Pungello, Miller-Johnson, Burchinal, & Ramey, 2001; Reynolds, 2000; Schweinhart et al., 1993), and support for the motivational and social adjustment hypothesis is growing (Heckman, 2000; Reynolds, Ou, and Topitzes, 2003).

To the extent that high-quality child care, state-funded preschools, and federal early intervention programs impact any or all of these five intervention hypotheses, long-term effects on educational attainment and social behavior are more likely to occur. For instance, based on the cognitive advantage hypothesis of early education, findings that these programs resulted in cognitive gains parallel to those from the intensive preschool programs that served children from very low-income families strongly indicate the possibility of persistent effects. This evidence bodes well for the effectiveness of universal access programs provided they are good in quality. Of course, knowledge about the effects of preschool participation for children with low levels of risk is limited

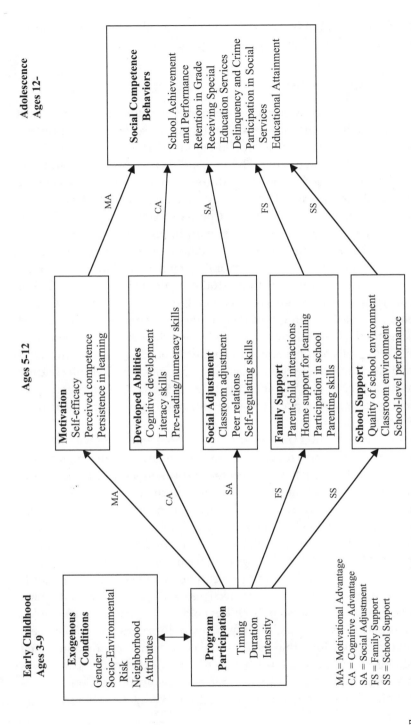

Early Childhood
Ages 3-9

Ages 5-12

Adolescence
Ages 12-

Social Competence Behaviors

School Achievement
and Performance
Retention in Grade
Receiving Special
Education Services
Delinquency and Crime
Participation in Social
Services
Educational Attainment

Motivation
Self-efficacy
Perceived competence
Persistence in learning

Developed Abilities
Cognitive development
Literacy skills
Pre-reading/numeracy skills

Social Adjustment
Classroom adjustment
Peer relations
Self-regulating skills

Family Support
Parent-child interactions
Home support for learning
Participation in school
Parenting skills

School Support
Quality of school environment
Classroom environment
School-level performance

Exogenous Conditions
Gender
Socio-Environmental
Risk
Neighborhood
Attributes

Program Participation
Timing
Duration
Intensity

MA= Motivational Advantage
CA = Cognitive Advantage
SA = Social Adjustment
FS = Family Support
SS = School Support

FIGURE 3.2.   Paths from Early Childhood Education to Social Competence (see Chapter 5), but our review of the best available information from child care and state-run programs suggests some likely benefits.

POLICY IMPLICATIONS

Our review has considered the economic benefits of investments in preschool education that extend throughout the school years into adulthood. Findings from extensive longitudinal studies of the Chicago Child-Parent Centers, the High/Scope Perry Preschool, and the Abecedarian Project show that the economic returns to society of preschool can far exceed costs. They range from about $4 to $10 per dollar invested, a return of 300 to 900 percent on investment. The demonstrated benefits were driven primarily by improved social competence, which led to lower rates of remedial education and crime and greater educational attainment and economic well-being. While the generalizability of the findings of these studies is limited by the low SES of participants, two strengths are evident. First, substantial benefits were found for all three programs despite their differences in content and focus, timing and duration, geography, and decade of implementation (1960s to 1980s and beyond). Second, evidence from recent studies of child care and state-funded preschool programs, which enroll children from more economically and ethnically diverse populations, shows a similar pattern of impacts on school readiness, the major precursor of long-term effects.

We also compared the benefits of preschool education with those of other social programs for children and youth. Investments in preschool had substantially higher net benefits and benefit-cost ratios than several education, job training, and health service interventions. The estimated economic return of grade retention policy was actually negative. It was relatively modest for youth job training and class size reductions and relatively high for WIC and the Prenatal/Early Infancy Project. Most other social programs, from child welfare treatment to delinquency and child abuse prevention, have even weaker records of effectiveness, let alone cost-effectiveness (Durlak, 1997; Guterman, 1999; MacLeod & Nelson, 2000; Reynolds & Robertson, 2003; Zigler, Taussig, & Black, 1992). Certainly, many of these programs fill a need, but preventive investments in early education have demonstrated the largest and most enduring benefits. Yet of the total expenditures on social programs, less than 1 percent goes to prevention services (National Science and Technology Council, 1997). Our review strongly indicates that early education programs deserve a greater share of public investments.

Will the economic benefits of preschool education for children from wealthier homes be equivalent to those for children from low-income families? Based on the findings reviewed here, the answer is no; expected benefits could be lower. Current research does indicate, however, that programs of good quality can enhance children's school readiness and early achievement patterns regardless of socioeconomic circumstances. To the extent that participation in high-quality child care and state-run preschool programs impacts any or all five hypotheses of how early education improves competence, enduring effects can be expected. These effects could translate into significant economic returns. Thus, even with a return of one-half of that found for Perry, Abecedarian, and Child-Parent Centers, scaled-up programs would be well worth the investment and could provide a greater return than most other social programs.

The findings for the Child-Parent Centers add significantly to the literature by showing that larger-scale public programs run by schools can produce the same pattern of benefits as model programs. Because the CPC study is the first cost-benefit analysis of a public preschool program, the findings are indicative of what is possible from high-quality programs that are not carefully controlled models, including universal access programs.

GUIDING PRINCIPLES FOR PRESCHOOL INVESTMENTS

Findings reviewed in this chapter indicate that greater investments in high-quality preschool programs are warranted. Today, nearly two in five children do not enroll in center-based preschool programs, and the quality of services that many receive is not high. In the rush to expand, critical program elements can be left out, reducing potential benefits. Research on the Child-Parent Centers, Perry Preschool, Abecedarian Project, and other interventions reveals five major principles that can enhance the effectiveness of preschool education and increase the chances of long-term economic benefits.

The first principle is that a coordinated system of early education must be in place at least by age three and continue through the early school grades. Program implementation within a single administrative system can promote stability in children's learning environments and ensure smooth transitions between levels of schooling so the child isn't "starting all over" each year. The three major programs we reviewed were either housed in elementary schools or provided continuity of services between preschool and formal schooling. This is a "first decade" strategy for promoting children's learning (Reynolds, Wang, & Walberg, 2003). Today, most preschool programs are not integrated within public schools and children usually change schools more than once by the early grades. Further, community programs that provide coordinated or "wrap-around" services may be more effective under a centralized leadership structure rather than under a case-management framework. To promote developmental continuity, schools could take a leadership role in partnership with community agencies. This is certainly doable. The CPC program, for example, is an established program in the third largest school system in the nation. Findings from the CPC give a good indication of the effects that could be possible in public schools, the largest administrative system of any universal access program. The School of the 21st Century, which includes schools that provide family and early childhood services from birth to age 12, is a more comprehensive exemplar of this approach (see Chapter 10).

Several recommendations are apparent from this principle of system coordination. First, the share of Title I funds that go to preschool should be increased. In 2000 only 5 percent of $10 billion allocated to schools under Title I went to preschool programs (U.S. General Accounting Office, 2000). Second, more Head Start grants should be awarded to public schools. Only about one-third of Head Start grantees are schools, despite the obvious benefits of communication and program coordination. Third, more full-day programs in both preschool and kindergarten are needed. Research in the CPC and Abecedarian programs indicates that as program length increases, so does children's school performance.

A second major principle of effective preschool education is that the teaching staff should be trained and compensated well. Teachers should have bachelor's degrees, certification in early childhood, and ongoing professional training. Competitive salaries are needed to attract and retain teachers with such qualifications. These characteristics are much more likely under a public school model of universal access, notwithstanding the need for established partnerships with community child care agencies. It is no coincidence that the three major programs reviewed in the chapter followed this principle. Being located in public schools, the Perry and CPC programs were implemented by credentialed teachers. They were paid on the public school salary scale, and Perry teachers received a 10 percent bonus for working in the program. In the Abecedarian program, teachers were compensated at a level that was highly competitive with public schools. Staff turnover was relatively low in all three programs. In most other early education programs, from child care to Head Start, staff do not have this level of education, training, and compensation, and turnover is often significantly higher.

Third, educational content should be responsive to all of children's learning needs, but special emphasis should be given to cognitive and school readiness skills through a structured but diverse set of learning activities. All three cost-effective programs reviewed here had a strong emphasis on the development of cognitive and language skills necessary to do well in school. Child-to-staff ratios of less than 9 to 1 in preschool certainly helped as well. The specific curriculum appeared to be less important, because the programs employed quite different approaches. Extrapolating these findings, early childhood programs are more likely to have enduring effects if they provide services that are intensive and focused on educational and social skills (Heckman, 2000; Zigler & Berman, 1983).

A fourth principle for effective preschool education is that comprehensive family services should be provided to impact the child's total rearing environment. As child development programs, preschool services must be tailored to family circumstances and thus promote opportunities for positive learning experiences in school and at home (Zigler & Styfco, 1993). Each of the cost-effective preschool programs discussed in this chapter provided family services. Abecedarian provided medical and nutritional services. The Perry Preschool had weekly home visits by teachers. In the CPC program, parent involvement is more intensive. Each center has a parent resource room run by a certified teacher and provides school-community outreach. Parents' own education and personal development are important program goals.

Finally, greater commitment to ongoing evaluations of program effectiveness and cost-effectiveness is needed. Cost-benefit analyses are rarely conducted, which limits full consideration of alternative programs. Paramount in conducting cost-benefit analyses is the availability of longitudinal data. Yet many programs for children and youth are not evaluated at all, or scores are collected at the beginning and end of the program to assess the instant return rather than potentially lasting impacts of participation. In addition, more studies are needed that address the differential effects of participation across a range of child, family, and program attributes. The identification of the mediators of the effects of program participation and the environmental conditions necessary to promote lasting effects also is a high priority. To carry out these activities, research funding must be increased. Of the approximately $550–600 billion spent on K–16 education and social programs for children and youth each year, only one-third of 1 percent goes to research and development (National Science and Technology Council, 1997). Research spending on investments in children should approximate the 2 to 3 percent of total expenditures that go to biotechnology, energy, and transportation.

CONCLUSION

The major challenge for the future is how the principles derived from the knowledge base on early education can be used to best meet the needs of children and families. Unlike a decade ago, scientific support for the benefits of a wide variety of programs, both pilot and large-scale, is strong. Clear guidelines have emerged as to what makes early childhood programs effective. They should be well organized with attention to transitions, sufficiently focused on promoting school readiness, have the resources necessary to employ and retain well-trained staff, and provide comprehensive services. The tension between targeting limited resources to the most disadvantaged children and providing a coherent system for all will continue, but attention to these empirically supported principles will help achieve a better balance between the two goals. As investments increase for expanding programs for young children, understanding their effects and how to improve quality will be paramount. As reviewed in this chapter, however, the demonstrated benefits of these investments have never been clearer.

References

Alexander, K. L., Entwisle, D. R., & Dauber, S. L. (2003). *On the success of failure: A reassessment of the effects of retention in the primary grades* (2nd ed.). Cambridge: Cambridge University Press.

Avruch, S., & Cackley, A. P. (1995). Savings achieved by giving WIC benefits to women prenatally. *Public Health Reports, 110,* 27–34.

Barnett, W. S. (1995). Long-term effects of early childhood programs on cognitive and school outcomes. *The Future of Children, 5*(3), 25–50.

Barnett, W. S. (1996). *Lives in the balance: Age 27 benefit-cost analysis of the High/Scope Perry Preschool Program.* Ypsilanti, MI: High/Scope Press.

Berreuta-Clement, J. R., Schweinhart, L., Barnett, W. S., Epstein, A., & Weikart, D. (1984). *Changed lives: The effects of the Perry Preschool Program on youths through age 19.* Ypsilanti, MI: High/Scope Educational Research Foundation.

Campbell, F. A., Pungello, E. P., Miller-Johnson, S., Burchinal, M., & Ramey, C. T. (2001). The development of cognitive and academic abilities: Growth curves from an early childhood educational experiment. *Developmental Psychology, 37*, 231–242.

Campbell, F. A., & Ramey, C. T. (1995). Cognitive and school outcomes for high risk African-American students at middle adolescence: Positive effects of early intervention. *American Educational Research Journal, 32*, 743–772.

Carroll, Ochshorn, Kagan, S., & Fuller, B. (2003). Effective investments in early care and education: What can we learn from research? *NCSL Policy Brief I.* Denver: National Conference of State Legislators.

Chicago Longitudinal Study. (1999). *Chicago Longitudinal Study: User's guide* (Vol. 6). Madison: Waisman Center, University of Wisconsin.

Clarke, S. H., & Campbell, F. A. (1998). Does intervention early prevent crime later? *Early Childhood Research Quarterly, 13*, 319–343.

Cohen, M. A. (1998). The monetary value of saving a high-risk youth. *Journal of Quantitative Criminology, 14*, 5–33.

Committee for Economic Development. (2002). *Preschool for all: Investing in a productive and just society.* New York: Author.

Consortium for Longitudinal Studies. (1983). *As the twig is bent . . . lasting effects of preschool programs.* Hillsdale, NJ: Erlbaum.

Durlak, J. A. (1997). *Successful prevention programs for children and adolescents.* New York: Plenum.

Gilliam, W. S., & Zigler, E. F. (2001). A critical meta-analysis of all impact evaluations of all state-funded preschool from 1977 to 1998: Implications for policy, service delivery, and program evaluation. *Early Childhood Research Quarterly, 15*, 441–473.

Governor's Task Force on Universal Access to Preschool. (2002). *Ready set grow: Illinois preschool.* Springfield, IL: Author.

Guterman, N. B. (1999). Enrollment strategies in early home visitation to prevent child physical abuse and neglect and the "universal versus targeted" debate: A meta-analysis of population-based and screening-based programs. *Child Abuse & Neglect, 23*, 863–890.

Hanushek, E. (1999). Some findings from an independent investigation of the Tennessee STAR experiment and from other investigations of class size effects. *Educational Evaluation and Policy Analysis, 21*, 143–163.

Haveman, R., & Wolfe, B. (1984). Schooling and well-being: The role of nonmarket effects. *Journal of Human Resources, 19*, 377–407.

Heckman, J. (2000). Policies to foster human capital. *Research in Economics, 54*, 3–56.

Heubert, J. P., & Hauser, R. M. (Eds.). (1999). *High stakes: Testing for tracking, promotion, and graduation.* Washington, DC: National Academy Press.

Karoly, L. A. (2002). Reducing poverty through human capital investments. In S. H. Danziger & R. H. Haveman (Eds.), *Understanding poverty.* Cambridge, MA: Harvard University Press.

Karoly, L. A., Greenwood, P. W., Everingham, S. S., et al. (1998). *Investing in our children: What we know and don't know about the costs and benefits of early childhood interventions.* Santa Monica, CA: RAND.

Kruger, A. (1999). Experimental estimates of educational production functions. *Quarterly Journal of Economics, 114*, 497–532.

Kruger, A. (2003). Economic considerations and class size. *Economic Journal, 113*, F34–F63.

Levin, H. M., & McEwan, P. J. (2001). *Cost-effectiveness analysis: Methods and applications* (2nd ed). Thousand Oaks, CA: Sage.

Lipscomb, J., Weinstein, M. C., & Torrance, G. W. (1996). Time preference. In M. R. Gold, L. B. Russell, J. E. Siegel, & M. C. Weinstein (Eds.), *Cost-effectiveness in health and medicine* (pp. 214–246). New York: Oxford University Press.

Long, D., Maller, C., & Thorton, C. (1981). Evaluating the benefits and costs of the Job Corps. *Journal of Policy Analysis and Management, 81*, 55–76.

MacLeod, J., & Nelson, G. (2000). Programs for the promotion of family wellness and the prevention of child maltreatment: A meta-analytic review. *Child Abuse & Neglect, 24*, 1127–1149.

Masse, L. N., & Barnett, W. S. (2002). *A benefit-cost analysis of the Abecedarian early childhood intervention*. New Brunswick, NJ: National Institute for Early Education Research.

Mosteller, F. (1995). The Tennessee study of class size in the early school grades. *The Future of Children, 5*, 113–27.

National Science and Technology Council. (1997, April). *Investing in our future: A national research initiative for America's children for the 21st century*. Washington, DC: Executive Office of the President, Office of Science and Technology Policy, Committee on Fundamental Science, and the Committee on Health, Safety, and Food.

Olds, D. L., Eckenrode, J., Henderson, C. R., et al. (1997). Long-term effects of home visitation on maternal life course and child abuse and neglect. Fifteen-year follow-up of a randomized trial. *Journal of the American Medical Association 278*, 637–643.

Oppenheim, J., & McGregor, T. (2003). *The economics of education: Public benefits of high-quality preschool education for low-income children*. Entergy Corporation, New Orleans.

Ou, S. (2003). *The effects of an early childhood intervention on educational attainment*. Unpublished doctoral dissertation, Madison, University of Wisconsin.

Peisner-Feinberg, E. S. (1999). *The children of the Cost, Quality, and Child Outcomes Study go to school: Technical report*. Chapel Hill: Frank Porter Graham Child Development Center, University of North Carolina.

Peltzman, S. (1997). Class size and earnings. *Journal of Economic Perspectives, 11*, 225–226.

Ramey, C. T., Campbell, F. A., & Blair, C. (1998). Enhancing the life course for high risk children: Results from the Abecedarian Project. In J. Crane (Ed.), *Social programs that work* (pp. 163–183). New York: Russell Sage.

Ramey, C. T., Campbell, F. A., Burchinal, M., Skinner, M. L., Gardner, D. M., & Ramey, S. L. (2000). Persistent effects of early intervention on high-risk children and their mothers. *Applied Developmental Science, 1*, 2–14.

Reynolds, A. J. (1999). Educational success in high-risk settings: Contributions of the Chicago Longitudinal Study. *Journal of School Psychology, 37*, 345–354.

Reynolds, A. J. (2000). *Success in early intervention: The Chicago Child-Parent Centers*. Lincoln: University of Nebraska Press.

Reynolds, A. J., Ou, S., & Topitzes, J. W. (2003). *Paths of effects of early intervention on educational attainment and juvenile arrest: A confirmatory analysis of the Chicago Child-Parent Centers*. University of Wisconsin, Madison. Unpublished manuscript.

Reynolds, A. J., & Robertson, D. L. (2003). School-based early intervention and later child maltreatment in the Chicago Longitudinal Study. *Child Development, 74,* 3–26.

Reynolds, A. J., Temple, J. A., Robertson, D. L., & Mann, E. A. (2001). Long-term effects of an early childhood intervention on educational achievement and juvenile arrest: A 15-year follow-up of low-income children in public schools. *Journal of the American Medical Association, 285,* 2339–2346.

Reynolds, A. J., Temple, J. A., Robertson, D. L., & Mann, E. A. (2002). Age 21 cost-benefit analysis of the Title I Chicago Child-Parent Centers. *Educational Evaluation and Policy Analysis, 24,* 267–303.

Reynolds, A. J., Wang, M. C., & Walberg, H. J. (Eds.). (2003). *Early childhood programs for a new century*. Washington, DC: CWLA Press.

Schweinhart, L. J., Barnes, H. V., & Weikart, D. P. (1993). *Significant benefits: The High-Scope Perry Preschool study through age 27*. Ypsilanti, MI: High/Scope Press.

Schweinhart, L. J., Montie, J., Xiang, Z., Barnett, W. S., Belfield, C. R., & Nores, M. (2005). *Lifetime effects: The High/Scope Perry Preschool study through age 40*. Monographs of the High/Scope Educational Research Foundation (No. 14). Ypsilanti, MI: High/Scope Press.

Scrivner, S., & Wolfe, B. (2003). *Universal preschool: Much to gain but who will pay?* Discussion paper. Madison: Institute for Research on Poverty, University of Wisconsin.

Sullivan, L. M. (1971). *Let us not underestimate the children*. Glenview, IL: Scott, Foreman.

Temple, J. A., Reynolds, A. J., & Ou. S. (2003). Grade retention and school dropout: Another look at the evidence. In H. J. Walberg, A. J. Reynolds, & M. C. Wang (Eds), *Can unlike students learn together?: Grade retention, tracking, and grouping* (pp. 35–69). Greenwich, CT: Information Age.

U.S. General Accounting Office. (1992). *Early intervention: Federal investments like WIC can produce savings. Report no. HRD-92-18*. Washington, DC: Author.

U.S. General Accounting Office. (2000). *Title I preschool education: More children served but gauging effect on school readiness unclear. Report no. HEHS-00-171*. Washington, DC: Author.

Vandell, D. L., & Pierce, K. M. (2003). Child care quality and children's success at school. In A. J. Reynolds, M. C. Wang, & H. Walberg (Eds.), *Early childhood programs for a new century* (pp. 115–139). Washington, DC: CWLA Press.

Weisbrod, B. A. (1965). Costs and benefits of preventing high school dropouts. In R. Dorfman (Ed.), *Measuring benefits of government investments* (pp. 117–149). Washington, DC: Brookings Institution.

White House. (2003, February). *Head Start policy book*. Washington, DC: Office of the President. http://www.whitehouse.gov/infocus/earlychildhood/hspolicybook/hs_policy_book.pdf. Accessed July 11, 2003.

Yoshikawa, H. (1994). Prevention as cumulative protection: Effects of early family support and education on chronic delinquency and its risks. *Psychological Bulletin, 115*, 27–54.

Zigler, E., & Berman, W. (1983). Discerning the future of early childhood intervention. *American Psychologist, 38*, 894–906.

Zigler, E., & Styfco S. J. (1993). *Head Start and beyond: A national plan for extended childhood intervention*. New Haven, CT: Yale University Press.

Zigler, E., Taussig, C., & Black, K. (1992). Early childhood intervention: A promising preventive for juvenile delinquency. *American Psychologist, 47*, 997–1006.

4

The Need for Universal Prekindergarten for Children in Poverty

With Marguerite Malakoff

Forty years of research have convinced scholars and policy makers that quality preschool experiences benefit children from impoverished environments and help prepare them for school entry (see reviews by Barnett, 1995; Brooks-Gunn, 2003; Frede, 1995; Haskins, 1989; National Research Council, 2000, 2001; Yoshikawa, 1995). Yet public preschool programs for disadvantaged children remain sparse and underfunded. Although the United States was among the first industrialized nations to offer 12 years of free public education to rich and poor alike, it still does not ensure that poor children receive the preschool experience necessary to get ready for school. Despite our democratic ideals, nonpoor children in the United States have greater access to quality preschool programs than those whose families have less money. Indeed, evidence indicates that the most at-risk children are the least likely to attend preschool (Hofferth, West, Henke, & Kaufman, 1994; West, Hausken, & Collins, 1993).

In 1965, as part of the Johnson administration's War on Poverty, the federal government created a nationwide, community-based preschool intervention to promote school readiness among economically disadvantaged children. Since its inception, Head Start has grown from a six-week summer school to an academic-year program that by now has served more than 22 million preschoolers and their families (U.S. Department of Health and Human Services, 2005). To be eligible for Head Start, children must live in homes that are below the federal poverty threshold ($18,244 for a family of four in 2002). Although the law does allow up to 10 percent of slots to be open to children from families with higher incomes, this is rarely possible. Due to lack of funding, the more

69

than 900,000 preschoolers Head Start serves annually are only about 50–60 percent of those eligible (Children Now, 2002). And although Head Start was designed to serve three- and four-year-olds, in 2002 71 percent of children attended for only a single year prior to kindergarten (Schumacher & Irish, 2003).

State-funded prekindergarten systems, operating in 40 states, serve more than 980,000 children annually. With the exception of Georgia and Oklahoma, which have implemented universal prekindergarten for all four-year-olds, most states limit their preschool enrollment to targeted groups of children deemed most in need of school readiness programming. Although there is wide variation among the states in who may be served and how many seats are available, in general public prekindergartens enroll only about half of their eligible populations (Gilliam & Ripple, 2004). The Department of Education also funds preschool in high-poverty school districts through Title I of the Elementary and Secondary Education Act (now called the No Child Left Behind Act). These programs are located in about 9 percent of America's poorest schools and serve only some 100,000 preschoolers annually (Clifford, Early, & Hills, 1999). Reliable estimates of the total number of preschoolers served across Head Start, state-funded prekindergartens, and Title I preschool are elusive because the blended funding that often occurs between these programs can result in double and triple counting of the same children. Therefore, a straight sum of these numbers would provide an overestimate of the number enrolled.

In comparison to America's targeted approach, many nations provide broad access to public preschool. Belgium, Italy, and France (mostly through the public *école maternelle* system) serve almost all three- and four-year-olds. In Spain, the Netherlands, England, and Luxembourg nearly all four-year-olds are provided prekindergarten, and more than 70 percent of all four-year-olds are served in Denmark, the Czech Republic, Germany, Austria, and Greece (Boocock, 2003; Merrow, 2002). By contrast, access to quality preschool in the United States is typically linked to socioeconomic status, geographic location, and the simple availability of openings, with no true national system that allows equal opportunity to attend.

Today, the need for universal access to high-quality preschool programs is all the more pressing. First, as more and more mothers have entered the work force, there are large numbers of preschoolers in out-of-home care that is simply not good enough to provide them with the early educational experiences they need to prepare for school. Second, there is now overwhelming evidence that high-quality early childhood programs have a significant positive impact on the lives of poor children. Given that we know the importance of early childhood experiences for lifelong achievement (see National Research Council, 2000), simple social equity demands that all children have access to preschool, not just those whose families can afford it.

Effect of Early Education on Poor Children's School Readiness and Long-Term Outcomes

Decades of research have shown that family income is associated with children's cognitive development, educational achievement, and social behavior from the earliest years through elementary school and beyond (Brooks-Gunn, 2003; Duncan & Brooks-Gunn, 1997, 2000; Lee & Burkman, 2002; Pagani, Boulerice, Vitaro, & Tremblay, 1999; Smith, Brooks-Gunn, & Klebanov, 1997). The adverse effects of poverty on children's development are apparent by 18 to 24 months of age, with the developmental gap between poor and nonpoor children increasing over time (McCall, 1979). By preschool age, children living in persistent poverty already show pronounced effects on their intelligence test scores and vocabulary (Brooks-Gunn, Klebanov, Liaw, & Spiker, 1993; Duncan, Brooks-Gunn, & Klebanov, 1994; Klebanov, Brooks-Gunn, McCarton, & McCormick, 1998), although the negative effects of inadequate rearing environments are not limited to children living below the poverty threshold (Brooks-Gunn, 2003). Childhood poverty is also associated with poor social development and with adverse outcomes that include low self-esteem, underachievement, and antisocial behavior (Huston, 1994; McLoyd, 1989; National Research Council, 2000; Ramey & Campbell, 1991; Yoshikawa, 1995). The unique importance of early childhood experiences is underscored by the finding that family income during the preschool and early childhood years, but not later years, is associated positively with rates of high school completion (Duncan, Brooks-Gunn, Yeung, & Smith, 1998).

Democratic and Republican policy makers alike have placed education and school readiness squarely on their agendas, and research findings clearly back up the political rhetoric: children who enter kindergarten without the requisite school skills are more likely to experience early school failure (Dauber, Alexander, & Entwisle, 1993; May & Kundert, 1997, Morrison, Griffith, & Alberts, 1997; National Research Council, 2000, 2001), which, in turn, is associated with lower educational achievement and higher delinquency rates (Reynolds, Temple, Robertson, & Mann, 2001). Although school readiness is not, alone, a "magic pill" that will ensure academic success, the research is clear that it plays a critical role in both short- and long-term educational outcomes (Brooks-Gunn, 2003; Gruendel, Oliveira, & Geballe, 2003; National Research Council, 2000, 2001).

Quality early childhood education programs are proven to positively impact the educational achievement of low-income children (Barnett, 1995; Brooks-Gunn, 2003; Haskins, 1989; Hertzman & Wiens, 1996; Miller, Shieh, & Lavagna, 2002; Peisner-Feinberg et al., 1999; Ramey et al., 2000; Schweinhart, Barnes, Weikart, Barnett, & Epstein, 1993). These programs also have been successful in providing broader services to improve children's nutrition and access to medical and dental care (Barnett & Brown, 2000; Fosburg, Goodrich, & Fox, 1984; Hale, Seitz, & Zigler, 1990; O'Brien, Connell, & Griffin, 2004). Good physical health is critical for school readiness (Zigler & Trickett, 1978). Gains from quality preschool programs have been shown to impact a range of school-related skills, including intelligence and cognitive abilities (Barnett, 1995; Broburg, Wessels, Lamb, & Hwang, 1998; NICHD, 2000), language (Feagans & Farran, 1994; McCartney, 1984; Vandell, Henderson, & Wilson, 1988), preliteracy skills (Whitehurst, 1997; Whitehurst et al., 1999), math skills (Johnson & Walker, 1991; Peisner-Feinberg et al., 1999), and social development (Campbell & Ramey, 1994; Yoshikawa, 1995). The average size of the immediate effect of preschool programs on cognitive development and school achievement is about one-half of a standard deviation (Barnett, 1998), a magnitude of impact that is educationally meaningful.

Findings from Model Programs for Poor Children

The findings that have been used to justify public investment in early education came mostly from model programs that had extremely high quality and were delivered under nearly ideal conditions. This being the case, they likely represent high-end estimates of the benefits of early education for low-income children. Conventional wisdom is that public preschool services will not have the same impact as the models because they have less intensity and quality and much less funding (Besharov & Hartle, 1987; Haskins, 1989). However, it seems reasonable to expect that the positive effects of these high-quality programs can be obtained in a universal prekindergarten system as long as quality and intensity are sufficiently high, even if not optimally so (see Reynolds & Temple, Chapter 3; Zigler & Styfco, 1994).

Longitudinal findings have captured the most public attention. There are several long-term studies that together provide convincing evidence of the effectiveness of high-quality early education services as a means for improving children's success not just in school but in later life. Three of these studies – the High/Scope Perry Preschool Project, the Carolina Abecedarian Program, and the Chicago Child-Parent Centers – were described in detail by Reynolds and Temple in Chapter 3. Because the findings so strongly relate to the argument of this chapter, we very briefly summarize them here.

All three studies employed rigorous research methods and followed participants through the school years into adulthood. The Perry Preschool and Abecedarian studies used random assignment of children to treatment and comparison conditions. Both programs were implemented in well-controlled laboratory settings, while the Chicago Child-Parent Centers operate in the public schools. As such, the Chicago study may provide some of the best estimates of the effects of a well-implemented universal prekindergarten system, because many such programs likely will be based in the schools.

The Abecedarian Project provided intensive early intervention services to four cohorts of at-risk children and their families. Children entered the program in infancy and attended all day, year-round, for five years (Campbell & Ramey, 1994). By age 15, the intervention group had significantly higher scores than the control group on the Woodcock Johnson Reading and Mathematics subtests and had significantly fewer grade retentions and special education placements (Ramey et al., 2000). The positive impacts have lasted into adulthood, with program participants continuing to outpace controls in educational achievement, college attendance (36 vs. 13 percent), and earnings from employment (Campbell, Ramey, Pungello, Sparling, & Miller-Johnson, 2002). A recent cost-benefit analysis shows a four-to-one return on every dollar spent on the program in terms of societal gains and cost aversions (Masse & Barnett, 2003).

The High/Scope Perry Preschool Program has provided the most extensive longitudinal data on the effectiveness of a preschool intervention. Varied outcome data have been collected on program graduates through the age of 40. As compared with the control group, graduates of the preschool remained in school longer and were 31 percent more likely to have graduated from high school or earned a general educational development diploma. In school, they were 56 percent less likely to need special education services, and they achieved significantly higher grade point averages and language, reading, and arithmetic scores on the California Achievement Test (Schweinhart et al., 1993). By age 27, preschool graduates were 80 percent less likely to have been arrested than the control group, were earning 59 percent more in monthly incomes, and were 26 percent less likely to be relying on social welfare services. Males, if married, were more likely to remain married than men in the control group. Cost-benefit analysis indicated that every dollar invested in the program yielded more than $7 in cost aversion and savings to society (now raised to $17 by age 40; Schweinhart et al., 2005). The bulk of these benefits were related to reduced costs stemming from lower delinquency and crime rates (Schweinhart et al., 1993).

Studies of other model early intervention programs support these findings for low-income children. The Syracuse University Family Development Research Program (Honig, 1977; Honig & Lally, 1982) documented long-term educational impacts of preschool, including better grades, higher test scores in reading and math, improved attendance and classroom behavior, less grade retention, and increased likelihood of high school graduation. Results were significantly more pronounced and lasting for girls, relative to boys. Participants in the Harlem Project (Deutsch, 1985) were 200 percent more likely to be employed, 33 percent more likely to earn a GED or high school diploma, and 30 percent more likely to go on to postsecondary educational training.

It is important to note that in all of these studies, program participants had much better outcomes relative to children from similar backgrounds who did not attend. Compared with data for middle-class children, however, there was still a sizable achievement gap. Early intervention is clearly successful in reducing that gap, but it alone is not enough to erase the harmful effects of growing up in poverty.

Findings from Large-Scale Programs for Poor Children

The findings from these model programs have been supported by studies of a large-scale public preschool program, the Chicago Child-Parent Centers, described by Reynolds and Temple in Chapter 3. Funded by Title I, the program is located in 24 centers in high-poverty neighborhoods. Children attend preschool for two years and receive school-age services through third grade. Parents are heavily involved in the program. Compared with peers who attended an alternative full-day kindergarten, preschool participants showed greater cognitive skills at school entry and scored higher in mathematics and reading achievement at the end of elementary school (Reynolds, 1995). At age 20, participants had significantly higher rates of high school completion, lower rates of grade retention and special education placement, and fewer juvenile arrests (Reynolds et al., 2001). Similar to cost savings found for model preschool programs, these positive impacts translated into a return of nearly $7 for every dollar spent on the program by age 21 (Reynolds & Temple, Chapter 3). Summarizing cost-benefit findings and accounting for lifetime benefits, the total return on investment may exceed $9 for each dollar spent (Oppenheim & MacGregor, 2003).

Head Start, which serves more than 900,000 preschoolers each year, is the largest federal preschool program for children living in poverty. Although hundreds of studies have been conducted on Head Start over four decades, the research is not as organized and rigorous as that of the Chicago and model programs. Nonetheless, it is sufficient to show that the program increases readiness skills, improves children's outcomes when they enter kindergarten, and enhances academic adjustment (Barnett 1995; Currie & Thomas, 1995; Lee, Brooks-Gunn, & Schnur, 1988; Lee, Brooks-Gunn, Schnur, & Liaw, 1990; U.S. Department of Health and Human Services, 2003). A large meta-analysis of research from the first two decades of Head Start (McKey et al., 1985) found educationally meaningful overall impacts on participants' school readiness and academic test scores at school entry. Longer-term studies have shown that Head Start graduates are less likely to be retained in grade or to be placed in special education (Barnett, 1995). Because both grade retention and special education are costly, these reductions undoubtedly provide appreciation of cost savings associated with Head Start. Unfortunately, cost-benefit analyses have not been conducted.

The Head Start effectiveness research is limited by several methodological and implementation issues. For one, a paltry research budget has not permitted extensive national evaluations until very recently. Limited funding, as well as a policy to serve the most needy applicants, means that children who attend Head Start tend to be from more at-risk backgrounds than eligible children who are not enrolled (Hebbler, 1985; Lee & Loeb, 1995; Schnur, Brooks-Gunn, & Shipman 1992). This difference would underestimate the program effects found in studies that compare children who did or did not attend Head Start. Unlike the model and Chicago programs, Head Start centers typically offer only a half-day program for one year prior to kindergarten. And whereas the model programs were implemented under well-controlled conditions, Head Start is delivered in more than 20,000 centers (U.S. Department of Health and Human Services, 2005). Local grantees adapt services to meet the needs of their clientele, although they must stay within the parameters of Head Start's national performance standards. This means that children who attend Head Start do not experience the same program, making it difficult to compare results from different studies. In addition, Head Start graduates commonly attend elementary schools that are of a much lower quality, both in terms of academics and safety, than the national norm (Lee & Loeb, 1995). Given these caveats, the long-term benefits of Head Start that have been found are even more impressive.

The final two decades of the 20th century marked dramatic growth in state-funded prekindergarten programs, with the number of states providing preschool services increasing eightfold – from 5 states to 40. Currently, there are 55 unique state-funded prekindergarten systems operating in 40 states and serving more than 980,000 preschoolers annually (Gilliam & Ripple, 2004, as updated by unpublished data from the ongoing National Prekindergarten Study). Many of these programs are restricted to low-income preschoolers. However, financial eligibility criteria are typically 30 to 85 percent less restrictive than Head Start's (Gilliam & Ripple, 2004), meaning that children from working poor families can attend. Further, children in some states can qualify for services on the basis of risk factors other than low income such as being in a single-parent family or speaking a language other than English. In Georgia, Oklahoma, and the District of Columbia, preschool is theoretically available to all children. Other states are making great strides in opening access to their state-funded prekindergartens to all age-eligible children. There are significant differences in policies and procedures among the states, so state-run preschools are far more variable in intensity and quality than Head Start (Barnett, Robin, Hustedt, & Schulman, 2004; Gilliam & Ripple, 2004; Schulman, Blank, & Ewen, 1999).

A review of the research conducted on state preschool programs through 1998 shows a pattern of findings that supports their effectiveness (Gilliam & Zigler, 2000). The most robust effects were increased academic readiness at kindergarten entry and reduced grade retention during elementary school. Literally every state program in which these outcomes were measured found a significant impact. Positive results were also documented for school attendance rates and educational test scores. The least robust effects were reported in the areas of special education placement and parent involvement. Although serious methodological limitations were present in several of these evaluations, the overall pattern and magnitude of results clearly favored prekindergarten participation. Each of the 10 states reviewed by Gilliam and Zigler targeted services to children who were from low-income families or were considered at-risk for school failure because of some other reason.

PRESCHOOL AND THE DEVELOPMENT OF LITERACY SKILLS

Many children from low-income families enter kindergarten well behind their more affluent peers in vocabulary, letter naming, and phonological awareness, skills that are foundational to learning to read (National Center for Educational Statistics, 2003; National Research Council, 1998). Scores from the 2002 National Assessment of Educational Proficiency show that this literacy gap continues throughout the public school years (Grigg, Daane, Jin, & Campbell, 2003). Research has shown that rich language and literacy experiences in the preschool years support the acquisition of skills required for reading. Being read to in the first years of life is especially important, and contributes to the development of phonemic awareness and narrative and comprehension skills (Fletcher & Lyon, 1998; National Research Council, 1998; Pfannenstiel, Seitz, & Zigler, 2002).

An unfortunate fact is that fewer than half of low-income preschoolers are read to on a daily basis, compared with 61 percent of children in families above the poverty line (Federal Interagency Forum on Child and Family Statistics, 2002). This deficit places poor children at risk for later reading difficulties and delays. Quality preschool programs can provide the level of language and print stimulation necessary for school readiness, preferably in a way that facilitates the family's role in supporting language and literacy development in the home. The George W. Bush administration established the educational goal that all children learn to read by the end of grade three (U.S. Department of Education, 2002). Recognizing the need to provide the language and print experiences that support the development of literacy, the No Child Left Behind Act of 2001 includes funds specifically targeted toward early education programs through the Early Reading First Act. Access to quality preschool settings and home literacy supports must be greatly expanded, however, for such goals and mandates to make a meaningful difference for all children.

Successful entry into kindergarten also requires particular learning behaviors and social skills. These include the abilities to get along with peers and teachers, delay gratification, control impulses, rely on intrinsic rewards, work independently, and follow directions (Blair, 2002; Huston, McLoyd, & Garcia-Coll, 1994; Malakoff, Underhill, & Zigler, 1998; Raver & Zigler, 1997, 2004). The ability to regulate emotions, impulses, and attention are predictors of whether a child will be held back in kindergarten (Agostin & Bain, 1997). Because children without these abilities tend to participate less in classroom activities than their more prosocial peers and tend to receive less instruction and positive feedback from teachers, social and emotional difficulties early in school may compound over time (McEvoy & Welker, 2000).

Low family income, low maternal education, and low English proficiency are all considered key demographic risk factors for the development of social and emotional problems (Halpern, 2000; Raver & Knitzer, 2002). The stressors associated with living in high-poverty environments also place children at higher risk for problems in the social and emotional domains. In one survey, Head Start teachers reported that approximately 40 percent of their students exhibited, on a daily basis, at least one aggressive behavior such as kicking, hitting, and threatening, while 10 percent exhibited six or more aggressive behaviors daily (Kupersmidt, Bryant, & Willoughby, 2000).

Although Head Start was designed to facilitate children's physical, cognitive, and socioemotional development – all features of overall social competence – the role of preschool interventions in enhancing competent behavior remains underinvestigated (Raver & Zigler, 1997). One study of the program's effects on learning behaviors found that Head Start students showed greater curiosity, were more likely to select a challenging task, worked more independently and persistently on difficult tasks, and were more interested in the type of symbolic rewards typically used in school than children who were wait-listed but had not attended a Head Start Center (Malakoff et al., 1998). Earlier work has shown improved motivation and self-image from attendance (e.g., Zigler, Abelson, Trickett, & Seitz, 1982; Zigler & Butterfield, 1968).

Cognitive and social-emotional development are tightly intertwined. Universal prekindergarten programs that focus on one without the other will fall short in achieving school readiness. There have been some efforts to develop specific preschool curricula to promote the development of social competence and self-regulation (Fox & Little, 2001; Raver & Knitzer, 2002). In addition to this type of instruction, universal preschool can aid the early identification of serious emotional and behavioral disabilities. Although parents may recognize behavioral problems in the preschool years, services are typically not provided until later in elementary school (Raver & Knitzer, 2002). By this time, the problems have intensified and the child has failed academically and socially. Prekindergarten is a good venue for universal screening systems to identify younger children who might benefit from support services in order to make a successful transition to school (Gilliam, Meisels, & Mayes, 2005).

THE PROBLEM OF ACCESS FOR POOR AND NEAR-POOR CHILDREN

Although federal and state subsidies have greatly improved children's access to preschool programs in recent years, low-income children are still significantly underenrolled. Data suggest, in fact, that children who most need quality early education and care are the least likely to be attending such programs (Kagan & Neuman, 1997). Among families with incomes less than $15,000, only 37 percent of three- and four-year-olds were enrolled in prekindergarten programs, as compared with 54 percent of those in families with incomes between $50,000 and $75,000, and 68 percent of those in families with incomes greater than $75,000 (U.S. Census Bureau, 1999). Low-income Hispanic preschoolers have particularly low levels of enrollment in preschool programs (U.S. Census Bureau, 1999; West et al., 1993).

Working-class families have particular difficulty accessing preschool for their children. Many do not qualify for publicly funded programs, or even child care subsidies, but they cannot afford the tuition on their limited incomes (Phillips, Voran, Kisker, Howes, & Whitebook, 1994; Whitebook, Howes, & Phillips, 1989). Head Start is permitted to allot 10 percent of seats to students from families above the poverty threshold; however, limited funds do not allow many programs to serve all area children below the poverty line, much less accept children from families with higher incomes. Furthermore, the preschool programs that children from low-income families attend frequently are not of optimal quality. The U.S. General Accounting Office (1995) found that 59 percent of the children from low-income families enrolled in preschool were in programs that did not offer the full range of services necessary to have the desired effects on school readiness.

There are other barriers that prevent low-income children from attending quality preschool. Access to prekindergarten programs is often limited by the neighborhoods in which low-income families live, because lower-income neighborhoods tend to have a more sporadic supply of quality early education programs relative to wealthier areas (Policy Analysis for California Education, 2002). Preschool participation is also strongly related to maternal education – children with the least educated mothers are the least likely to be enrolled in prekindergarten programs. In 1998, only 28 percent of three- to five-year-olds whose mothers had less than a high school degree attended preschool, as compared with 63 percent of children whose mothers had graduated from a four-year college; enrollment in prekindergarten programs among just four-year-olds whose mothers have a bachelor's degree or higher has remained above 80 percent since 1991, and attained 85 percent in 1999 (National Center for Educational Statistics, 2000). If one assumes that children with the most educated mothers also have more educational experiences at home, preschool attendance gives them a double advantage over children with the least educated mothers.

The Promise of Universal Prekindergarten for Low-Income Preschoolers

Early education services that address the full range of academic, social, and health needs of low-income children are vital for their success in school. If preschool programs were universally available, and funded at levels that maintain high quality, many of the participation barriers for poor children would be overcome.

Universal prekindergarten would also end the segregation of poor children from their wealthier peers that characterizes preschool programs today. There is emerging evidence that the beneficial impacts of early education for poor children can be enhanced when they attend school with a mixed socioeconomic group. In one study, receptive vocabulary skills in a sample of 50 low-income preschoolers who attended programs consisting of all poor children were compared with those of 31 similar children attending preschool with children across the socioeconomic spectrum (Schechter, 2003). All programs were accredited by the National Association for the Education of Young Children, providing some marginal evidence of similarity of quality across the settings. Results indicated that the low-income preschoolers in the more heterogeneous settings increased their vocabularies over the course of the year at a rate that significantly exceeded their low-income peers in homogeneous settings. Although the study is small and preliminary, and children were not randomly assigned to treatment conditions, these results suggest that the more diverse mix of income levels present in a universal prekindergarten program may be more effective at promoting school readiness for low-income children than our traditionally targeted systems. Whether this might be due to the middle-class children modeling more advanced skills to their lower-income classmates or to subtle differences in the quality of the settings or instruction is unclear. Certainly, more research in this area is needed.

The evidence is clear, however, that high-quality early education for low-income children is effective at increasing school readiness and laying a solid foundation for later success in school and life. Unfortunately, low-income children often do not have access to preschool services, and if they do participate in a center-based program, it may not be of high enough quality. Universal prekindergarten holds the promise of addressing both of these related concerns by reducing participation barriers and by providing low-income children with a program that is at the level of quality necessary to meaningfully impact their school readiness.

References

Agostin, T. M., & Bain, S. (1997). Retention in kindergarten. *Psychology in the Schools, 34*, 219–228.

Barnett, W. S. (1995). Long-term effects of early childhood programs on cognitive and school outcomes. *The Future of Children, 5*(3), 25–50.

Barnett, W. S. (1998). Long-term cognitive and academic effects of early childhood education on children in poverty. *Preventive Medicine, 27*, 204–207.

Barnett, W. S., & Brown, K. C. (2000). *Issues in children's access to dental care under Medicaid. Dental Health Policy Analysis Series.* Chicago: American Dental Association.

Barnett, W. S., Robin, K. B., Hustedt, J. T., & Schulman, K. L. (2004). *The state of preschool: 2003 state preschool yearbook.* New Brunswick, NJ: National Institute for Early Education Research.

Besharov, D. J., & Hartle, T. W. (1987). Head Start: Making a popular program work. *Pediatrics, 79*, 440–441.

Blair, C. (2002). School readiness: Integrating cognition and emotion in a neurobiological conceptualization of children's functioning at school entry. *American Psychologist, 57*, 111–127.

Boocock, S. S. (2003). Lessons from Europe: European preschools revisited in a global age. In A. J. Reynolds, M. C. Wang, & H. J. Walberg (Eds.), *Early childhood programs for a new century* (pp. 299–328). Washington, DC: Child Welfare League of America Press.

Broberg, A. G., Wessels, H. R., Lamb, M. E., & Hwang, C. P. (1998). Effects of day care on the development of cognitive abilities in 8-year-olds: A longitudinal study. *Developmental Psychology, 33,* 62–69.

Brooks-Gunn, J. (2003). Do you believe in magic?: What we can expect from early childhood intervention programs. *Social Policy Report, 17,* 3–14.

Brooks-Gunn, J., Klebanov, P. K., Liaw, F., & Spiker, D. (1993). Enhancing the development of low birth weight, premature infants: Changes in cognition and behavior over the first three years. *Child Development, 64,* 736–753.

Campbell, F. A., & Ramey, C. T. (1994). Effects of early intervention on intellectual and academic achievement: A follow-up study of children from low-income families. *Child Development, 65,* 684–698.

Campbell, F. A., Ramey, C. T., Pungello, E., Sparling, J., & Miller-Johnson, S. (2002). Early childhood education: Young adult outcomes from the Abecedarian Project. *Applied Developmental Science, 6,* 42–57.

Children Now. (2002). *California report card.* www.childrennow.org/california/rc2002/rc-2002.pdf.

Clifford, R. M., Early, D. M., & Hills, T. W. (1999). Almost a million children in school before kindergarten: Who is responsible for early childhood services? *Young Children, 54*(5), 48–51.

Currie, J., & Thomas, D. (1995). Does Head Start make a difference? *American Economic Review,* 341–364.

Dauber, S. L., Alexander, K., & Entwisle, D. R. (1993). Characteristics of retainees and early precursors for retention in grade: Who is held back? *Merrill-Palmer Quarterly, 39,* 326–343.

Deutsch, M. (1985). *Long-term effects of early intervention: Summary of selected findings.* New York: Institute for Developmental Studies, New York University.

Duncan, G. J., & Brooks-Gunn, J. (1997). Income effects across the lifespan: Integration and interpretation. In G. J. Duncan & J. Brooks-Gunn (Eds.), *Consequences of growing up poor* (pp. 596–610). New York: Russell Sage.

Duncan, G. J., & Brooks-Gunn, J. (2000). Family poverty, welfare reform, and child development. *Child Development, 71,* 188–196.

Duncan, G. J., Brooks-Gunn, J., & Klebanov, P. K. (1994). Economic deprivation and early childhood development. *Child Development, 65,* 296–318.

Duncan, G. J., Brooks-Gunn, J., Yeung, W. J., & Smith, J. R. (1998). How much does childhood poverty affect the life chances of children? *American Sociological Review, 63,* 406–423.

Feagans, L. V., & Farran, D. C. (1994). The effects of daycare intervention in the preschool years on the narrative skills of poverty children in kindergarten. *International Journal of Behavioral Development, 17,* 503–523.

Federal Interagency Forum on Child and Family Statistics. (2002). *America's children: Key national indicators of well-being, 2002.* Washington, DC: U.S. Government Printing Office. www.childstats.gov/ac2002/index.asp.

Fletcher, J. M., & Lyon, G. R. (1998). Reading: A research-based approach. In W. M. Evers (Ed.), *What's gone wrong in America's classrooms.* Stanford, CA: Hoover Institution Press.

Fosburg, L. B., Goodrich, N., & Fox, M. (1984). *The effects of Head Start health services: Report of the Head Start Health Evaluation.* Cambridge, MA: Abt Associates.

Fox, L., & Little, N. (2001). Starting Early: Developing school-wide support in a community preschool. *Journal of Positive Behavior Interventions, 3,* 251–254.

Frede, E. C. (1995). The role of program quality in producing early childhood program benefits. *The Future of Children, 5,* 115–132.

Gilliam, W. S., Meisels, S., & Mayes, L. (2005). Screening and surveillance in early intervention systems. In M. J. Guralnick (Ed.), *A developmental systems approach to early intervention: National and international perspectives.* Baltimore: Paul H. Brookes.

Gilliam, W. S., & Ripple, C. H. (2004). What can be learned from state-funded prekindergarten initiatives? A data-based approach to the Head Start devolution debate. In E. Zigler & S. J. Styfco (Eds.), *The Head Start debates* (pp. 477–497). Baltimore: Paul H. Brookes.

Gilliam, W. S., & Zigler, E. F. (2000). A critical meta-analysis of all evaluations of state-funded preschool from 1977 to 1998: Implications for policy, service delivery and program evaluation. *Early Childhood Research Quarterly, 15,* 441–473.

Grigg, W. S., Daane, M. C., Jin, Y., & Campbell, J. R. (2003). *The nation's report card: Reading 2002* (NCES No. 2003-521). Washington, DC: U.S. Department of Education.

Gruendel, J. M., Oliveira, M., & Geballe, S. (2003). *All children ready for school: The case for early care and education. A guide for policy makers.* New Haven, CT: Connecticut Voices for Children. info.med.yale.edu/chldstdy/CTvoices/kidslink/kidslink2/reports/PDFs/ResourceChallenges.pdf.

Hale, B., Seitz, V., & Zigler, E. (1990). Health services and Head Start: A forgotten formula. *Journal of Applied Developmental Psychology, 11,* 447–458.

Halpern, R. (2000). Early childhood intervention for low-income children and families. In J. P. Shonkoff & S. J. Meisels (Ed.), *Handbook of early childhood intervention* (2nd ed., pp. 361–386). Cambridge: Cambridge University Press.

Haskins, R. (1989). Beyond metaphor: The efficacy of early childhood education. *American Psychologist, 44,* 274–282.

Hebbler, K. (1985). An old and new question on the effects of early education for children from low income families. *Educational Evaluation and Policy Analysis, 7,* 207–216.

Hertzman, C., & Wiens, M. (1996). Child development and long-term outcomes: A population health perspective and summary of successful interventions. *Social Science and Medicine, 43,* 1083–1095.

Hofferth, S. L., West, J., Henke, R., & Kaufman, P. (1994). *Access to early childhood programs for children at risk.* Washington, DC: U.S. Department of Education. (ERIC Reproduction Service No. ED 370 715).

Honig, A. S. (1977). The Children's Center and the Family Development Research Program. In B. M. Caldwell & D. J. Stedman (Eds.), *Infant education: A guide for helping handicapped children in the first three years* (pp. 81–99). New York: Walker.

Honig, A. S., & Lally, J. R. (1982). The Family Development Research Program: Retrospective review. *Early Child Development and Care, 10*, 41–62.

Huston, A. C. (1994). Children in poverty: Designing research to affect policy. *Social Policy Report, 8*, 1–12.

Huston, A. C., McLoyd, V. C., & Garcia-Coll, C. (1994). Children and poverty: Issues in contemporary research. *Child Development, 65*, 275–282.

Johnson, D., & Walker, T. A. (1991). A follow-up evaluation of the Houston Parent Child Development Center: School performance. *Journal of Early Intervention, 15*, 226–236.

Kagan, S. L., & Neuman, M. (1997). Defining and implementing school readiness: Challenges for families, early care and education, and schools. In R. P. Weissberg (Ed.), *Establishing preventive services* (pp. 61–96). Thousand Oaks, CA: Sage.

Klebanov, P. K., Brooks-Gunn, J., McCarton, C., & McCormick, M. C. (1998). The contribution of neighborhood and family income to developmental test scores over the first three years of life. *Child Development, 69*, 1420–1436.

Kupersmidt, J. B., Bryant, D., & Willoughby, M. (2000). Prevalence of aggressive behaviors among preschoolers in Head Start and community child care programs. *Behavioral Disorders, 26*, 42–52.

Lee, V., Brooks-Gunn, J., & Schnur, E. (1988). Does Head Start Work? A 1-year follow-up comparison of disadvantaged children attending Head Start, no preschool and other preschool programs. *Developmental Psychology, 24*, 210–222.

Lee, V., Brooks-Gunn, J., Schnur, E., & Liaw, F. (1990). Are Head Start effects sustained? A longitudinal follow-up comparison of disadvantaged children attending Head Start, no preschool, and other preschool programs. *Child Development, 61*, 495–507.

Lee, V., & Loeb, S. (1995). Where do Head Start attendees end up? One reason why preschool effects fade out. *Educational Evaluation and Policy Analysis, 17*, 62–82.

Lee, V. E., & Burkman, D. T. (2002). *Inequality at the starting gate: Social background differences in achievement as children begin school*. Washington, DC: Economic Policy Institute.

Malakoff, M. E., Underhill, J. M., & Zigler, E. (1998). The effect of inner-city environment and Head Start experience on effectance motivation. *American Journal of Orthopsychiatry, 68*, 630–638.

Masse, L. N., & Barnett, W. S. (2003). *A benefit cost analysis of the Abecedarian Early Childhood Intervention*. New Brunswick, NJ: National Institute for Early Education Research. nieer.org/resources/research/AbecedarianStudy.pdf. Accessed September 22, 2003.

May, D. C., & Kundert, D. K. (1997). School readiness practices and children at-risk: Examining the issues. *Psychology in the Schools, 34*, 73–84.

McCall, R. B. (1979). The development of intellectual functioning in infancy and the prediction of later I.Q. In J. D. Osofsky (Ed.), *Handbook of infant development* (pp. 707–741). New York: Wiley.

McCartney, K. (1984). Effect of quality of day care environment on children's language development. *Developmental Psychology, 20*, 244–266.

McEvoy, A., & Welker, R. (2000). Antisocial behavior, academic failure, and school climate: A critical review. *Journal of Emotional and Behavioral Disorders, 8*, 589–598.

McKey, R. H., Condelli, L., Ganson, H., Barrett, B. J., McConkey, C., & Plantz, M. C. (1985). *The impact of Head Start on children, families, and communities* (DHHS Publication No. [OHDS] 90-31193). Washington, DC: U.S. Government Printing Office.

McLoyd, V. C. (1989). Socio-economic disadvantage and child development. *American Psychologist, 53*, 185–204.

Merrow, J. (2002, September 25). The "failure" of Head Start. *Education Week, 22*(4), 52.

Miller, D. C., Shieh, Y., & Lavagna, K. (2002, April). Preschool attendance as a long-term predictor of postsecondary educational attainment: Findings from the National Educational Longitudinal Study. Paper presented at the annual meeting of the American Educational Research Association, New Orleans.

Morrison, F. J., Griffith, E., & Alberts, D. (1997). Nature-nurture in the classroom: Entrance age, school readiness, and learning in children. *Developmental Psychology, 33*, 254–262.

National Center for Educational Statistics. (2000). *The condition of education: 2000*. Washington, DC: U.S. Department of Education. www.nces.ed.gov/pubs2000/coe2000.

National Center for Educational Statistics. (2003). *The condition of education: 2003* (NCES No. 2003-067). Washington, DC: U.S. Department of Education.

National Research Council. (1998). Preventing reading difficulties. In C. E. Snow, M. S. Burns, & P. Griggin (Eds.), *Commission on Behavioral and Social Sciences and Education* (pp. 137–171). Washington, DC: National Academy Press.

National Research Council. (2000). *From neurons to neighborhoods: The science of early childhood development*. Washington, DC: National Academy Press.

National Research Council. (2001). *Eager to learn: Educating our preschoolers*. Washington, DC: National Academy Press.

NICHD Early Child Care Research Network. (2000). The relation of child care to cognitive and language development. *Child Development, 71*, 960–980.

O'Brien, R. W., Connell, D. B., & Griffin, J. (2004). Head Start's efforts to improve child health. In E. Zigler & S. J. Styfco (Eds.), *The Head Start debates* (pp. 161–178). Baltimore: Paul H. Brookes.

Oppenheim, J., & MacGregor, T. (2003). *The economics of education: Public benefits of high-quality preschool education for low-income children*. New Orleans, LA: Entergy.

Pagani, L., Boulerice, B., Vitaro, F., & Tremblay, R. E. (1999). Effects of poverty on academic failure and delinquency in boys: A change and process model approach. *Journal of Child Psychology & Psychiatry, 40*, 1209–1219.

Peisner-Feinberg, E. S., Burchinal, M. R., Clifford, R. M., Culkin, M. L., Howes, C., Kagan, S. L., Yazejian, N., Byler, P., Rustici, J., & Zelazo, J. (1999). *The children of the cost, quality, and outcomes study go to school: Technical report.* Chapel Hill: University of North Carolina, Frank Porter Graham Child Development Center.

Pfannenstiel, J. C., Seitz, V., & Zigler, E. (2002). Promoting school readiness: The role of the Parents as Teachers Program. *NHSA Dialog, 6*, 71–86.

Phillips, D., Voran, M., Kisker, E., Howes, C., & Whitebook, M. (1994). Childcare for children in poverty: Opportunity or inequality? *Child Development, 65*, 440–456.

Policy Analysis for California Education (PACE). (2002). *A stark plateau: California families see little growth in child care centers.* Berkeley, CA: Author.

Ramey, C. T., & Campbell, F. A. (1991). Poverty, early childhood education, and academic competence: The Abecedarian experiment. In A. Huston (Ed.), *Children reared in poverty* (pp. 190–221). Cambridge: Cambridge University Press.

Ramey, C. T., Campbell, F., Burchinal, M., Skinner, M., Gardner, D., & Ramey, S. L. (2000). Persistent effects of early childhood education on high-risk children and their mothers. *Applied Developmental Science, 4*, 2–14.

Raver, C. C., & Knitzer, J. (2002). *Ready to enter: What research tells policymakers about strategies to promote social and emotional school readiness among three- and four-year old children.* New York: National Center for Children in Poverty.

Raver, C. C., & Zigler, E. F. (1997). Social competence: An untapped dimension in evaluating Head Start's success. *Early Childhood Quarterly, 12*, 363–385.

Raver, C. C., & Zigler, E. F. (2004). Another step back? Assessing readiness in Head Start. *Young Children, 59*(1), 58–63.

Reynolds, A. J. (1995). One year of preschool intervention or two? Does it matter? *Early Childhood Quarterly, 10*, 1–31.

Reynolds, A. J., Temple, J. A., Robertson, D. L., & Mann, E. A. (2001). Long-term effects of an early childhood intervention on educational achievement and juvenile arrest: A 15-year follow-up of low-income children in public schools. *Journal of the American Medical Association, 285*, 2339–2346.

Schechter, C. (2003). *Learning in mixed company.* St. Joseph's College, West Hartford, CT. Unpublished manuscript.

Schulman, K., Blank, H., & Ewen, D., (1999). *Seeds of success: State prekindergarten initiatives, 1998–1999.* Washington, DC: Children's Defense Fund.

Schnur, E., Brooks-Gunn, J., & Shipman, V. C. (1992). Who attends programs serving poor children? The case of Head Start attendees and nonattendees. *Journal of Applied Developmental Psychology, 13*, 405–421.

Schumacher, R., & Irish, K. (2003). What's new in 2002? A snapshot of Head Start children, families, teachers, and programs. *CLASP Policy Brief*, Head Start Series, No. 2.

Schweinhart, L. I., Barnes, H. V., Weikart, D. R., Barnett, W. S., & Epstein, A. S. (1993). *Significant benefits: The High/Scope Perry Preschool study through age 27.* Ypsilanti, MI: High/Scope Press.

Schweinhart, L. J., Montie, J., Xiang, Z., Barnett, W. S., Belfield, C. R., & Nores, M. (2005). *Lifetime effects: The High/Scope Perry Preschool study through age 40*. Monographs of the High/Scope Educational Research Foundation (No. 14). Ypsilanti, MI: High/Scope Press.

Smith, J. R., Brooks-Gunn, J., & Klebanov, P. K. (1997). Consequences of living in poverty for young children's cognitive and verbal ability and early school achievement. In G. J. Duncan & J. Brooks-Gunn (Eds.), *Consequences of growing up poor* (pp. 132–189). New York: Russell Sage.

U.S. Census Bureau. (1999, October). *School Enrollment in the United States – Social and Economic Characteristics* (P20-533). Washington, DC: Author.

U.S. Department of Education. (2002). *No Child Left Behind: A desktop reference*. Washington, DC: Author. http://www.ed.gov/offices/OESE/reference.html.

U.S. Department of Health and Human Services. (2003). *Head Start FACES 2000. Fourth progress report*. Washington, DC: Author.

U.S. Department of Health and Human Services. (2005). *Head Start Statistical Fact Sheet 2005*. Washington, DC: Author.

U.S. General Accounting Office. (1995). *Early childhood programs: Services to prepare children for school often limited* (Report N, 95-21). Washington, DC: Author.

Vandell, D. L., Henderson, V. K., & Wilson, K. S. (1988). A longitudinal study of children with day-care experiences of varying quality. *Child Development, 59*, 1286–1292.

West, J., Hausken, E. G., & Collins, M. (1993). *Profile of preschool children's child care and early education program participation: National Household Education Survey* (NCES 93-133). Washington, DC: National Center for Education Statistics, Office of Educational Research and Improvement, U.S. Department of Education.

Whitebook, N., Howes, C., & Phillips, D. (1989). *Who cares? Child care teachers and the quality of care in America: Final report of the National Child Care Staffing Study*. Oakland, CA: Child Care Employee Project.

Whitehurst, G. J. (1997). Language processes in context: Language learning in children reared in poverty. In L. B. Adamson & M. A. Romski (Eds.), *Research on communication and language disorders: Contribution to theories of language development* (pp. 233–266). Baltimore: Paul H. Brookes.

Whitehurst, G. J., Zevenbergen, A., Crone, D. A., Schultz, M. D., Velting, O. N., & Fischel, J. E. (1999). Outcomes of an emergent literacy intervention from Head Start through second grade. *Journal of Educational Psychology, 91*, 261–272.

Yoshikawa, H. (1995). Long-term effects of early childhood programs on social outcomes and delinquency. *The Future of Children, 5*, 51–75.

Zigler, E., Abelson, W. D., Trickett, P., & Seitz, V. (1982). Is an intervention program really necessary to raise disadvantaged children's IQ scores? *Child Development, 53*, 340–348.

Zigler, E., & Butterfield, E. C. (1968). Motivational aspects of changes in IQ test performance of culturally deprived nursery school children. *Child Development, 39*, 1–14.

Zigler, E., & Styfco, S. J. (1994). Is the Perry Preschool better than Head Start? Yes and no. *Early Childhood Research Quarterly, 9,* 269–287.

Zigler, E., & Styfco, S. J. (2001). Extended childhood intervention prepares children for school and beyond. *Journal of the American Medical Association, 285,* 2378–2380.

Zigler, E., & Trickett, P. (1978). IQ, social competence, and evaluation of early childhood intervention programs. *American Psychologist, 33,* 789–798.

5

The Need for Universal Preschool Access for Children Not Living in Poverty

With Marguerite Malakoff

The United States was among the first of all nations in the world to provide children and youth equal access to 12 years of public education. Democracy requires government by the people, so our early leaders believed that all people had to be educated if they were to participate effectively. As the young states began to build their universal school systems, many set the entrance age at six or seven years old (Zigler & Lang, 1991). Some two centuries later, a great deal has been learned about cognitive development in the first five years of life. Modern studies of neural patterns and brain growth suggest that learning experiences very early in life influence the capacity and motivation to learn throughout the life cycle. By preschool age, children are enormously capable of pre-academic and social training. Further, early learning experiences build the foundation for later achievement of academic skills. Despite these advances in knowledge, most young children in the United States still do not have access to public preschool education (Beatty, 1995). In fact, as of the year 2000, ten states did not even require that school districts offer kindergarten (Vecchiotti, 2003). By 2004, 42 states and the District of Columbia did mandate that school districts provide at least half-day kindergarten programs, but only 14 states and the District of Columbia required that age-eligible children attend (Education Commission of the States, 2004).

This is not the case in most industrialized nations, where universal access to high-quality public preschool is an established reality. John Merrow (2002) emphasized how far behind the United States is in this regard. In France, virtually all three- to five-year-olds attend high-quality preschool, most through the public *école maternelle* system.

Nearly three-quarters of German, Danish, and Greek four-year-olds attend public school, and almost all do in England, Luxembourg, and the Netherlands. Likewise, most four- and five-year-olds in Italy and Spain attend public school. The wide availability of public preschool in Europe and elsewhere stands in sharp contrast to the situation in the United States, where access to preschool is linked to socioeconomic status, geographic location, and the simple availability of seats, and quality is not guaranteed.

Preschool education in this country is sharply divided into public and private systems. The national Head Start program serves children from extremely low-income families, but it has never been funded to enroll more than 50–60 percent of those eligible. Federal law dictates that states make public programs available to all preschoolers with disabilities. Beyond that, state and local governments choose whether to fund prekindergarten. With a few exceptions, those which do so generally offer these programs only to children deemed unlikely to succeed in school because of low family income or other risk factors. Children without apparent risks attend preschool in the private sector *if* their parents can afford it and can negotiate barriers such as transportation and school schedules that interfere with work schedules. The result is a haphazard, two-tiered preschool system where poor children attend one set of schools and wealthy children another, and many in both groups and the majority of the vast group in between may or may not get the chance to receive high-quality early education. This inequality of opportunity is a poor start to preparing young citizens to participate fully in the democracy that our founding fathers envisioned.

While there have been increasing calls from educators and policymakers to offer preschool to children living in poverty, to date universal access to preschool for all three- and-four-year-old children has received far less attention. In this chapter, we argue that all children can benefit from high-quality, developmentally appropriate educational experiences prior to entering kindergarten. In a major report, the prestigious National Research Council concluded that preschool programs have the potential "to have a powerful impact on child development" because the years from three to five represent a period of such tremendous cognitive, language, and social-emotional development – development that can be substantively influenced by environmental factors (Bowman, Donovan, & Burns, 2000, p. 58). We concur. We also see value in the potential of high-quality preschool programs to support the healthy development and school readiness of children who spend much of the work week in child care settings. The quality of child care in America is highly variable.

While some care is excellent, the majority is mediocre, and some is so poor that it can actually harm children's development. Indeed, research has indicated that children from middle-income families are more likely than those from high- or low-income families to attend child care centers of poor quality (Whitebrook, Howes, & Phillips, 1989).

Finally, our interest in public funding of voluntary, high-quality preschool programs available to all children arises from the need to win public support for such programs. The social reality is that programs meant for a select group are not as easy to sell to taxpayers as those that benefit a broader constituency. For example, elementary school classes for gifted students are often disdained by parents whose children are not selected to attend, and these programs are usually the first to go when education budgets are cut. By the same token, although at-risk preschoolers may benefit more from high-quality early childhood experiences than their age-mates, we do not believe they will gain access unless all children are invited to participate.

WHO GOES TO PRESCHOOL?

The opportunity to attend preschool was not always dictated by family wealth or place of residence. In fact, the case for publicly funded early education programs open to all children has been periodically advanced since the early 20th century (Vinovskis, 1993). For example, in the 1920s there were a number of experimental preschool programs funded through local public school systems that were open to children regardless of family income. Federal involvement in public preschool became widespread during the New Deal era and the Second World War. In both cases, however, the purpose was not to promote child development but to advance national agendas. During the Great Depression, preschool programs were set up to create work for unemployed teachers. During World War II, women were needed in the war effort at a time when huge numbers of men were fighting overseas. Children needed care while their mothers and grandmothers worked, so child care centers were opened for children of all ages. Although early education may have been provided to preschool-age children, the centers existed for the convenience of mothers and employers, and most closed promptly when the war ended.

The War on Poverty in the mid-1960s saw the beginning of a longer-lasting commitment of the federal government to preschool services for disadvantaged preschoolers. The Head Start program was created to break the cycle of poverty by helping young children from low-income families gain the skills they would need to succeed in school (see Chapter 11). Currently enrolling more than 900,000 children each year, Head Start has served 22 million children and their families over the past four decades. Most are three- and four-year-olds who attend half-day, center-based preschool. To be eligible, children must live in families with incomes below the federal poverty level. The only exceptions are children with disabilities and those whose family incomes have risen above the line after they enrolled. The law does allow up to 10 percent of seats to be offered to children from families with incomes above the poverty level, but funding constraints have limited this possibility. It should be noted that Head Start is much more than a traditional preschool; it is a two-generation program that offers health, education, and support services to children and their families.

Welfare reform in the 1990s created further government involvement in preschool services but only because of their role in providing child care. Time limits were placed on the receipt of welfare assistance, but recipients could not join the work force without a place to leave their children. Hence states supported early care and education services not for their value to children but as a means of enabling their parents to work.

Beginning with a summit of the 50 state governors and the first President Bush in 1989 (see National Education Goals Panel, 1999), there has been a growing interest in school readiness among state decision makers. The emphasis in early care and education is starting to be placed on the education side of the phrase instead of on the needs of parents for child care. As explained in Chapter 1, the majority of states now offer prekindergarten in at least some school districts. Most of these programs are targeted to at-risk groups. Currently, only Georgia and Oklahoma offer free public preschool to all four-year-olds. Despite the fact that Georgia was the first state to offer universal preschool, only 55 percent of Georgian four-year-olds were served in the 2002–2003 school year (Barnett, Robin, Hustedt, & Schulman, 2003). However, not all children in Georgia have access to a high-quality program. Quality varies across the state, and parents line up the night before registration opens to secure a place in the best programs (Merrow, 2002). Other states have shown public commitment to future universal programs, but their progress varies. West Virginia, for example, mandates that prekindergarten be universal by the year 2012 (Barnett et al., 2003).

These state initiatives are a start. However, it is clear that children have unequal opportunities to benefit from quality early care and education. Current federal and state initiatives generally target children considered most in need of early education, or parent groups considered most in need of child care services so they can be self-supporting. The needs of middle-class children and parents for both services are largely ignored in public planning, but they are no less real.

A Portrait of Preschool Attendance in the United States

Many children in the United States enter kindergarten without prior experience in preschool. According to the U.S. Census Bureau, in 2001 about 65 percent of four-year-old children were enrolled in a preschool program. Three-year-olds were far less likely to attend – only 39 percent were enrolled in preschool, and more than half of these were in private programs (U.S. Census, 2001).

Among middle-class families, preschool enrollment is closely linked to socioeconomic level, whether measured by family income or mother's education. In families with incomes above $75,000, two-thirds of children ages three to five attended preschool in 2001. Just over half of children from families making between $50,000 and $75,000, and 40 percent of children from families with incomes between $30,000 and $50,000, attended preschool programs (U.S. Census, 2001). These percentages are roughly the same when maternal education is used instead of family income. That is, children whose mothers have at least a bachelor's degree are more likely to attend preschool than those whose mothers have some college, and the latter are more likely to attend than children whose mothers have a high school diploma.

The census data further suggest that attendance is related to the availability of *public* preschool programs. Of children who attended preschool, the proportion enrolled in public programs was inversely related to income. For example, among families with incomes below $20,000, 82 percent of the children attending preschool were in public programs. By contrast, among families earning between $40,000 and $75,000, only 37 percent of children in preschool attended public programs, and among families earning more than $75,000, the proportion dropped to 21 percent. The same trend is evident when children are grouped by maternal education. Although the impact of the financial burden associated with private preschool was not directly assessed, these data suggest that the scarcity of universal public prekindergarten limits the ability of middle-class families to choose preschool for their children.

Preschool versus Child Care

Arguments in favor of universal access to public preschools are typically made in the context of school readiness, overlooking contributions to the same goal of high-quality, developmentally appropriate, out-of-home care for children of working parents. Today, they are the majority of children. In 1999 less than 25 percent of families with children under the age of six had one parent who stayed at home (U.S. Census Bureau, 2000). Welfare reform in 1996 certainly increased the proportion of single mothers with jobs among low-income households. Yet the rise in the number of working mothers has affected families of all socioeconomic levels. Economic necessity, higher consumption, rises in home ownership and accompanying mortgage payments, increasing numbers of divorced or never-married parents, and more professional opportunities for women in the work force are prominent reasons why middle- and upper-middle-class mothers also work outside the home. Not surprisingly, in 1995, 68 percent of three-year-olds and more than three-quarters of four-year-olds received some form of child care on a regular basis (West, Wright, & Hausken, 1995). These numbers are similar today (National Child Care Information Center, 2004).

As might be expected, children of working mothers are somewhat more likely to attend preschool programs than are children whose mothers are not in the work force. In 2001 just over half of three- and four-year-old children of mothers employed full-time attended preschool, compared with 44 percent of children whose mothers did not work outside the home (U.S. Census, 2001). While some working parents rely on preschools for child care, many preschool-age children are in alternative forms of care that are available for the length of the workday, all year long. The Federal Interagency Forum on Child and Family Statistics (2002) reported that in 2001, 56 percent of prekindergarten children were in some form of center-based care, although the survey did not distinguish between educational and noneducational programs. Three-year-olds, however, were more likely to be in family day care or relative care (National Center for Education Statistics, 2002), settings that are far less regulated than center-based care. One national study found that the quality of one-third of family day care programs was rated to be so poor as to endanger children's development (Galinsky, Howes, Kontos, & Shinn, 1994); in another study, only 13 percent were rated to be of good quality (National Center for Early Development and Learning, 2002).

Center-based care, however, does not in itself ensure high quality. In fact, a number of studies suggest that most center-based child care in the

United States is generally of mediocre quality – children's basic needs are met, but there are limited opportunities for learning and language activities (e.g., Bowman et al., 2000; Peisner-Feinberg et al., 2001). One multistate study found only 14 percent of center-based classrooms were of high-quality, while 12 percent provided less than *minimum* quality; that is, the care was so poor it could endanger children's healthy development (Cost, Quality and Child Outcomes Study Team, 1995).

The general lack of quality in available child care raises serious concerns about children's developmental outcomes. High-quality care is needed to build the cognitive, language, and social-emotional foundations necessary for successful entry into kindergarten and achievement in later schooling. The work of Vandell and Wolfe (2000) suggests that a change in caregiver quality from poor or mediocre to high would increase young children's school readiness and language skills by 50 percent.

The issue of high-quality early care and education cannot be separated from its costs. Full-day, center-based care (which may include preschool) for a four-year-old in an urban area costs, on average, between $4,000 and $6,000 per year. Costs can range up to $10,000, depending on the age of the child, the type and quality of the program, and the level of subsidy available (Schulman, 2000). While there is not a perfect correlation between cost and quality, there is no doubt that the features that contribute to good care can be expensive. For example, one indicator of quality is better-trained teachers, who command higher salaries than teachers with less education (see Maxwell & Clifford, Chapter 9). Better salaries and benefits reduce employee turnover, another element of quality. Good programs also have smaller group sizes and fewer children per adult, and there are more educational toys and activities. These all add to the price. Research has shown that middle-class families are the *least* likely to be able to afford high-quality care because they do not have the financial resources to pay for good private programs, but they are not eligible for public or subsidized programs that mostly target low-income families (Phillips, Voran, Kisker, Howes, & Whitebook, 1994).

In sum, the basic statistics about working parents and the comprehensive body of research on the quality of child care in the United States reveal two findings. (1) For a variety of reasons, an ever-growing number of parents are working outside the home, underscoring that both low- *and* middle-income families have a clear need for affordable, high-quality child care environments. (2) The child care that is commonly available, whether center-based or more informal, generally is not of high enough quality to promote children's healthy development and school readiness. We believe that publicly funded, high-quality preschool for three- and four-year-old children has the potential to meet the child care needs of working families as well as the need for educationally meaningful preschool experiences that help all children prepare for school.

UNIVERSAL NEED FOR SCHOOL READINESS

Assuring that all children are ready for school was the first of the National Education Goals adopted by all 50 states (National Education Goals Panel, 1996; also see Chapter 2). The goals were codified in the Goals 2000: Educate America Act of 1994 but were not reauthorized during the George W. Bush administration. Although the mandate for the goals has expired, the need for efforts to promote school readiness has not. As we discussed in Chapter 2, kindergarten teachers report that one-third or more of their students do not have the abilities necessary to succeed in kindergarten, lacking not only specific academic skills but behaviorial skills like knowing how to follow directions and work independently. This is too high a ratio to attribute poor school readiness to the usual suspects like low-income and English-language learners.

Statistics confirm that higher socioeconomic background and maternal education do not ensure that children arrive at school with all the relevant early learning experiences they need. Considering only preschool-aged children without major risk factors in their family backgrounds, the National Center for Education Statistics (2002) reported that fewer than two-thirds were taught words, letters, or numbers at home at least three times a week, and only about half were taught songs or music or did arts and crafts that often. Among all children above the poverty level, only 61 percent were read to on a daily basis. Mothers who work 35 hours or more per week were less likely to read to their children every day than mothers who worked less, and children in single-parent families were less likely to be read to than children in two-parent families. Experience with early literacy activities is of special concern when one considers that for more than half of children entering school, learning to read presents a tremendous challenge (Lyon, 1999), and failing at this task means they will struggle throughout their academic careers.

Estimates by the National Institute for Early Education Research show in stark reality what the authors aptly describe as a "school readiness gap." Middle-income children's scores on a variety of indicators at kindergarten entry (including both social skills and academic skills such as reading, math, and general knowledge) fall well below the richest 20 percent of children, but above those in the lowest 20 percent of income (Barnett, Brown, & Shore, 2004). This work replicates that described in a report by the Economic Policy Institute entitled, "Inequality at the Starting Gate" (Lee & Burkam, 2002). Clearly, there is a continuum of functioning on school readiness tasks that is tied to family income, and "there is substantial room for the vast majority of children to improve school readiness through better preschool education" (Barnett et al., 2004, p. 5).

In addition to providing a broad range of experiences that help children prepare for school, preschool programs also provide a mechanism for the early identification of developmental problems and delays that can affect children in all income groups. Children who enter kindergarten with developmental difficulties are more vulnerable to poorer grades and lower academic attainment (Horn & Packard, 1985; Pianta & McCoy, 1997). The earlier that specific learning disabilities and delays are identified, the earlier that intervention can be provided and the better the subsequent learning outcomes (Bowman et al., 2000; Snow, Burns, & Griffin, 1998). By way of example, in a study of a preschool program in a mostly middle-class community, Wheeler (undated) found that children who did not attend were almost three times as likely to require special education and more than four times as likely to be retained at the end of their kindergarten year than children who did participate.

Preschool programs also have a nearly exclusive role in the early identification of serious emotional and behavioral disorders. Although parents may recognize behavioral problems in the preschool years, children are rarely linked to mental health services until later in elementary school after prolonged social and academic failure (Raver & Knitzer, 2002). Like deficits in preacademic skills, emotional and behavioral problems are not the exclusive domain of children from poor families. Research on affluent youth is revealing that they are a heterogeneous group of children both at low and high risk for delinquent behavior and depression (Luthar, 2003; Luthar & Becker, 2002). A growing body of evidence demonstrates that attendance in high-quality preschool plays a significant role in delinquency prevention among low-income children (Ramey et al., 2000; Reynolds, Temple, Robertson, & Mann, 2001; Schweinhart, Barnes, & Weikart, 1993; Yoshikawa, 1995), but research to date has not addressed whether it has similar value for wealthier groups. Nonetheless, the possibility of crime reduction benefits is strong enough that Fight Crime: Invest in Kids (a group of more than 2,500 police chiefs, sheriffs, prosecutors, and victims of violence) has endorsed public investments in "school readiness child care and development programs" for all children (Newman et al., 2000, p. ii).

The Benefits of Preschool for Middle-Income Children

We know from a large body of research on the impact of child care quality (some noted previously and described in more detail in Chapter 6) that participation in high-quality child care can have genuine and long-lasting benefits for children across socioeconomic backgrounds. With regard to participation in preschool, there is solid evidence that attendance helps low-income and at-risk children prepare for school (as documented in Chapters 3 and 4). However, research on the impact of preschool for middle-income children is sparse. One relevant study was conducted by Larsen and Robinson (1989), who used a rigorous, experimental design with a low-risk, educationally advantaged sample. They found that for boys, preschool attendance had a significant positive impact on achievement scores in second and third grade, and in particular, on language indicators such as vocabulary and reading. Research using data gathered as part of a nationally representative study of kindergarten children found that participation in preschool had a positive impact on reading and math skills, even after accounting for a variety of family background characteristics (including income), and that these effects persisted into the first grade (Magnusson, Meyers, Ruhm, & Waldfogel, 2004).

Evidence from evaluations of state universal prekindergarten programs is somewhat more mixed. To date only two states, Georgia and Oklahoma, have implemented truly universal programs. In the Georgia evaluation, positive impacts of program participation were seen for disadvantaged children compared with nonparticipants, but no significant differences were found among middle-class children who did or did not attend. It should be noted that middle-class children did not do worse as a result of their participation, and that a variety of factors including poor design of the study could explain the lack of findings for this group (Henry et al., 2003). In contrast, a more rigorous evaluation of Oklahoma's pre-K program indicated that attendance resulted in positive impacts on several subtests of the Woodcock-Johnson achievement test for children from all socioeconomic backgrounds (Gormley, Gayer, Phillips, & Dawson, 2004). In Maryland, the superintendent of schools for Montgomery County has embarked on a campaign to reduce the achievement gap between children from different economic backgrounds by offering full-day kindergarten. In a longitudinal study of 16,000 participants, children of all socioeconomic backgrounds showed sustained improvement through the second grade. Most importantly for our purposes, middle-income children continued to improve, even when grouped with low-income children (Hodgkinson, 2003; Weast, 2004).

In discussions of universal access to high quality preschool for all three- and four-year-old children, an often overlooked benefit is the potential to bolster academic outcomes by improving the learning environment in the classroom. As we have made clear in this chapter, differences in school readiness are quite apparent among middle-class children. In a survey conducted by Fight Crime: Invest in Kids, 86 percent of kindergarten teachers said "poorly prepared students in the classroom negatively affect the progress of all children, even the best prepared" (2004, p. 1). With universal preschool, all children would arrive at school with two years of similar experiences and more equal levels of school readiness, creating a better-prepared kindergarten class. The transition to school would be smoother – less time would be needed for children to adapt to the school environment before formal instruction begins. For example, the introduction to formal literacy is less difficult when children have already experienced literacy activities that resemble those in the kindergarten classroom (Snow et al., 1998). Children would also be better socialized, knowing more about taking turns, sharing, respecting others' space, and how to express needs appropriately. Classes would thus be less likely to be disrupted by behavior and discipline problems, which have been linked to language and cognitive delays (Raver & Knitzer, 2002). Although teachers will always be required to teach to a range of individual differences, two years of preschool experience will diminish the degree of differences in academic and social preparation evident at kindergarten entry and will permit teachers to begin the curriculum sooner in the school year.

Integration of All Children

Another argument in favor of providing universal access to preschool for all three- and four-year-olds is to promote integration of children from different ethnic and socioeconomic backgrounds, as well as the integration of students with and without disabilities. John Dewey long ago argued that public education does more than impart academic learning – it prepares children to be future citizens who participate fully in a diverse society.

Currently, the two-tiered preschool system – publicly funded preschools for children from low-income families and private preschools for children from wealthier homes – ensures socioeconomic segregation. Because of the confounding of ethnicity and immigrant status with socioeconomic status, there is also a de facto segregation according to race and culture. Merrow (2002) argues that we need to design a national preschool program in the same manner that we designed our interstate highway system. He notes that we created one interstate system that is "good enough for people behind the wheel of a Cadillac or a Lexus" and is equally available to drivers of less expensive vehicles.

The case for socioeconomic integration is certainly one of equity and preparation for responsible citizenship. There is also some research showing there are developmental benefits of integrating children in the classroom. As is the case for research on the effects of preschool, most studies of heterogeneous grouping have looked at the impact on students from low-income families. Decades ago, Coleman (1966) found that the achievement of economically disadvantaged students was greater when they were in educational settings with middle-class children; Henderson et al. (1969) found similar results when disadvantaged Mexican American children attended school with middle-class Anglo classmates.

More recent research with elementary school students has further shown that socioeconomic integration significantly improves the achievement of disadvantaged children and does not hurt the academic performance of more affluent students. On the other hand, segregation appears to depress the performance of disadvantaged students (Gottlieb, 2002). At the preschool level, research has shown that low-income children showed greater gains in language development when they were in programs with middle-class children than when they were in economically segregated programs (Schechter, 2002). Specifically, the investigators found that low-income children who attended integrated programs showed six times the gain in vocabulary compared with their peers in economically segregated programs (who also showed a marked improvement). Evidence in support of integration also comes from research on the inclusion of children with disabilities in mainstream classrooms. In high-quality programs, the inclusion of children with disabilities with typically developing children resulted in increased social skills among both groups. Nondisabled children in inclusion classes were found to be more accepting of children with disabilities, to show greater sensitivity to their limitations, and to have a greater appreciation for diversity (Diamond, Hestenes, Carpenter, & Innes, 1997; Hanline, 1993; Okagaki, Diamond, Kontos, & Hestenes, 1998).

Although research on the benefits of integration to middle-class children is scant, common sense tells us they have much to gain from interactions with children from a range of backgrounds. Exposure to other languages is the most obvious plus. Further, people of various heritages have different sets of strengths and skills that are emphasized and passed on through child-rearing practices. Children model these abilities to one another. The more diverse the setting, the more experiences there are for children to learn from one another.

The heterogeneous grouping of children has received broad support among early childhood educators and policy makers both because of its educational benefits and because it is the "right thing to do" (Bailey, McWilliam, Buysse, & Wesley, 1998, p. 29). Just as it is no longer acceptable to segregate children and adults by race, it is against democratic principles to impose discrimination in preschool. Yet this is exactly what our current two-tiered system of early care and education does. Equal opportunity has come a long way since *Brown vs. Board of Education* in 1954, the landmark ruling that ended the practice of separate schools for blacks and whites. Unfortunately, the meaning of the ruling has yet to filter to the preschool. Federal and state governments continue to practice reverse discrimination, funding programs that are deliberately segregated. Early exposure to diversity in preschool can only ease the transition into the public school system, where desegregation and diversity are more likely, and, ultimately, the transition into a multicultural and diverse adult society and work force.

CONCLUSION

Children from middle-class homes are commonly considered to be "low-risk," at least compared with low-income children. This is the reason why public preschool efforts are directed largely to children who are poor or have certain features in their backgrounds that deem them in need of extra help to get ready for school. However, the literature reviewed in this chapter indicates that family income and maternal education are not guarantees of school readiness.

All children need rich language and literacy experiences, exposure to early math concepts, and the many skills gained through arts and play to adequately prepare for school. They also need good physical and mental health and age-appropriate social and emotional traits to adapt to and thrive in the school setting. Parents, child caregivers, and early childhood teachers share responsibility for providing the environmental nutrients needed to promote development in all these areas. Yet the alarming lack of readiness among preschoolers tells us something is missing from young children's environments regardless of their family incomes. Poor-quality child care experiences are a prime suspect, but so are overly academic preschool programs and work schedules that leave parents too busy to offer enough learning opportunities at home. High-quality, universal preschool can help close the "readiness gap" by providing all children with developmentally appropriate programs that target healthy growth in the physical, cognitive, and social and emotional domains. The substantial research cited here shows that at-risk children are not the only ones in need of such attention.

It is clear that middle-class parents very much want quality preschool for their children. That is why Georgia parents spend all night in line to enroll their children in the best programs. Families in Georgia have a clear advantage over those in most other places because preschool is available to all state residents. Parents can afford to be "fussy." In 48 other states, middle-class children may be more likely than those in lower-income families to attend preschool, but high-quality private programs can cost more than their parents can afford to pay. The same is true of the child care environments where many spend a significant part of their formative years.

A sign of the value that middle-class parents place in high-quality programs that are available to everyone is that they support funding them – but *only* if they are available to everyone. Policy makers in Georgia, Oklahoma, Florida, and other places that have passed legislation to build universal systems were initially concerned with providing prekindergarten to children from groups who traditionally do not do well in school. As described in more detail in Chapter 12, these leaders understood it would be difficult to summon support for a program by asking other groups who want and need it to vote in favor of providing it to someone else. They won voter support by making their programs universal.

All parents want the best for their children. The society wants and needs all children to succeed in school so they grow up to become responsible, contributing citizens. Wide disparities in school readiness thwart this goal at the starting gate. These disparities are evident not just *between* social and economic classes but *within* them. Just as children from lower-income families face obstacles in preparing for school, so do middle-class children. These obstacles are the same: poor-quality child care and lack of preschool education, or preschool that is too brief or uninspiring to build the solid base needed for the long educational journey that lies ahead. Universal access to voluntary, high-quality preschool for all three- and four-year-old children will ease differences in school readiness and begin to address the child care crisis that affects many American families. Universal preschool will also extend equal opportunity to our youngest citizens and give every child a better chance to realize his or her full potential.

References

Bailey, D. B., Jr., McWilliam, R. A., Buysse, V., & Wesley, P. W. (1998). Inclusion in the context of competing values in early childhood education. *Early Childhood Research Quarterly, 13*, 27–47.

Barnett, W. S., Brown, K., & Shore, R. (2004). The universal vs. targeted debate: Should the United States have preschool for all? *Preschool Policy Matters,* 6. New Brunswick, NJ: National Institute for Early Education Research, Rutgers University.

Barnett, W. S., Robin, K., Hustedt, J., & Schulman, K. (2003). *The state of preschool: 2003 state preschool yearbook*. New Brunswick, NJ: National Institute for Early Education Research.

Beatty, B. (1995). *Preschool education in America: The culture of young children from the colonial era to the present*. New Haven, CT: Yale University Press.

Bowman, B., Donovan, M. S., & Burns, M. S. (Eds.). (2000). *Eager to learn: Educating our preschoolers*. National Research Council, Committee on Early Childhood Pedagogy. Washington, DC: National Academy Press.

Coleman, J. S. (1966). *Equality of educational opportunity*. Washington, DC: U.S. Government Printing Office.

Cost, Quality and Child Outcomes Study Team. (1995). *Cost, quality, and child outcomes in child care centers: Executive summary*. Denver: Author, University of Colorado.

Diamond, K. E., Hestenes, L. L., Carpenter, E. S., & Innes, F. K. (1997). Relationships between enrollment in an inclusive class and preschool children's ideas about people with disabilities. *Topics in Early Childhood Special Education, 17*, 520–536.

Education Commission of the States. (2004). State statutes regarding kindergarten. Updated June 2004. *ECS StateNotes*. http://www.ecs.org/clearinghouse/49/99/4999.htm.

Federal Interagency Forum on Child and Family Statistics. (2002). *America's children: Key national indicators of well-being, 2002*. Washington, DC: U.S. Government Printing Office.

Fight Crime: Invest in Kids. (2004, August 11). *Law enforcement group calls for more federal investment in pre-K to cut crime*. Press release. Washington, DC: Author. http://www.fightcrime.org.

Galinksy, E., Howes, C., Kontos, S., & Shinn, M. (1994). *The study of children in family child care and relative care: Highlights of findings*. New York: Families and Work Institute.

Gormley, W. T., Gayer, T., Phillips, D., & Dawson, B. (2004). *The effects of universal pre-K on cognitive development*. Center for Research on Children in the United States, Georgetown Public Policy Institute & the Georgetown University Department of Psychology, Washington, DC. Unpublished manuscript.

Gottleib, A. (2002). Economically segregated schools hurt poor kids, study shows. *The Term Paper, 1*(2), 1–2, 5–6.

Hanline, M. F. (1993). Inclusion of preschoolers with profound disabilities: An analysis of children's interactions. *Journal of the Association for Persons with Severe Handicaps, 18*(1), 28–35.

Henderson, R. W., et al. (1969). *Positive effects of a bicultural preschool program on the intellectual performance of Mexican-American Children*. Washington, DC: Office of Education, Arizona Research and Development Center.

Henry, G. T., Henderson, L. W., Ponder, B. D., Gordon, C. S., Mashburn, A. J., & Rickman, D. K. (2003). *Report of the findings from the Early Childhood Study: 2001–02*. Altanta: Georgia State University, Andrew Young School of Policy Studies.

Hodgkinson, H. L. (2003). *Leaving too many children behind: A demographer's view on the neglect of America's youngest children*. Washington, DC: Institute for Educational Leadership.

Horn, W. F., & Packard, T. (1985). Early identification of learning problems: A meta-analysis. *Journal of Educational Psychology, 77*, 597–607.

Larsen, J. M., & Robinson, C. C. (1989). Later effects of preschool on low-risk children. *Early Childhood Research Quarterly, 4*, 133–144.

Lee, V. E., & Burkam, D. T. (2002). *Inequality at the starting gate: Social background differences in achievement as children begin school*. Washington, DC: Economic Policy Institute.

Luthar, S. S. (2003). The culture of affluence: Psychological costs of material wealth. *Child Development, 74*, 1581–1593.

Luthar, S. S., & Becker, B. E. (2002). Privileged but pressured? A study of affluent youth. *Child Development, 73*, 1593–1610.

Lyon, G. R. (1999, July 27). Statement to the Committee on Education and the Workforce, U.S. House of Representatives, Hearing on Title I of the Elementary and Secondary Education Act. Washington, DC.

Magnuson, K., Meyers, M., Ruhm, C., & Waldfogel, J. (2004). Inequality in preschool education and school readiness. *American Educational Research Journal, 41*, 115–157.

Merrow, J. (2002, September 25). The "failure" of Head Start. *Education Week, 22*(4), 52.

National Center for Early Development and Learning. (2002). Regulation of child care. *Briefs, 2*(1), 1–2.

National Center for Education Statistics. (2002). *Digest of educational statistics, 2001.* Washington, DC: U.S. Department of Education.

National Child Care Information Center. (2004). *Number of children in early care and education programs.* Washington, DC: Child Care Bureau, Administration for Children and Families, DHHS.

National Education Goals Panel. (1996). *National Education Goals report: Building a nation of learners.* Washington, DC: U.S. Government Printing Office. (1996-415-143/60328)

National Education Goals Panel. (1999). *National Education Goals report: Building a nation of learners.* Washington, DC: U.S. Government Printing Office.

Newman, S., Brazelton, T. B., Zigler, E., Sherman, L., Bratton, W., Sanders, J., & Christeson, W. (2000). *America's child care crisis: A crime prevention tragedy* (2nd ed.). Washington, DC: Fight Crime: Invest in Kids. http://www.fightcrime.org.

Okagaki, L., Diamond, K. E., Kontos, S. J., & Hestenes, L. L. (1998). Correlates of young children's interactions with classmates with disabilities. *Early Childhood Research Quarterly, 13,* 67–86.

Peisner-Feinberg, E. S., Burchinal, M. R., Clifford, R. M., Culkin, M. L., Howes, C., Kagan, S. L., & Yazejian, N. (2001). The relation of preschool child-care quality to children's cognitive and social developmental trajectories through second grade. *Psychological Science, 13,* 1534–1553.

Phillips, D., Voran, M., Kisker, E., Howes, C., & Whitebook, M. (1994). Child care for children in poverty: Opportunity or inequity? *Child Development, 65,* 472–492.

Pianta, R. C., & McCoy, S. J. (1997). The first day of school: The predictive validity of early school screening. *Journal of Applied Developmental Psychology, 18,* 1–22.

Ramey, C. T., Campbell, F., Burchinal, M., Skinner, M., Gardner, D., & Ramey, S. L. (2000). Persistent effects of early childhood education on high-risk children and their mothers. *Applied Developmental Science, 4,* 2–14.

Raver, C. C., & Knitzer, J. (2002). *Ready to enter: What research tells policymakers about strategies to promote social and emotional school readiness among three- and four-year old children.* New York: National Center for Children in Poverty.

Reynolds, A. J., Temple, J. A., Robertson, D. L., & Mann, E. A. (2001). Long-term effects of an early childhood intervention on educational achievement and juvenile arrest: A 15-year follow-up of low-income children in public schools. *Journal of the American Medical Association, 285,* 2339–2380.

Schechter, C. (2002). *Language growth in low income children in economically integrated versus segregated preschool programs.* West Hartford, CT: St. Joseph's College.

Schulman, K. (2000). *Issue brief: The high cost of child care puts quality care out of reach for many families.* Washington, DC: Children's Defense Fund.

Schweinhart, L. I., Barnes, H. V., & Weikart, D. R. (1993). *Significant benefits: The High/Scope Perry Preschool study through age 27.* Ypsilanti, MI: High/Scope Press.

Snow, C., Burns, M. S., & Griffin, P. (Eds.). (1998). *Preventing reading difficulties in young children*. National Research Council, Committee on the Prevention of Reading Difficulties in young Children. Washington, DC: National Academy Press.

U.S. Census Bureau. (2000). Money income in the United States: 1999. *Current Population Reports, P60-209*. Washington, DC: Author.

U.S. Census Bureau. (2001). Table 4. Preprimary enrollment of people 3 to 6 years old, by control of school, mother's labor force status and education, family income, race and hispanic origin. Internet Release http://www.census.gov/population/socdemo/school/ppl-148/tab04.txt. Accessed June 1, 2001.

Vandell, D., & Wolfe, B. (2000). *Child care quality: Does it matter and does it need to be improved?* (Special Report 78). Madison: University of Wisconsin, Institute for Research on Poverty. http://www.ssc.wisc.edu/irp/.

Vecchiotti, S. (2003). Kindergarten: The overlooked school year. *Social Policy Report, 17*(3).

Vinovskis, M. A. (1993). Early childhood education: Then and now. *Daedalus, 122*, 151–176.

Weast, J. D. (2004). *Early success: Closing the opportunity gap for our youngest learners*. Rockville, MD: Montgomery County Public Schools.

West, J., Wright, D., & Hausken, E. G. (1995). *Child care and early education program participation of infants, toddlers, and preschoolers*. Washington, DC: U.S. Department of Education, National Center for Education Statistics. http://nces.ed.gov/pubs/95824.html.

Wheeler, C. (undated). Assessing the effectiveness of high-quality preschool as a promoter of school readiness and school success in middle-income children at risk for academic failure. Yale University, Department of Psychology, New Haven, CT. Unpublished manuscript.

Whitebook, M., Howes, C., & Phillips, D. (1989). *Who cares? Child care teachers and the quality of care in America*. (Final report of the National Child Day Care Staffing Study). Oakland, CA: Child Care Employee Project.

Yoshikawa, H. (1995). Long-term effects of early childhood programs on social outcomes and delinquency. *The Future of Children, 5*(3), 51–75.

Zigler, E., & Lang, M. E. (1991). *Child care choices: Balancing the needs of children, families, and society*. New York: Free Press.

6

Program Quality, Intensity, and Duration
in Preschool Education

Up to this point, we have described the growing national momentum toward universal preschool, as well as the developmental and economic rationales for early education and its role in the lives of children across the income spectrum. In the next several chapters, we turn our attention to issues regarding the content of effective preschool services. In this chapter we discuss issues of program intensity and duration. We also focus on the various components of quality associated with lasting benefits and strategies for how programmatic quality can be facilitated and maintained during large-scale implementation.

The effectiveness of any preschool program is related directly to the quality of that program and the amount of the program that is actually received. Beneficial impacts are most appreciable when services are delivered at reasonably high levels of quality and received in sufficient quantity by those who need the services (Brooks-Gunn, 2003; Ramey & Ramey, 1998). Aspects of program delivery can be described as program duration, intensity, and quality. An analogous description is used in medicine: when describing medication effects physicians often refer to how long the patient receives the medication, how often the patient receives it, and the amount of active ingredient it contains. Although everyone in the medical community would agree that these components are of paramount importance to good medical care, decision makers and administrators responsible for implementing social and educational programs often seem to skimp on these features and end up with a ghost of the originally planned intervention. We therefore offer specific recommendations for the delivery of effective preschool services drawn from the knowledge base and the positions of researchers and early childhood experts.

PROGRAM QUALITY

After more than 40 years of research on the effects of early childhood education and child care programs, two overall findings are clear. First, as previously discussed in this book, high-quality preschool programs can have a remarkable, long-lasting impact on the lives of children, both educationally and in terms of life-long productivity (see Chapter 3, 4, and 5). Second, these impacts are dependent on the quality of the program actually experienced by the child and family. In numerous studies, high-quality programs have been found to be related to beneficial outcomes, whereas low-quality programs are often associated with disappointing results (Berlin, O'Neal, & Brooks-Gunn, 1998; Gilliam, Ripple, Zigler, & Leiter, 2000; Love, Schochet, & Meckstroth, 1996). This relation has been demonstrated in both child care and early childhood education programs, such as Head Start and state-funded prekindergarten programs (Cost, Quality, and Child Outcomes Study Team, 1999; Gilliam & Zigler, 2000, 2004).

Because many young children spend about as much time in their day with teachers and child care providers as they do with their families, it is not surprising that the quality of their experiences and personal relationships away from home affect their development. Indeed, the influence of quality in early childhood settings on academic and social learning appears to be independent of the child's home environment (Bryant, Burchinal, Lau, & Sparling, 1994). In other words, quality matters whether you are rich or poor.

There are many ways to characterize the quality of early care and education programs, but the most commonly accepted framework differentiates between structural and process features (Phillips & Howes, 1987). *Structural characteristics* include variables such as the number of children in the group or class, the ratio of children to teachers or caregivers, and the educational level of the teachers and directors. In recent years, researchers have been paying increasing attention to related features such as the specific type of training and experience teachers have, their wage levels, and staff turnover rates (Cryer, 2003; Phillipsen, Burchinal, Howes, & Cryer, 1997).

Process characteristics refer to such variables as the physical arrangement of the classroom, teacher-child interactions, and the degree of enrichment and developmental stimulation provided. While structural characteristics are straightforward and relatively easily measured, process variables are more subtle and typically require direct observation and careful documentation. However, process variables provide a clearer indication of what the child actually experiences in the classroom. Settings with high levels of process quality are characterized by warm interpersonal relationships between teachers and children and developmentally and individually appropriate curricular goals and pedagogic styles.

Structural and process characteristics are significantly interrelated (Phillipsen et al., 1997). Obviously, better structural quality (e.g., lower child-teacher ratios and higher levels of teacher training and education) facilitates increased levels of process quality (e.g., better and more frequent interactions between teachers and children). Although both sets of features are related to child outcomes, the process variables of quality appear to have the most direct impact. For example, the NICHD Study of Early Child Care assessed children who were four and a half years old and in out-of-home care for at least 10 hours per week (NICHD, 2005). Teacher training and child-teacher ratios (both structural features) were found to be related to the quality of interactions between adults and children, in terms of teacher availability and sensitivity, emotional appropriateness, and cognitive stimulation. In turn, the quality of these interactions was significantly related to children's cognitive and social-behavioral functioning. These findings are consistent with a sizable literature showing that responsive interpersonal relationships between teachers and children are associated with better developmental outcomes and enhanced motivation to learn.[1]

These findings on the relation between structural and process quality variables as predictors of child outcomes highlight the importance of the relationships between children and their teachers. Ample evidence shows that young children learn best through the intellectual and social stimulation they receive from adults and peers (Shonkoff & Phillips, 2000). However, the quality of interpersonal relationships is not something that is easily impacted by legislation or program guidelines. Rather than trying to achieve process quality through mandates, programs should be carefully designed to create a context in which these relationships can flourish.

---

[1] For examples, see Bowman et al., 2001; NICHD, 2005; Peisner-Feinberg & Burchinal, 1997; Raver & Knitzer, 2002; and Shonkoff & Phillips, 2000.

The Ingredients of a High-Quality Early Education Program

Over the past decades there has been a vast amount of research on quality indicators in child care and early education programs. Recently, an expert panel at the National Institute for Early Education Research (NIEER) synthesized the results and compiled a list of key aspects of high-quality preschool (Jacobson, 2004). These include physical space and materials; teacher qualifications, compensation, and supervision; group size and teacher-child ratios; positive teacher-child relationships filled with a high level of mutual, responsive, and stimulating communication; and parental involvement.

Of these characteristics, the structural variables of teacher qualifications and compensation, class size, and ratios are arguably the easiest to address through policy, with the expectation that high levels of the quality in these areas will enable children to have greater amounts of positive interactions with teachers and other children. These core features of quality are discussed in further detail here. Parental involvement, which is an important predictor of children's school readiness and subsequent academic performance, is the topic of Chapter 8.

Teacher Credentials

Considerable research on teacher education shows that preschoolers learn best in classes led by well-trained and well-compensated teachers (Bowman, Donovan, & Burns, 2001; Cost, Quality and Child Outcomes Study Team, 1999; NICHD, 2005). "Well trained" is usually defined as a minimum of a bachelor's degree with specialized training in early childhood education. Specifically, evidence suggests that teachers with higher educational levels and specific training in early childhood provide care that is warmer and more sensitive to children's needs and are able to create a more stimulating and language-rich learning environment (Clarke-Stewart, Vandell, Burchinal, O'Brien, & McCartney, 2002). Well-educated teachers are also more likely to endorse a child-centered approach to teaching, leading to increased educational stimulation.

As a result, children in these environments have been found to show higher levels of cognitive and language development. Indeed, Howes (2000) found that teachers with a bachelor's degree or a Child Development Associate (CDA) credential tended to elicit more language activity and higher levels of complex play from the children in their care relative to teachers who did not have either of these credentials.[2] Teachers whose bachelor's degrees were in early childhood education elicited even greater levels of complexity and creativity in children's play. In a study of Head Start classrooms, teacher educational level was found to be significantly related to children's school readiness outcomes, whereas years of experience teaching was not a significant factor (Wheeler, 2002). (See Chapter 9 for more information on teacher requirements and work force development issues.)

To date, research and reality have yet to meet. While the consensus of the fields of early education and developmental psychology is that preschool teachers should have a minimum of a bachelor's degree plus specialized training in early childhood, most early care and education classrooms in America are not taught by a teacher with these credentials. Of the 40 states with prekindergarten, only 20 require teachers to have a bachelor's degree, and only 16 of those 20 require content specific to early education (Barnett, Robin, Hustedt, & Schulman, 2003). Child care licensure is far behind even the modest requirements for prekindergarten. Only 1 state requires child care teachers to hold a bachelor's degree, and most (40 states) require no formal postsecondary education or credentials (e.g., the CDA) at all (Barnett et al., 2003).

Standards are equally lax regarding the qualifications of assistant teachers. Preschool classrooms typically consist of 16 to 20 children, a lead teacher, and one or more assistant teachers or aides who may have a variety of roles. Although researchers and decision makers have been paying increased attention to the qualifications of the lead teacher, the characteristics of assistant teachers are often overlooked. This is shortsighted for at least two reasons. First, the purpose of having assistant teachers in preschool classrooms is to allow for a more advantageous ratio of staff to children. This enables the adults to provide more supervision and have more individual interactions with the children, and it gives children more access to adults who can help facilitate their learning. Second, it is not uncommon for assistant teachers eventually to become lead teachers. Because these assistants may represent a sizable portion of the lead teachers of tomorrow, investing in their skills today

---

[2] The CDA requires teachers to possess at least: (1) a high school diploma or equivalent; (2) 480 clock-hours of appropriate preschool experience; (3) 120 clock-hours of formal early childhood education training; (4) documented competency through formal observation of their teaching, satisfactory confidential evaluations from parents, and an approved professional resource file; and (5) passing scores on the CDA written and oral examinations (Council for Early Childhood Professional Recognition, 1996).

may reap benefits later in terms of developing the preschool teacher work force.

Amazingly, few state-funded prekindergarten programs require any level of training for assistant teachers. Of the state systems that report having requirements for assistant teachers, more than two-thirds require no more than a high school diploma or general educational development (GED) diploma; only two states require an associate's degree, and seven require assistant teachers to have a CDA credential (Barnett et al., 2003).

To provide an optimal learning environment for preschoolers and to build an infrastructure for career development that leads to a stronger and more professionalized work force in the future, it seems prudent that state planners should consider the level of training that assistant teachers should possess. Currently, 40 states recognize the CDA as a legitimate credential for teaching staff in early education and child care programs. We recommend that they require a CDA or an associate's degree in early education as a minimum level of training for assistant teachers. Of course, as Maxwell and Clifford explain in Chapter 9, more research is needed to determine the relative differences in quality of work between staff trained at the CDA, AA, and BA levels in order to make better-informed policy decisions. At this time, however, the evidence is so strong that teacher qualifications make a difference on child outcomes that we believe it is wise to err on the side of caution and require more rather than less training.

The issue of teacher training is paramount now that the states are rapidly moving toward universal preschool. Recently, increased national attention has been given to issues of accountability in schools. Even early education programs, such as Head Start and state-funded prekindergarten systems, are being scrutinized regarding the amount of student learning. If the purpose of these programs is to improve student outcomes, they must be equipped with the tools needed to achieve this goal. The most essential tool in every preschool classroom is a highly qualified staff. Teachers with specialized training in how to educate young children are more likely to have the skills necessary to provide a rich learning environment, facilitate active learning, and ultimately achieve greater levels of school readiness among their young students.

Compensation

Higher education and specialized training in early childhood are important ways teachers gain the skills necessary to work effectively with young children, facilitate learning, manage active classroom environments, and engage parents. For a college student to undertake the level of training and education needed to be an effective preschool teacher, the end result must be worthwhile. New teachers rightfully expect to be compensated for the efforts they put into their long course of study and the expenses incurred. In the early childhood field, however, compensation generally falls very short of what a skilled worker is worth – and what a person needs to support a decent standard of living. Currently, the average pay for a child care provider in America is barely above $8 per hour, often with no health, vacation, and retirement benefits. The average salary of a preschool teacher is less than half that of the average elementary school teacher (Olsen, 2002). Furthermore, salaries in early education tend to not increase much over time, even during periods when public expenditures for early education and salaries in other fields are rising (Blau, 1992). The situation is worse for preschool teachers who work in areas of concentrated poverty, serving the most at-risk populations (Sachs, 2000). An exception is preschool teachers in public school settings. They are generally more educated and better compensated relative to their peers in community-based child care programs (Bellm, Burton, Whitebook, Broatch, & Young, 2002) and Head Start (Gilliam & Ripple, 2004). Not surprisingly, their turnover rates more closely match those of elementary school teachers rather than the much higher rates found in community-based child care programs (Bellm et al., 2002).

With salary structures this poor and inconsistent across the field of early education, program directors often cannot attract highly qualified teachers (i.e., those with a bachelor's degree in early education). And when current teachers attain higher qualifications, they very often leave for jobs in public schools or other fields where pay is a lot higher. In the preschool setting, where quality and learning depend on interpersonal relationships, high teacher turnover can disrupt children's attachments and educational progress. Studies have in fact shown that staff stability is associated with better educational and developmental outcomes for children, especially those at greatest risk for educational failure (Cost, Quality and Child Outcomes Study Team, 1995; Peisner-Feinberg et al., 1999).

The link between wages and turnover is understandable and undeniable, and both are clearly associated with quality. Indeed, teacher salaries are one of the most robust predictors of the overall quality of the classroom learning environment (Phillipsen et al., 1997). For example, in a study of 104 child care centers in Boston, Atlanta, and central Virginia, teacher wages were found to be the strongest single predictor of classroom quality for both infant and toddler programs and preschools (Phillips, Mekos, Scarr, McCartney, & Abbott-Shim, 2000). In fact, teacher wages significantly predicted classroom process quality even after teacher-child ratio, group size, and teacher education and training were controlled. In a nutshell, higher wages allow directors to staff their programs with higher-skilled teachers and improve work force stability. It is also important to note that better credentialed directors, who can provide better supervision to teachers, are also associated with lower staff turnover rates (Cost, Quality and Child Outcomes Study Team, 1995; Phillips et al., 2000; Whitebook, Sakai, Gerber, & Howes, 2001; Whitebook, Sakai, & Howes, 1997).

Of course, staff salaries account for the greatest part of the overall cost of child care programs (Cost, Quality and Child Outcomes Study Team, 1995). Therefore, policies regarding teacher qualifications and salary structures are costly issues. Advocating only for greater funding for early education programs will not solve the problem of inadequate quality in preschool settings. Our position is that investments in early education should be made at a level that is likely to pay dividends in terms of increased school readiness. This means that all preschool classrooms should be staffed with a lead teacher who holds a bachelor's degree in early education and at least one assistant teacher with a minimum of a CDA or associate's degree in early education. Although these requirements will increase the overall cost of prekindergarten, our belief is that any level of cost that is not likely to yield measurable benefits to children is a waste of resources. Cost and access must always be balanced in policy decisions such as this, but when access is maximized at the expense of providing a sufficiently stimulating environment for learning, the result may be little or no return on the investment.

Some efforts have been mounted to increase teacher qualifications by making training more available and affordable. Programs such as the highly successful T.E.A.C.H. in North Carolina and other states (see Chapter 9) attempt to make higher education and specialized training in early education more affordable to a work force of preschool teachers and caregivers who earn salaries so low that subsidizing their own education is financially difficult (Roseman, 1999). Unfortunately, there are few mechanisms in early education by which wages and benefits are kept in line with increased qualifications, and there is some evidence that when preschool teachers achieve more marketable credentials they leave the field of early education for jobs where they can earn more money for fewer hours of work, such as in elementary schools (Bellm et al., 2002). Clearly, policy strategies for increasing teacher qualifications must be matched with strategies to reward higher credentials with higher salaries and benefits in order to keep these professionals in the field.

Group Size and Child-Teacher Ratios

Even well-trained and adequately compensated teachers will not be very effective educators if they have little time to interact with the individual children in their classroom. Sound early childhood pedagogy is largely a function of responsive, supportive, and stimulating interactions between adults and children. The better the quality of these interactions and the more frequently they occur, the greater the opportunity for children to learn. Obviously, the more children the teacher is responsible for, the fewer opportunities for individual attention each child will have. However, teacher qualifications, group size, and child-teacher ratios may be interactive. It may be true that better-educated teachers can effectively manage larger numbers of children, relative to teachers with less training. In France, for example, where teachers hold the equivalent of a master's degree, class sizes are surprisingly large.

Group size refers to the number of children in the classroom. It is generally assumed that regardless of the number of adults present, large numbers of children in the room increase noise levels and can create an overstimulating, chaotic environment not very conducive to learning. Research, however, does not strongly support this assumption *if* child-teacher ratios are low. Although studies have shown that smaller group sizes are associated with more positive caregiving in infant and toddler programs (Clarke-Stewart et al., 2002; Phillips et al., 2000), this seems to be less true for programs serving preschoolers (Phillips et al., 2000). Group size was related to quality only in infant and toddler classrooms, and even then the effects of group size vanished once child-teacher ratios were considered. In contrast, lower child-teacher ratios are associated with better classroom quality across all age ranges of young children – infants, toddlers, and preschoolers (Phillips et al., 2000; Phillipsen et al., 1997). Additionally, lower child-teacher ratios are related to increased responsiveness by teachers, leading to a host of positive outcomes for young children, such as improved language skills, social-emotional functioning, behavior, and play skills (Howes, Smith, & Galinsky, 1995; Love et al., 1996; NICHD, 2005; Phillips et al., 2000).

Given these data, it seems best to focus efforts primarily on reducing child-teacher ratios, because group size – which typically ranges from 16 to 20 preschoolers – seems to matter less.

What is the ideal child-teacher ratio to maximize children's learning opportunities? This is a potent question because reducing the number of children per teacher increases the overall cost of providing the program and may limit the number of children who can be served. Research to date offers suggestions but no definitive answers. We do know that highly effective, model early education programs, such as the Perry Preschool, the Abecedarian Project, and the Chicago Child-Parent Centers, had teacher-child ratios that ranged between one to six and one to eight – much higher than most widely implemented programs mandate (Duncan & Magnuson, 2004).

A study of 123 state-funded prekindergarten classes in Connecticut (Gilliam, 2000) revealed a direct link between ratios and quality. Classrooms with child-staff ratios of seven to one or less scored significantly higher on a measure that primarily assesses the quality of the learning opportunities in the classroom. Additionally, classrooms with three or four teachers present in the room (regardless of the number of children) scored significantly higher than classrooms where only one teacher was present. Given these data, a reasonable child-teacher ratio might be no fewer than three teachers for a class of 20 preschool children. The only state prekindergarten system that approaches this ratio is the New Jersey Abbott Preschool Program, which follows a court-ordered mandate of no more than 15 children for two teachers (Barnett et al., 2003).

Further research is obviously needed to examine the cost-benefit relationship between ratios and student learning, and how teacher and assistant teacher credentials might interact with ratios. While we already know that lower child-teacher ratios are better than higher ones, we need to learn at what point does further reduction in the number of children per teacher lead to diminishing returns in terms of children's learning opportunities. As is the case with other components of preschool quality, we must balance the often-competing issues of quality and effectiveness at the individual child level on the one hand with program cost and access on the other.

INTENSITY AND DURATION

In addition to issues of quality, the effectiveness of early education programs is also a function of intensity and duration. Intensity refers to the amount of the program the children receive on a daily basis. The extant range of intensity in preschool programs is great, ranging from about 2 hours long for a couple of days per week to programs that are 6 to 10 hours in length five days a week. Duration refers to how long children attend the program. For preschool programs, this is typically one academic year or, less often, two years. As previously discussed, the effectiveness of any early education program depends on how much of the integral ingredients (i.e., stimulating interactions with adults, other children, and classroom materials that facilitate learning) participants receive. The more intensity and the longer the duration of the program, the more contact with these ingredients children have.

Surprisingly, little is known about the degree of intensity needed to achieve beneficial outcomes for preschoolers. Although research supports the conventional wisdom that intensity is related to child outcomes across a variety of early intervention programs for at-risk infants and young children with developmental disabilities (see Shonkoff & Phillips, 2000, for a review), less is known about intensity effects in educational programs for preschoolers in the general population. One relevant study of intensity examined the effects of full-day versus half-day kindergarten (Elicker & Mathur, 1997). The study employed a rigorous design in which both teachers and students were randomly assigned to the longer or shorter sessions. Children who attended the full-day kindergarten scored significantly higher than half-day participants on school readiness indicators, as rated by their first-grade teachers. The mechanism by which the full-day students achieved greater levels of school readiness appeared to be at least somewhat related to the effects of the longer day on the teacher's pedagogical style. Specifically, children in full-day kindergarten spent more time engaged in child-initiated learning activities and stimulating interactions with their teachers. Children in half-day kindergarten spent a higher proportion of their time in more passive teacher-directed activities aimed at the entire group.

Several studies of early intervention programs for at-risk children have shed some light on the relative roles of duration and timing. The Carolina Abecedarian Project (Campbell & Ramey, 1994) was one of the few rigorous studies to randomly assign both duration and the exact timing of the intervention. The results indicated that earlier intervention was more beneficial than later, and a longer duration was associated with better child outcomes that tended to last longer. In a study of the effects of the Chicago Child-Parent Program (CPC), Reynolds (1995) found that two years of preschool were significantly more effective than one at increasing children's cognitive school readiness at kindergarten entry. This has also been found in a study of Head Start classrooms (Wheeler, 2002). In a careful review of dose-effect issues, Reynolds (2003) concluded that evidence from the early intervention literature supports the theory that longer durations, including follow-through programming into elementary school, are associated with increased educational achievement beyond the immediate effects of the preschool experience. For example, children who received four years or more of services through the Chicago CPC had higher educational achievement when they were 12 to 15 years old, relative to children who did not attend CPC. Because the Chicago CPC is implemented in public school settings, these results are particularly relevant to the issue of duration in universal prekindergarten. A caveat is that the program operates in low-income, inner-city districts, so the results may not generalize to other populations.

Reynolds (2004) proposed three reasons why increased duration might be associated with more optimal child outcomes. First, because effective early education programs often coordinate several key support services for children and families, time is needed for the effects of these services to reach a critical mass. Second, many children at risk of educational failure lack social stability in their homes and communities, and a longer program can provide a measure of the stability they need for optimal development. Third, longer programs serve children for a greater portion of the time when language and social skills are undergoing periods of rapid development.

However, the cost-benefit question remains: is it cost-effective to provide two years of preschool rather than one? Although preschool programs that have greater intensity and duration appear to be more effective at increasing school readiness, some shorter and less intense model programs have also been found to be highly effective. Because it seems highly unlikely that preschool programs in the real world will ever consistently match the quality of model programs implemented under near ideal conditions, increasing their intensity and duration might be viewed as one way of increasing their overall effectiveness.

The cost-benefit decision might be easier to decide if the data clearly indicated that two years of preschool are actually more than twice as effective as one year. If this were true, then the cost of doubling the duration would be easily offset by the results. However, Reynolds (1995) found that the effects on school readiness of two years of preschool were about 40 percent greater than one year – significantly greater, but not twice as great. The question, then, becomes whether a 40 percent increase in school readiness outcomes is worth essentially doubling the cost of the service. Because preschool programs implemented in large-scale contexts are on average nearly half as effective as the model programs that provide the level of results used to justify preschool (see Chapter 3) – and are less expensive per child per year to operate – the increased cost of enrolling children for two years appears justifiable.

WHY QUALITY MATTERS

The evidence is clear that children in high-quality preschool programs show better developmental outcomes than children who attend lower-quality programs. The importance of program quality cuts across all income levels, but it is particularly salient for children from low-income families. While preschool settings differ from home settings for all children, the difference is often greater for children who live in poverty (Frede, 1998). Because their home environments often do not strongly support their cognitive, language, and social development, they are particularly vulnerable to the effects of low-quality preschool. Children in poor-quality care are more likely to show delays in language, reading, and other cognitive skills and more likely to display aggressive behaviors (Bowman et al., 2001).

Quality preschool programs, on the other hand, enhance school readiness, particularly for children affected by poverty and other risk factors. In several rigorous studies, high-quality programs have been shown to improve language development, emergent literacy, and cognitive and social skills, even after controlling for family factors.[3] These effects are immediate, in terms of improved school readiness at kindergarten and first-grade entry, and sustained, as evidenced by improved academic success throughout the elementary school years (Broburg, Wessels, Lamb, & Hwang, 1998; Peisner-Feinberg et al., 2001; Vandell, Henderson, & Wilson, 1988).

Quality in Model Programs

Often, arguments for public investment in early education are made on the basis of results from highly successful and well-publicized

---

[3] See Clarke-Stewart & Allhusen, 2002; Howes, 2000; NICHD, 2005; Peisner-Feinberg & Burchinal, 1997; Peisner-Feinberg et al., 2001; Peth-Pierce, 1998.

programs, such as the Perry Preschool and the Abecedarian programs. Results from "model" preschools such as these are quite impressive, and data showing the cost-savings associated with these impacts can be very compelling to decision makers. However, it is important to realize that these model programs were thoughtfully designed, implemented at extremely high levels of quality, and studied using rigorous methods of evaluation. Frede (1998) found that effective models all shared six factors: (1) a strong focus on language; (2) a curriculum that supports learning processes, school-related skills, and knowledge; (3) qualified staff who use reflective teaching practices and are supported by highly qualified supervisors; (4) small class sizes with a high teacher-child ratio; (5) intense, coherent, and thoughtful program planning; and (6) close collaborative relationships with parents. Additionally, the scientifically scrutinizing environments in which these programs were implemented may well have kept the quality of instruction at levels that are rarely seen in real-world settings, where the work of teachers is monitored to a far lesser degree.

As Reynolds and Temple (Chapter 3) show, these model programs demonstrate much stronger effects than those typically achieved by widely implemented efforts staged in nonscientific, real-world settings (e.g., child care and state-funded prekindergarten systems). The quality of these model services may be a root cause for this difference, as is the fact that children were selected to participate on the basis of exacting criteria. (Children with the highest needs may show the most progress from early intervention.) Of course, it is not realistic to expect public early care and education systems to achieve the level of quality observed in model demonstrations. In public programs, funding is lower, attention from program designers is less intense, and admission standards are much broader. But this does not mean programs have to be perfect to produce desired outcomes. A reasonable threshold of quality may be enough to deliver benefits. We now turn to a discussion of state prekindergartens to look at how quality issues play out in more typical early childhood settings.

Quality in State-Funded Preschool Systems

Due to the growing role states are playing to support early education efforts, and the wide range of settings in which these programs are delivered, state-funded prekindergarten systems provide a good vantage point from which to appreciate issues of program quality. Unfortunately, apart from several studies of state policies and aspirational statements, few data exist to give a clear picture of actual classroom quality in the states. As of 2003, only 17 of the 40 states funding prekindergarten services have been evaluated statewide. (See Gilliam & Zigler, 2000, 2004, for descriptions of these evaluations and their findings.) Further, few of these studies used measures of process quality which, as already noted, document what children actually experience in the classroom.

Outcome data are also sparse. Exceptions occurred in South Carolina and Michigan, where significant relationships were found between classroom quality, as measured by standardized observational instruments, and child developmental outcomes. Specifically, in South Carolina preschool teachers' classroom management skills were related to children's later reading scores in kindergarten. However, only after classrooms with low-quality ratings were removed from the statistical analyses were positive program impacts found. The Michigan evaluation also revealed a significant relation between program quality in several areas and children's subsequent developmental level in kindergarten.

At least one state evaluation underscores the value of including process quality indicators in addition to measures of classroom structural quality. The New Jersey Abbott Preschool Program was launched after a State Supreme Court mandate to provide greater educational opportunities to students from low-income families. In partial response, in 1998 New Jersey began funding preschool for three- and four-year-old children in 30 of the state's poorest districts. The court ordered that these classes have a teacher with a bachelor's degree and certification in early education, an assistant teacher, and no more than 15 children per classroom (Barnett, Tarr, Lamy, & Frede, 2002). Although these teacher education and child-teacher ratio requirements are among the most stringent for state prekindergarten systems, process quality was still rated as "minimal" overall. In a representative sample of Abbott classrooms (Barnett et al., 2002), the average score was only 3.86 on the Early Childhood Environment Rating Scale–Revised (ECERS-R), a popular scale of classroom quality that ranges from a low of 1 to a high of 7. About one in five classrooms scored in a range suggestive of "inadequate" quality (1.00–2.99) that might actually be harmful to children's physical or developmental well-being, and only 2 percent scored in the "excellent" range (6.00–7.00), suggestive of levels of quality that facilitate children's development.[4] It is important to note that all of these Abbott preschool classrooms were located in high-poverty neighborhoods and targeted low-income children.

The situation in the Abbott schools is indicative of the general lack of high-quality early care and education available, particularly for children who most need the highest-quality programs. The U.S. General Accounting Office (1995) found that nearly 60 percent of children from low-income families who were enrolled in preschool attended programs that did not offer the level of quality necessary to optimally impact school readiness. A more recent study of five state preschool initiatives found that all reported a shortage of resources, particularly personnel shortages, needed to run a quality prekindergarten program (Gallagher, Clayton, & Heinemeier, 2001). And as we have seen, although the New Jersey Abbott Preschool Program maintains high levels of mandated structural quality, the process quality of the services received by the children remains disappointingly low. This problem is not limited to preschool programs targeted to low-income families. In Georgia, where the universally accessible prekindergarten system reaches more than half of all four-year-olds, parents are reported to line up the night before registration opens to enroll their children in the better programs (Merrow, 2002).

The Connecticut School Readiness Initiative (CSRI) serves three- and four-year-old children from low-income families, but the neighborhood income criteria are not as stringent as in the Abbott program. Teacher education and child-staff requirements are also not as strict, but the overall level of observable quality (as rated with the ECERS-R) was found to be much higher (Gilliam, 2000). In Connecticut, parents of children who qualify for the program can enroll them in any preschool that participates in the system, provided they can find an opening. In theory, this allows parents to be picky about the quality of preschool education their children receive. Although there are advocates of parental choice as a mechanism for facilitating program quality (Blau, 2001), consumer choice alone apparently is not sufficient for ensuring high-quality services. In a sample of 110 CSRI classrooms, process quality

---

[4] Barnett (personal communication) suggests that in order to achieve levels of quality similar to "model" programs, classrooms should score in the 6.00–7.00 range on the ECERS-R.

as rated by the ECERS-R was negatively related to the proportion of CSRI-subsidized children in those classes (Gilliam, 2000). In other words, even with a mechanism in place to encourage low-income children's access to higher-quality programs, the better programs were the least likely to serve the children with greatest need.

Although there may be several reasons for this, it seems likely that the primary cause lies in the funding mechanism for this prekindergarten system. All participating preschool sites receive the same funding level, regardless of the level of quality provided. Thus, many high-quality programs that are more expensive to operate choose not to participate, and those that do are forced fiscally to limit the number of public-supported children they enroll. Further, many of the higher-quality programs ultimately drop out of the public system because they cannot maintain their quality standards with the available public dollars (Gilliam, 2000). There is no question that quality costs money. For example, a significant part of the cost of preschool is spent on personnel. Well-trained teachers cost more to attract and retain than teachers with less training, who may deliver a lower-quality educational experience.

In the private sector, it is widely accepted that you "get what you pay for." Indeed, the spending choices of consumers exert considerable market influence over service supply and quality. However, this is not always the case when the consumer is the general public, and public funds are allocated in ways that may be unrelated to the quality of the service being purchased. One solution is tiered reimbursement, which gives higher-quality programs compensation reflective of their relatively higher costs and provides a financial incentive for other programs to boost quality. Systems of differential or tiered reimbursement have been found to be effective means for improving quality, but they are rarely used by states (Gormley, 2002; Gormley & Lucas, 2000). Rather than just purchasing any preschool services, funding systems need to support efforts to encourage, improve, and sustain quality. According to data from the Cost, Quality and Child Outcomes Study (1995), quality can be increased from minimal to good levels with a surprisingly small increase in funds.

ACHIEVING ADEQUATE LEVELS OF QUALITY

How can public-funded early education programs be implemented at a level of quality similar to the "model" programs that are so often used to justify their existence? This should be the question that guides efforts to provide public systems of early care and education. Unfortunately, when there are many unmet needs competing for limited public funds, decision makers often pay more attention to program budgets than they do to whether the program is strong enough to achieve the goals they mounted it for in the first place.

Duncan and Magnuson (2004) identify three motivations for the development of social policies: compassion, justice, and "social investment." Given the challenges faced by children living in poverty or otherwise at-risk for educational failure, early intervention is indeed a very compassionate endeavor. However, the children who most need early education are typically the least likely to attend, and when they do participate, their program is typically of lower quality than what children from more affluent families receive and far less than what is needed to prepare them for school success. This certainly builds the case for a social justice rationale for universally available preschool that is of relatively uniform quality. Ample evidence from a variety of model programs also makes the case that early education is an economic investment that can pay attractive dividends for society. But if our early education efforts are of a quality that is less than adequate for achieving school readiness, then they are neither truly compassionate, just, nor economically wise.

After decades of hearing about the impressive effects of model preschool programs that had nearly ideal conditions of quality, many decision makers and advocates have come to expect that any preschool program implemented with any level of quality and funding will achieve the same results. Although this expectation is enticing, it is not realistic (Brooks-Gunn, 2003). It is time to move beyond cheap funding of quick and dirty solutions for complex social problems.

Based on this review of the literature on quality in early childhood education programs, the following actionable recommendations are offered. To provide children with the level of quality optimally needed to support their development and school readiness, preschool programs should:

1. Be led by a qualified teacher with a bachelor's degree or higher that includes specialized training in early childhood education, and an assistant teacher who has at least a CDA credential or associate's degree in early education

2. Have a system of continuous in-service training for all staff, similar to what is provided for elementary school teachers

3. Be led by teachers who are compensated at a rate that is competitive with elementary school teachers at the same level of training, experience, and work hours
4. Have no more than 10 preschoolers per teacher or assistant teacher, and fewer if children with special needs are in the class
5. Have full-day and two-year program options
6. Implement a curriculum with empirically demonstrated effectiveness at increasing children's school readiness
7. Have clearly articulated plans for parental involvement
8. Have a monitoring system in place that includes on-site observation of the quality of education and care, with results used for tangible quality-enhancement efforts
9. Have funding levels adequate to support high-quality programs

After four decades of experimentation, the promise of early education to help all America's children get ready for school is largely unfulfilled. Most public (and indeed the majority of private) preschool programs fall short of what is needed to have a meaningful impact on children's chances for educational success. This is not only a waste of resources, it is a false promise. Policy makers and taxpayers should not be content that they have launched an early education program if that program is not good enough to meaningfully improve school readiness. Research has shown what is needed, and this knowledge should guide the gaining momentum toward universal preschool in the states. The thrust of this book is to present a vision of what should and could be.

References

Barnett, W. S., Robin, K. B., Hustedt, J. T., & Schulman, K. L. (2003). *The state of preschool: 2003 state preschool yearbook.* New Brunswick, NJ: National Institute for Early Education Research.

Barnett, W. S., Tarr, J. E., Lamy, C. E., & Frede, E. C. (2002). *Fragile lives, shattered dreams: A report on implementation of preschool education in New Jersey's Abbott districts.* New Brunswick, NJ: National Institute for Early Education Research.

Bellm, D., Burton, A., Whitebook, M., Broatch, L., & Young, M. P. (2002). *Inside the pre-k classroom: A study of staffing and stability in state-funded prekindergarten programs.* Washington, DC: Center for the Child Care Workforce. http://www.ccw.org/pubs/ccw_pre-k_10.4.02.pdf. Accessed October 27, 2003.

Berlin, L. J., O'Neal, C. R., & Brooks-Gunn, J. (1998). What makes early intervention programs work? The program, its participants, and their interaction. *Zero to Three, 18*(4), 4–15.

Blau, D. M. (1992). The child care labor market. *Journal of Human Resources, 27*(2), 9–39.

Blau, D. M. (2001). *The child care problem: An economic analysis.* New York: Russell Sage.

Bowman, B. T., Donovan, M. S., & Burns, M. S. (Eds.). (2001). *Eager to learn: Educating our preschoolers.* Washington, DC: National Academy Press.

Broberg, A. G., Wessels, H. R., Lamb, M. E., & Hwang, C. P. (1998). Effects of day care on the development of cognitive abilities in 8-year-olds: A longitudinal study. *Developmental Psychology, 33*, 62–69.

Brooks-Gunn, J. (2003). Do you believe in magic? What we can expect from early childhood intervention programs. *Social Policy Report, 17*, 3–14.

Bryant, D. M., Burchinal, M., Lau, L. B., & Sparling, J. J. (1994). Family and classroom correlates of Head Start children's developmental outcomes. *Early Childhood Research Quarterly, 9*, 289–309.

Campbell, F. A., & Ramey, C. T. (1994). Effects of early intervention on intellectual and academic achievement: A follow-up study of children from low-income families. *Child Development, 65*, 684–698.

Clarke-Stewart, K. A., & Allhusen, V. (2002). Nonparental caregiving. In M. Bornstein (Ed.), *Handbook of parenting. Vol. 3: Being and becoming a parent* (2nd ed., pp. 215–252). Mahwah, NJ: Erlbaum.

Clarke-Stewart, K. A., Vandell, D. L., Burchinal, M., O'Brien, M., & McCartney, K. (2002). Do regulable features of child-care homes affect children's development? *Early Childhood Research Quarterly, 17*, 52–86.

Cost, Quality and Child Outcomes Study Team. (1995). *Cost, quality and child outcomes in child care centers* (Public Report, 2nd ed.). Denver: Economics Department, University of Colorado.

Cost, Quality and Child Outcomes Study Team. (1999). *The children of the cost, quality, and outcomes study go to school: Technical report.* Chapel Hill: University of North Carolina, Frank Porter Graham Child Development Center.

Council for Early Childhood Professional Recognition. (1996). *The Child Development Associate assessment system and competency standards: Preschool caregivers in center-based programs.* Washington, DC: Author.

Cryer, D. (2003). Defining program quality. In D. Cryer & R. Clifford (Eds.), *Early childhood education and care in the USA* (pp. 31–46). Baltimore: Paul H. Brookes.

Duncan, G. J., & Magnuson, K. (2004). *Can society profit from investing in early education programs?* Northwestern University, Evanston, IL. Unpublished manuscript.

Elicker, J., & Mathur, S. (1997). What do they do all day? Comprehensive evaluation of a full-day kindergarten. *Early Childhood Research Quarterly, 12*, 459–480.

Frede, E. C. (1998). Preschool program quality in programs for children in poverty. In W. S. Barnett & S. S. Boocock (Eds.), *Early care and education for children in poverty: Promises, programs, and long-term outcomes* (pp. 77–98). Buffalo, NY: SUNY Press.

Gallagher, J. J., Clayton, J. R., & Heinemeier, S. E. (2001). *Education for four-year-olds: State initiatives. Technical report #2.* Chapel Hill: University of North

Carolina, FPG Child Development Center, National Center for Early Development & Learning.

Gilliam, W. S. (2000). *The School Readiness Initiative in South-Central Connecticut: Classroom quality, teacher training, and service provision. Final report of findings for fiscal year 1999.* New Haven, CT: Yale University Child Study Center. http://nieer.org/resources/research/CSRI1999.pdf.

Gilliam, W. S., & Ripple, C. H. (2004). What can be learned from state-funded prekindergarten initiatives? A data-based approach to the Head Start devolution debate. In E. Zigler & S. J. Styfco (Eds.), *The Head Start debates* (pp. 477–497). Baltimore: Paul H. Brookes.

Gilliam, W. S., Ripple, C. H., Zigler, E. F., & Leiter, V. (2000). Evaluating child and family demonstration initiatives: Lessons from the Comprehensive Child Development Program. *Early Childhood Research Quarterly, 15,* 41–59.

Gilliam, W. S., & Zigler, E. F. (2000). A critical meta-analysis of all evaluations of state-funded preschool from 1977 to 1998: Implications for policy, service delivery and program evaluation. *Early Childhood Research Quarterly, 15,* 441–473.

Gilliam, W. S., & Zigler, E. F. (2004). *State efforts to evaluate the effects of prekindergarten: 1977 to 2003.* Yale University, New Haven, CT. Unpublished manuscript.

Gormley, W. T. (2002). *Differential reimbursement policies and child care accreditation.* Georgetown University, Washington, DC. Unpublished manuscript.

Gormley, W. T., & Lucas, J. K. (2000). *Money, accreditation, and child care center quality.* Working Paper Series, Foundation for Child Development, New York.

Howes, C. (2000). Social-emotional classroom climate in childcare, child-teacher relationships and children's second grade peer relations. *Social Development, 9,* 191–204.

Howes, C., Smith, E., & Galinsky, E. (1995). *The Florida Child Care Improvement Study: Interim report.* New York: Families and Work Institute.

Jacobson, L. (2004, April 24). *Early childhood education: States moving toward universal coverage.* Education Reform. Washington, DC: Education Writers Association. www.ewa.org/offers/publications/earlychildhoodreform.pdf. Accessed August 5, 2004.

Love, J. M., Schochet, P. Z., & Meckstroth, A. L. (1996). *Are they in any real danger? What research does – and doesn't – tell us about child care quality and children's well-being.* Princeton, NJ: Mathematica.

Merrow, J. (2002, September 25). The "failure" of Head Start. *Education Week, 22*(4), 52.

NICHD Early Child Care Research Network. (2005). *Child care and child development: Results from the NICHD Study of Early Child Care and Youth Development.* New York: Guilford Press.

Olsen, L. (2002). Georgia, New York, and Oklahoma move toward "universal" preschool. Quality counts 2002: Building blocks for success. *Education Week, 21*(17), 14.

Peisner-Feinberg, E. S., & Burchinal, M. R. (1997). Relations between preschool children's child-care experiences and concurrent development: The Cost, Quality, and Outcomes Study. *Merrill-Palmer Quarterly, 43,* 451–477.

Peisner-Feinberg, E. S., Burchinal, M. R., Clifford, R. M., Culkin, M. L., Howes, C., Kagan, S. L., & Yazejian, N. (2001). The relation of preschool child-care quality to children's cognitive and social developmental trajectories through second grade. *Psychological Science, 13,* 1534–1553.

Peth-Pierce, R. (1998). *NICHD Study of Early Child Care.* Washington, DC: National Institute of Child Health and Human Development.

Phillips, D., & Howes, C. (1987). Indicators of quality in child care: Review of research. In D. Phillips (Ed.), *Quality in child care: What does research tell us?* (pp. 1–19). Washington, DC: National Association for the Education of Young Children.

Phillips, D., Mekos, D., Scarr, S., McCartney, K., & Abbott-Shinn, M. (2000). Within and beyond the classroom door: Assessing quality in child-care centers. *Early Childhood Research Quarterly, 15,* 475–496.

Phillipsen, L. C., Burchinal, M. R., Howes, C., & Cryer, D. (1997). The prediction of process quality from structural features of child care. *Early Childhood Research Quarterly, 12,* 281–303.

Ramey, C. T., & Ramey, S. L. (1998). Early intervention and early experience. *American Psychologist, 53,* 109–120.

Raver, C. C., & Knitzer, J. (2002). *Ready to enter: What research tells policymakers about strategies to promote social and emotional school readiness among three- and four-year-old children.* New York: National Center for Children in Poverty.

Reynolds, A. J. (1995). One year of preschool or two: Does it matter? *Early Childhood Research Quarterly, 10,* 1–31.

Reynolds, A. J. (2003). The added value of continuing early intervention into the primary grades. In A. J. Reynolds, M. C. Wang, & H. J. Walberg (Eds.), *Early childhood programs for a new century* (pp. 163–196). Washington, DC: CWLA Press.

Reynolds, A. J. (2004). Dosage-response effects and mechanisms of change in public and model programs. In E. Zigler & S. J. Styfco (Eds.), *The Head Start debates* (pp. 379–396). Batlimore: Paul H. Brookes.

Roseman, M. J. (1999). Quality child care: At whose expense? *Early Childhood Education Journal, 27*(1), 5–11.

Sachs, J. (2000). Inequities in early care and education: What is America buying? *Journal of Education for Students Placed at Risk, 5,* 383–395.

Shonkoff, J. P., & Phillips, D. A. (Eds.). (2000). *From neurons to neighborhoods: The science of early childhood development.* Washington, DC: National Academy Press.

U.S. General Accounting Office. (1995). *Early childhood programs: Services to prepare children for school often limited.* Washington, DC: Author. (Report N, 95-21)

Vandell, D. L, Henderson, V. K., & Wilson, K. S. (1988). A longitudinal study of children with day-care experiences of varying quality. *Child Development, 59,* 1286–1292.

Wheeler, C. M. (2002). A longitudinal investigation of preschoolers' Head Start experience and subsequent school readiness (Doctoral dissertation, Yale University). *Dissertation Abstracts International, 63*(03), 1592B.

Whitebook, M., Sakai, L., Gerber, E., & Howes, C. (2001). *Then & now: Changes in child care staffing, 1994–2000*. Washington, DC: Center for the Child Care Workforce.

Whitebook, M., Sakai, L., & Howes, C. (1997). *NAEYC accreditation as a strategy for improving child care quality: An assessment – Final report*. Washington, DC: Center for the Child Care Workforce.

7

A Whole Child Approach

The Importance of Social and Emotional Development

> We are witnessing a renewed emphasis on teaching the basic skills of read-
> ing, writing and arithmetic. No one can deny the importance of a literate
> population – one in which everyone can read, compute and communicate.
> The introduction of departmentalization of reading, math and language
> specialists earlier and earlier in schooling and the emphasis on reading
> and math in kindergarten may seem commonsensible approaches. But this
> press for basics overlooks the time-continuity, the self-organization and
> the basic responsiveness and rhythm patterns of the child. We *can* teach a
> three-year old to read, but what do the displacement of time demanded
> and the shift from other experiences do to the long-term development of
> the child?
>
> (Gordon, 1976, p. 126)

It may surprise some readers to learn that this statement was written
some 30 years ago. It could easily have been written today. Literacy has
become the buzzword not only in educational circles but in the halls of
the United States Congress. In kindergartens and first-grade classrooms
across the nation, arts and crafts and even recess are "out." Practice with
writing and all things related to words and spelling are "in." After-
school time that was once free for play and favorite activities is now
occupied by homework for children as young as five and six years old.
"Educational" toys and DVDs occupy increasing space on store shelves.

Not everyone, including your authors, agrees with this lopsided
view of child development. They believe that cognitive tasks are just
one part (albeit an important one) of what children need to accomplish as they grow and learn. Children also need to master physical
and motor skills, to learn healthy emotional responses to ordinary and

extraordinary situations, and to acquire the motivation and eagerness to try tackling new activities that demand new skills. This comprehensive view of a child's development is generally known as the "whole child" approach. During recent years, largely in the context of debates about school readiness, there has been a surge in the discourse about the relative value of emphasizing cognitive or preacademic skills versus taking a whole child approach to early learning and development. Those involved in this debate come from many realms, some of them not traditionally associated with early childhood issues. They include, among others, researchers in fields ranging from child development to neurobiology to economics; educators and curricula specialists; professionals from the medical and justice arenas; and an increasing number of policy makers at the local, state, and federal levels. We begin this chapter by briefly reviewing the history of this debate, for it is certainly not new, and by identifying what we see as the primary forces driving its resurrection today. We then summarize the most important concepts in the social-emotional domain, those that have been identified by research as being particularly important to successful functioning in preschool and beyond.

Our position, and that of the majority of scholars in child development, is that cognitive skills are not the sole determinant of how successful a child will be in school or in life. Nor does intelligence develop independently of social-emotional and other systems of human development. Think about the not-so-simple task of learning how to tie a shoe. A child must have the cognitive ability to memorize the steps involved and their order, the fine motor skills and eyesight needed, and the motivation to want to learn the task and to keep trying until he or she succeeds. Learning only the steps and content is not enough for the child to accomplish shoe-tying – or math, reading, or team sports for that matter.

We want to make clear at the outset that we are not discounting the importance of cognitive skills such as preliteracy or early math abilities. These are fundamental capabilities that certainly contribute to school readiness, and the preschool period is an opportune time to build them. Why, then, have we chosen to devote a chapter of this book to social-emotional skills and not one to cognitive skills? For one, the various intellectual tasks that must be presented and practiced in the preschool classroom are discussed throughout the book. Second, in today's social and political climate cognition is getting the lion's share of attention. Social and emotional development, by contrast, does not appear in media headlines or broadcast specials, and it has not been recognized by a White House conference. We have chosen to balance the debate by recognizing such development here, not to the exclusion of cognitive development but as a critical, if lately overlooked, component of everyday learning.

THE HISTORY OF THE DEBATE

The debate between the cognitive and whole child approaches to education has a long history (see Zigler & Bishop-Josef, 2004). At the turn of the 20th century, John Dewey's progressive movement provided invaluable approaches to pedagogy that centered on educating the whole child. Dewey (1938) emphasized fostering the imagination and early social relationships as one key path to promoting intellectual development. The Montessori movement, begun by Maria Montessori around the same time, essentially shared Dewey's view of the whole child but emphasized the development of the intellect as the path to success in social and emotional areas (Chattin-McNichols, 1981). In any case, both of these early 20th-century perspectives adopted an integrated view of development, one in which intellectual and social-emotional capabilities were seen as equally important.

The late 1950s saw a rapid shift to a preoccupation with cognitive skills. Although psychologists in Europe and other countries had been working on new models of intellectual development for some time, the attention of Americans was not grabbed until the Russians launched the satellite, Sputnik. "The Russians' feat was perceived by many as evidence that the more rigorous Soviet education system was more effective than ours. A return to the "3Rs" was touted as the way to build American superiority in the global arena" (Zigler & Bishop-Josef, 2004, p. 3). Soon cognition dominated the efforts of psychologists and educators, as if the rest of the child had ceased to exist. The focus on the cognitive system quickly gave rise to the "environmental mystique," the notion that a small amount of intervention in the early years of life could result in dramatic increases in children's intelligence test scores (Zigler, 1970).

A telling illustration comes from the history of Head Start, the comprehensive intervention program for economically disadvantaged children and their families. The program's goal was to help preschoolers from poor families prepare for elementary school. Environmentalists were elated when studies of Head Start and other early intervention programs showed that children's IQ scores went up considerably in as little as six to eight weeks. These increases were later found to be due to improvements in motivation and familiarity with the test content and school environment rather than rapid acquisition of cognitive skills (Seitz, Abelson, Levine, & Zigler, 1975; Zigler & Butterfield, 1968). Ironically, Head Start was designed to be a comprehensive program, with components to support physical and mental health, nutrition, social-emotional development, preschool education, support services for children and their families, and community and parent involvement. Yet largely in response to the zeitgeist of the times, researchers focused their studies on assessments of cognitive functioning, using IQ tests as their primary tools (Zigler & Trickett, 1978).

The 1970s saw the pendulum swing to a more moderate middle ground, and the movement toward the whole child perspective was again in ascendance. In the early 1970s the Office of Child Development (now the Administration on Children, Youth and Families) designated everyday social competence as the overriding goal of Head Start (Raver & Zigler, 1991). Around this time, researchers were beginning to think about what traits and skills help a child to function competently in school and elsewhere. Zigler and Trickett (1978) defined social competence broadly to include emotional and motivational factors, physical health and well-being, academic achievement, and formal cognitive ability. By the early 1980s the "naïve cognitive-environmental" view had been rejected, replaced by a renewed appreciation for the whole child in both the policy and research arenas (Zigler & Bishop-Josef, 2004).

In the past decade or so there has been an explosion of interest in ongoing research on the development of the human brain, and in particular, research linking early experience to neural growth. These exciting scientific advances captured a great deal of political, scholarly, and public attention. There were multiple reports in *Time* and *Newsweek* magazines, a nationally broadcast television special, professional conferences, hearings in Congress, and a flurry of books and "brain developing" activities and toys for sale to parents of infants and young children.

Much of this attention focused squarely on the possibility of enhancing cognitive growth and, specifically, on raising IQ scores. Yet this research, which in truth is only just beginning to be fully understood, is nowhere near the point of proving that intellectual capacity can be readily expanded, much less of providing a recipe for how to accomplish this end (Bruer, 1999). At this time, the work has shown that environmental factors in the early years do indeed influence neural growth patterns and the ultimate wiring of the brain, making the early years a period of special importance (Zigler, Finn-Stevenson, & Hall, 2002). So, while this work is promising and interesting, the potential application of the findings to date has been overblown. As Jones and Zigler (2002) have written elsewhere, this early, tentative research has been employed to back misguided, quick-fix solutions to more systemic, complex problems like school reform.

The attention to research on the developing brain began to push the pendulum swing away from the whole child perspective. The momentum was accelerated by President George W. Bush, who strongly emphasized cognition and literacy in his efforts to improve education – including preschool education. In July 2001 First Lady Laura Bush hosted a White House Summit on Early Childhood Cognitive Development to discuss "the latest research and ways to share information about developing strong cognitive skills in preschool programs, at home, and in other venues" (www.whitehouse.gov/firstlady/initiatives/education/earlychildhood.html). However, the emphasis of the summit was not on cognitive skills broadly construed but on literacy alone – one cognitive skill out of many related to success in school. Later, during the process of reauthorizing Head Start, language relating to social-emotional development was initially stricken from the bill passed in the House (H.R. 2210) and replaced with "literacy" (Schumacher, Greenberg, & Mezey, 2003). The change was eventually reversed, but the attempt underscores the Bush administration's narrow understanding of developmentally appropriate practice in the early years and of the skills young children need to succeed in school.

What is missed entirely in this newfound fascination with the brain is the obvious and correct assumption that the brain controls not only cognitive functions but emotions, the accompanying motivational systems, and so on. Indeed, these functions are likely intertwined and interrelated in the cortex. As Shonkoff (2004, p. 3) notes, "There isn't an exclusive brain area that determines intelligence, nor is there one for emotions or social skills. Scientific knowledge on this issue is crystal clear – cognitive, emotional, and social competence evolve hand in hand. When a supportive environment is provided, the emerging structure is sound, and all the parts work together."

ACCOUNTABILITY

While the period of zealous interest in research on early brain development might be called the "decade of the brain," the current and somewhat overlapping decade might be called "the decade of accountability." Even the staid Government Accounting Office has been renamed the Government Accountability Office. Dramatic school reform was imposed by the most radical changes to the Elementary and Secondary Education Act to occur in 40 years. The act itself was renamed the No Child Left Behind Act of 2001. This policy change was driven in large part by a desire for accountability in our public schools; accountability that would, in theory, result in better targeting of funds and programming to those schools and students that needed them the most. Federal policy makers had already mandated accountability for federal programs with the Government Performance and Results Act of 1993. With No Child Left Behind (NCLB), they extended their reach to public schools, which, although supported mostly by local and state taxes, do receive a small amount of federal funds (about 7 cents of every dollar spent). As we explain in the final chapter of this volume, there is nothing wrong with accountability. In fact, careful evaluation should be part of every programming effort, whether it is public schooling, intervention for at-risk children, universal preschool, or child care. Thoughtful and rigorous evaluation allows teachers and administrators to reflect on and revise their practices, and local and state governments to track the progress of children in their regions and determine whether further or different efforts are needed.

The darker side to accountability, and the side that is becoming more apparent as the impact of the NCLB legislation plays out, concerns what is chosen as an appropriate measure of success and what happens to those who don't meet predetermined benchmarks. To comply with NCLB, states must develop rigorous achievement tests that assess proficiency in academic areas like reading, math, and writing. The tests must be administered to almost all children in certain grades, including those with disabilities who receive special educational services. Schools that do not demonstrate consistent progress are to be given extra help. If student achievement still does not improve, a school can be closed, its administration taken over, or the students given vouchers to attend public or private schools elsewhere.

The Bush administration's focus on academic skills among public school students trickled down to preschoolers attending the federal Head Start program. The academic focus was endorsed by Congress in its Amendments to the Head Start Act in 1998, which ordered that children graduating from Head Start had to know 10 letters of the alphabet. It is unclear why 10 letters were chosen, instead of 9, or

26, or what exactly this knowledge has to do with eventual literacy. Legislators had never before acted as if they knew more about what young children should learn than do early childhood professionals, but they were apparently under a great deal of pressure to impose some form of accountability on Head Start instead of allowing it to be guided – as it always has – by its own acclaimed Program Performance Standards.

Accountability in Head Start was pushed a step further in 2003, when the National Reporting System (NRS) was instituted. The system imposes standardized testing twice per year to assess Head Start children's language, preliteracy, and premath skills. (To date, only children set to enter kindergarten are being tested; three-year-olds are thus far excluded.) This new system essentially tests whether children improve on a narrow set of cognitive skills and has been widely criticized as a result (e.g., Raver & Zigler, 2004). As described by experts in early childhood education and measurement, "This test teaches us very little about young children's preschool skills. It provides no authentic literacy evaluation and little information about math skills. Entire areas of development, such as social-emotional growth, physical development, science, social studies, the arts, and most of literacy and even phonemic awareness, are omitted" (Meisels & Atkins-Burnett, 2004, p. 3).

Other criticisms of the NRS center on the appropriateness of assessing such young children with formal, sit-down tests when they are first being introduced to school. Zigler and Styfco (2004) note that Head Start's goals are not limited to early education but include physical and mental health, social and emotional development, involving parents, and strengthening families and host communities, all of which are already being assessed through numerous mandatory reporting requirements. Testing whether a child can count the number of turtles in a picture does not begin to tap the purpose of Head Start. Furthermore, it remains unclear how and for what the test results will be used. One fear is that funding decisions will eventually be based on children's scores even though the test is considered inappropriate for preschoolers (Meisels & Atkins-Burnett, 2004; Stipek, 2004).

Accountability serves a valuable function. No program administrator should be given free use of public dollars without ever having to prove the money is going to good use. School performance and school readiness are complex but measurable results of publicly funded programs (see Chapter 2). To be useful, however, measures must be appropriate and realistic. They are best chosen by those who know what is appropriate and realistic. Otherwise, accountability assumes the role of dictating or inventing goals that are not embraced by those ordered to carry them out. School readiness was always the goal of Head Start, which has been joined in this mission by an increasing number of state prekindergarten programs. Head Start promotes readiness in the context of the whole child, but it is being held accountable only for academic goals. The danger here is the program is a model of effective early childhood services for the states as they develop their pre-K programs. If state planners see Head Start emphasizing cognition and striving to improve scores on the NRS, they will follow the model and design purely academic preschools. School readiness cannot and should not be defined by policy makers' needs for accountability but by early childhood experts' knowledge about what children need to succeed in school.

Despite these unfortunate developments, it is apparent the pendulum may again be moving to middle ground. Senators and even some officials in the Bush administration showed signs of listening to the calls of the research and practice communities and drafted legislation to acknowledge that cognitive and social-emotional development are synergistic, and that an integrated focus in early childhood programming and evaluation is the best way to achieve school readiness.

WHAT IS SOCIAL-EMOTIONAL DEVELOPMENT?

In an extraordinarily comprehensive synthesis of research in the early childhood field, the National Research Council defined two essential areas of social and emotional functioning: "learning to regulate one's emotions, behaviors, and attention," and "learning to relate well to other children and forming friendships" (Shonkoff & Phillips, 2000, p. 92). In this chapter, we describe these two domains more generally as emotional competence and social competence. Success in both depends in part on (1) the child's history of relationships with important caregivers and other children, and (2) the child's physical and mental health. We first describe the primary skills needed to progress in each of these areas and then discuss the links between these competencies and academic achievement.

Emotional Competence

Emotional competence is defined generally as a child's ability to manage emotions, to understand the feelings and emotions of others, and to take another's perspective. These skills are formed through an interplay of individual dispositions and experiences at home as well as in child care, preschool, and school. They are important predictors of a child's ability to get along with peers and the adults in their lives, to learn effectively, and ultimately to succeed in school.

The idea of emotional competence has been around for some time, although scientific interest in the concept periodically waxes and wanes. Younger readers were likely introduced to the term by Daniel Goleman's 1997 book, *Emotional Intelligence*. Goleman defines emotional intelligence as a combination of human competencies like self-awareness, self-discipline, persistence, and empathy. He argues that this type of intelligence is of greater consequence in life than formal cognitive skills. Not-quite-as-young readers will recall the study of emotions in children and their influence on development that surged decades ago (e.g., Izard, 1971). In fact, in the late 1970s researchers were placing emotional skills on equal footing with physical health, formal cognitive ability, achievement, motivation, and social skills (Zigler & Trickett, 1978). Then, as now, many child development experts believed growth and maturity in emotional skills to be a primary task of early childhood (Aber & Jones, 1997; Sroufe, 1979).

A complete and more scientific definition of emotional intelligence was developed by Mayer and Salovey: "Emotional intelligence involves the ability to perceive accurately, appraise, and express emotion; the ability to access and/or generate feelings when they facilitate thought; the ability to understand emotion and emotional knowledge; and the ability to regulate emotions to promote emotional and intellectual growth" (1997, p. 10). Thinking about this technical definition from the perspective of the preschool-aged child leaves us with something more general: the degree to which a child can use his or her emotional resources and abilities to meet the demands and opportunities of the school environment, including interactions with peers and adults and learning new academic skills.

In less technical terms, what are the emotional resources and abilities children need for success in preschool? They fall into four general categories: (1) emotion regulation: the ability to adjust emotional responses in a way that is appropriate to the context; (2) emotion knowledge: the ability to accurately identify and label a variety of emotions in oneself and others; (3) emotional expression: the ability to effectively use emotions in relationships with others; and (4) empathy or perspective taking: the ability to take another's point of view and understand their feelings (Cole, Martin, & Dennis, 2004; Raver & Zigler, 1997; Saarni, 1990).

These basic skills are, of course, interrelated. A child cannot understand another's feelings if he or she is unable to accurately recognize and label the emotions being expressed. Moreover, the appropriate use of different emotions in different contexts necessarily requires the ability to adjust emotional responses accordingly. In the preschool context, appropriately recognizing, using, and regulating emotions is a requirement of some of the most basic rhythms and tasks of the classroom. For example, children must manage the transition from home to school, including controlling anxiety and sadness associated with separating from their parents, and recognizing and understanding the same emotions in classmates as they too manage separation. Children must also be able to move emotionally from one task to another, such as from active outside play to a quiet lesson or naptime indoors. As a final example, in the school environment children must be able to divert attention away from noise and distractions in order to focus on the activity or lesson at hand. These examples each represent one of any number of instances in which children's knowledge of and ability to handle their emotions are likely to affect what and how much they learn. In the course of the day, these skills affect a child's ability to get along with others, solve problems, and negotiate conflicts that arise (Coie & Dodge, 1998; Lemerise & Arsenio, 2000).

Social Competence

While we endorse broad definitions of social competence that include the physical, cognitive, and social-emotional domains (e.g., Zigler & Trickett, 1978), in this section we focus on children's abilities to manage their interactions with peers and form friendships. This is a critical task of preschool and the early school years (Parker, Rubin, Price, & DeRosier, 1995) and is most relevant to our topic of social and emotional development. One set of skills necessary to positive interactions among children is social-cognitive in nature, meaning they are used when a child tries to understand a situation, reads and interprets the actions and intentions of others, and then decides on a course of action.

Kenneth Dodge is a scientist who has studied the factors that determine the nature of children's interactions with each other and, in particular, how and why some children develop aggressive behavior. He developed a model that describes a series of five social-cognitive steps that affect how a child will respond in different kinds of social situations (Dodge, 1986). Take, for example, a common social situation for a child in a preschool classroom: Bobby walks over to the book corner to find his favorite book for quiet time. When he gets there, he finds that Jesse has already taken the book he wanted. Does Jesse like this book too, or did she know that Bobby would be looking for it and grabbed it intentionally just to make him angry?

In Dodge's model, the progression from a social event (e.g., Jesse taking Bobby's book) to a particular response (e.g., Bobby either hitting Jesse or asking nicely to have the book back) follows a series of cognitive processing steps: attention to social and emotional signals, interpretation and understanding of those signals, thinking about possible responses to the situation, and deciding on a response (Crick & Dodge, 1994; Dodge 1986). An aggressive child confronted with a social problem-solving situation such as that between Bobby and Jesse, might immediately assume hostile intentions on the part of the other child. Seeing the classmate as mean makes it unlikely the child will choose a positive problem-solving strategy. Rather, the child will probably review a limited set of possible negative responses and choose an aggressive response as an effective solution. Children with this kind of biased perception are more likely to be disliked and rejected by their peers, to have difficultly forming and maintaining friendships, and to suffer academically (Dodge & Feldman, 1990; Ladd, Birch, & Buhs, 1999).

It is clear that the emotional and social competencies described here are interwoven (Lemerise & Arsenio, 2000). For example, a child must be able to recognize emotions to be able to read the social cues of peers accurately, and children must be able to regulate their own emotions and behavior when responding to the actions of others.

The Contexts of Emotional and Social Competence

Children's emotional and social skills arise from their inborn temperaments, but the development of these skills is strongly influenced by social histories of relationships with important caregivers and other adults, siblings, and peers. A major formulation in child development, called the ecological approach, views children's behavior as developing within a set of social systems ranging from close to far from the child's everyday world. The closest influence is of course the family system, followed by child care and schools, peer groups, and the neighborhood and community, extending eventually to broad societal norms and social policies (Bronfenbrenner, 1979). For instance, a child's sense of security or fear depends on how safe the family feels, which is influenced by crime rates in the neighborhood, which in turn are affected by community mores and law enforcement budgets, which are determined by policy makers' priorities and taxation policies. While it is accepted that all of these environments have an impact on child development, the family context is considered the most influential of these systems for very young children (Aber, 1994; Campbell, 1995; Zeanah, Boris, & Larrieu, 1997).

It is not surprising, then, that in the study of social and emotional development, no factor has received as much attention as the quality of the parent-child relationship. Decades of research have shown that this relationship establishes a critical foundation for the development of "virtually all aspects of development – intellectual, social, emotional, physical, behavioral, and moral. The quality and stability of a child's human relationships in the early years lay the foundation for a wide range of later developmental outcomes that really matter" (National Scientific Council on the Developing Child, 2004, p. 3).

Consider, for example, how the characteristics of the parent-child relationship are fundamentally important for literacy. The way parents talk to and respond to their children from the very beginning has a tremendous impact on social and emotional learning and motivation to achieve higher skills. In essence, reading begins with thousands of loving interactions between parent and child. It begins as a child develops a sense of self-worth by realizing that his or her accomplishments – whether they be smiling, learning to roll over, or reciting the alphabet – are important to significant others. It begins with sitting in a safe lap, hearing a bedtime story. It is evident that success in preschool, defined as the acquisition of the school readiness skills necessary for the next educational step, is determined in part by the child's history of relationships. Early relationships contribute to the skills and resources children bring with them to school, where relationships with teachers and friends expand those skills and resources.

When starting kindergarten, the resources children need most to adapt to the school environment derive from their mental health, socialization, and emotional maturity. Preschool is a good place to build on these resources and give children opportunities to practice using them. However, reports from the field suggest that an increasing number of young children require more than the usual amount of attention to their social and mental health needs (see Chapter 11). For example, studies have documented the presence of significant problems such as depression, aggression, and negative emotionality in children as young as toddlerhood, particularly among those at high risk due to socioeconomic factors (e.g., Carter, Briggs-Gowan, Jones, & Little, 2003). In a groundbreaking report on the mental health needs of children in Head Start, Yoshikawa and Knitzer (1997, p. 10) observe, "Staff report that children are showing more and more evidence of stress in the classroom, with a significant number exhibiting withdrawn, aggressive or 'out of control' behaviors that challenge the staff and sometimes threaten the overall classroom climate." Learning cannot proceed smoothly in such a climate. For these children, the preschool outcomes that really matter are their knowledge, use, and regulation of emotions and behavior, and their ability to apply these emotional skills effectively in their relationships with their teachers and peers.

THE CONNECTION BETWEEN SOCIAL-EMOTIONAL AND ACADEMIC FUNCTIONING

Research over the past two decades has revealed concrete links between the emotional and social competencies just described and academic success in preschool and beyond (see Raver, 2002; Raver & Zigler, 1991, 1997, 2004). Very early patterns of social-emotional and behavioral problems have been found to influence not only the course of social and emotional development later on but also to impact the acquisition of academic and cognitive skills (Jimerson, Egeland, & Teo, 1999; McLelland, Morrison, & Holmes, 2000; Shonkoff & Phillips, 2000). Raver (2002, p. 4) summarizes the literature with the simple statement, "Children who have difficulty paying attention, following directions, getting along with others, and controlling negative emotions of anger and distress, do less well in school." These problems are ascribed directly to children's emotional skills (e.g., their "ability to regulate their emotions in prosocial versus antisocial ways") and their social skills (e.g., the degree to which they get along with and are accepted by their peers, and elicit positive interactions with their teachers).

Raver (2002) goes on to list the serious academic consequences of social and emotional difficulties. Children with poor emotional and behavioral responses are likely to be rejected by their peers, so they may lose out on opportunities to learn from their classmates in play and group activities. They may miss academic lessons if they are always engaged in a conflict or daydreaming, or if they cannot focus their attention away from distracting thoughts, sights, and sounds and toward the task at hand. Due to a combination of these factors, they may grow to like school less and, as a result, participate less over time.

There is a mounting body of evidence that these problems in the early years are linked to later school adjustment and performance (e.g., Lynch & Cicchetti, 1997; Pianta, Steinberg, & Rollins, 1995; Wentzel, 2002). The clearest illustration that emotional status impacts academic outcomes can be drawn from data on students who have emotional disorders so serious that they are placed in special education services. Between 1992 and 2002, these students had high school dropout rates from 61 to more than 70 percent, far higher than any other special education grouping. In the 2002–2003 academic year, their dropout rate declined to a still shocking 56 percent (U.S. Office of Special Education Programs, 2004).

THE IMPACT OF INTERVENTION ON SOCIAL-EMOTIONAL SKILLS

Research strongly supports the possibility that high-quality, intensive, and coordinated efforts can have an impact on children's social and emotional skills. Not only has intervention been effective in reducing aggression and behavior problems in kindergarten, but in some programs these benefits have been found to extend to future problem behaviors like teenage delinquency and adult crime (e.g., Olds, 1997; Reynolds, 2000; Schweinhart, Barnes, & Weikart, 1993; Yoshikawa, 1995). The findings regarding the impact of early intervention on later delinquency have captured a great deal of national attention. The evidence is so compelling that there is now an advocacy group called Fight Crime: Invest in Kids, whose membership includes police chiefs, sheriffs, prosecutors, and crime victims. The group has issued policy statements calling for high-quality child care and universal prekindergarten programming as valuable crime prevention efforts (Fight Crime, 2004; Newman, Brazelton, Zigler, et al., 2000).

There is also growing evidence for the effectiveness of emotions-centered interventions on children's social-emotional skills in the early school years. For example, the PATHS (Promoting Alternative Thinking Strategies) curriculum has been evaluated with a variety of populations and has been shown to enhance children's fluency and comfort in discussing both positive and negative emotions, their understanding of the malleability of various emotion states, and their beliefs in their ability to control and manage their own emotions (Denham, 1998; Greenberg, Kusche, Cook, & Quamma, 1995). The PATHS intervention also has positive impacts on children's social-cognitive and interpersonal behavioral skills, assessed by teacher ratings of how children handle frustration, their assertive social skills, their attention and focus on tasks, and positive peer relations (Greenberg et al., 1995). Ways to build and use other emotion-centered curricula have also been published (e.g., Hyson, 2004).

The recent advances in neuroscience include one conceptualization emphasizing the neurobiological features underlying the integration of cognition and emotion – that is, both share certain areas and functions of the brain. Blair (2002) argues that because the development of these systems is integrated, early education should include curricula that specifically address social-emotional as well as cognitive skills. Head Start, which operationalized the whole child approach in the 1960s, has always had a service component devoted to mental health and a focus on social and emotional skills in addition to preschool education. Longitudinal research on Head Start is rare, but Blair identifies the similar whole child model used in the successful Chicago Child-Parent Centers as an example of how academic achievement is impacted by attention to social and emotional development.

CONCLUSION

The points we make here have been echoed in numerous research and policy reports over the past few years and are supported by a large and comprehensive body of research from the past several decades (e.g., Hyson, 2004; Raver & Zigler, 2004; Shonkoff, 2004). It is clear that relying on cognitive and academic functioning as the sole determinant of both curricular and evaluation choices in universal prekindergarten settings is shortsighted at best and developmentally inappropriate and potentially damaging to children's future life chances at worst. We must focus our efforts on the whole child: (1) the cognitive and early academic skills the child needs as a base on which to build later academic skills, (2) the social-emotional skills necessary to be an effective learner, (3) the physical and mental health of the child that influences his or her ability to do well in any of these domains, and (4) the "environment of relationships" (National Scientific Council, 2004) within which children construct their worlds. We agree with Jack Shonkoff's (2004, p. 9) eloquent statement:

Developmental scientists have concluded that you can't really separate these two domains [cognitive and social-emotional] of development within a child. And educators know that it doesn't matter how well you are able to read if you are pre-occupied with anxiety or fear or you can't control your behavior. Since a kindergartner who is emotionally healthy but has not mastered any pre-academic skills also is headed for difficulty in school, why are we wasting our time arguing about the relative importance of reading skills versus emotional well-being? Why can't we simply agree that they are both very important?

References

Aber, J. L. (1994). Poverty, violence and child development: Untangling family- and community-level effects. *Minnesota Symposium on Child Psychology, 27,* 229–272.

Aber, J. L., & Jones, S. M. (1997). Indicators of positive development in early childhood: Improving concepts and measures. In R. Hauser, B. Brown, W. Prosser, & M. Stagner (Eds.), *Indicators of children's well-being* (pp. 395–408). New York: Russell Sage.

Blair, C. (2002). School readiness: Integrating cognition and emotion in a neuro-biological conceptualization of children's functioning at school entry. *American Psychologist, 57,* 111–127.

Bronfenbrenner, U. (1979). *The ecology of human development: Experiments by nature and design.* Cambridge, MA: Harvard University Press.

Bruer, J. T. (1999). *The myth of the first three years: A new understanding of early brain development and life-long learning.* New York: Free Press.

Campbell, S. B. (1995). Behavior problems in preschool children: A review of recent research. *Journal of Child Psychology and Psychiatry, 36,* 113–149.

Carter, A. S., Briggs-Gowan, M., Jones, S. M., & Little, T. D. (2003). The Infant Toddler Social and Emotional Assessment: Factor structure, reliability, and validity. *Journal of Abnormal Child Psychology, 31,* 495–514.

Chattin-McNichols, J. P. (Ed.). (1981). *Montessori schools in America: Historical, philosophical and empirical research perspectives.* Lexington, MA: Ginn Custom Publishing.

Coie, J. D., & Dodge, K. A. (1998). Aggression and antisocial behavior. In N. Eisenberg (Ed.), *Handbook of child psychology. Vol. 3: Social, emotional and personality development* (pp. 779–862). New York: Wiley.

Cole, P. M., Martin, S. E., & Dennis, T. A. (2004). Emotional regulation as a scientific construct: Methodological challenges and directions for child development research. *Child Development, 75,* 317–333.

Crick, N. R., & Dodge, K. A. (1994). A review and reformulation of social-information processing mechanisms in children's social adjustment. *Psychological Bulletin, 115,* 74–101.

Denham, S. A. (1998). *Emotional development in young children.* New York: Guilford Press.

Dewey, J. (1938). *Experience and education.* New York: Touchstone.

Dodge, K. A. (1986). A social information processing model of social competence in children. *Minnesota Symposium in Child Psychology, 18,* 77–125.

Dodge, K. A., & Feldman, E. (1990). Issue in social cognition and sociometric status. In S. A. Asher & J. D. Coie (Eds.), *Peer rejection in childhood* (pp. 119–154). Cambridge: Cambridge University Press.

Fight Crime: Invest in Kids. (2004). Quality pre-kindergarten: Key to crime prevention and school success. *Research brief.* Washington, DC: Author.

Goleman, D. (1997). *Emotional intelligence.* New York: Bantam Books.

Gordon, I. J. (1976). *On the continuity of development.* Position paper of the Association for Childhood Education International, Washington, DC.

Greenberg, M., Kusche, C. A., Cook, E., & Quamma, J. P. (1995). Promoting emotional competence in school-aged children: The effects of the PATHS curriculum. *Development and Psychopathology, 7,* 117–136.

Hyson, M. (2004). *The emotional development of young children: Building an emotion-centered curriculum.* New York: Teachers College Press.

Izard, C. E. (1971). *The face of emotion.* New York: Appleton-Century-Crofts.

Jimerson, S., Egeland, B., & Teo, A. (1999). A longitudinal study of achievement trajectories: Factors associated with change. *Journal of Educational Psychology, 91,* 116–126.

Jones, S. M., & Zigler, E. (2002). The Mozart effect: Not learning from history. *Applied Developmental Psychology, 23,* 355–372.

Ladd, G. W., Birch, S. H., & Buhs, E. S. (1999). Children's social and scholastic lives in kindergarten: Related spheres of influence? *Child Development, 70,* 1373–1400.

Lemerise, E. A., & Arsenio, W. F. (2000). An integrated model of emotion processes and cognition in social information processing. *Child Development, 71,* 107–118.

Lynch, M., & Cicchetti, D. (1997). Children's relationships with adults and peers: An examination of elementary and junior high school students. *Journal of School Psychology, 35,* 81–99.

Mayer, J. D., & Salovey, P. (1997). What is emotional intelligence? In P. Salovey & D. J. Sluyter (Eds.), *Emotional development and emotional intelligence: Educational implications* (pp. 3–34). New York: Basic Books.

McLelland, M. M., Morrison, F. J., & Holmes, D. L. (2000). Children at risk for early academic problems: The role of leaning-related social skills. *Early Childhood Research Quarterly, 15,* 307–320.

Meisels, S. J., & Atkins-Burnett, S. (2004). The Head Start National Reporting System: A critique. *Young Children,* January 2004. http://www.journal.naeyc.org/bt,/200401/.

National Scientific Council on the Developing Child. (2004). *Young children develop in an environment of relationships.* Working Paper 1. Waltham, MA: Brandeis University.

Newman, S., Brazelton, T. B., Zigler, E., et al. (2000). *America's child care crisis: A crime prevention tragedy.* Washington, DC: Fight Crime: Invest in Kids.

Olds, D. (1997). Long-term effects of home visitation on maternal life-course and child abuse and neglect. *Journal of the American Medical Association, 27,* 637–643.

Parker, J. G., Rubin, K. H., Price, J. M., & DeRosier, M. E. (1995). Peer relationships, child development, and adjustment: A developmental psychopathology perspective. In D. Cicchetti & D. J. Cohen (Eds.), *Developmental psychopathology. Vol. 2: Risk, disorder, and adaptation* (pp. 96–161). New York: Wiley.

Pianta, R. C., & Steinberg, M. S., & Rollins, K. B. (1995). The first two years of school: Teacher-child relationships and deflections in children's classroom adjustment. *Development and Psychopathology, 7*, 295–312.

Raver, C. C. (2002). Emotions matter: Making the case for the role of young children's emotional development for early school readiness. *Social Policy Report, 16*(3), 3–18.

Raver, C. C., & Zigler, E. (1991). Three steps forward, two steps back: Head Start and the measurement of social competence. *Young Children, 46*, 3–8.

Raver, C. C., & Zigler, E. (1997). Social competence: An untapped dimension in evaluating Head Start's success. *Early Childhood Research Quarterly, 12*, 363–385.

Raver, C. C., & Zigler, E. (2004). Another step back? Assessing readiness in Head Start. *Young Children*, January 2004. http://www.journal.naeyc.org/btj/200401/.

Reynolds, A. (2000). *Success in early intervention: The Chicago Parent-Child Centers.* Lincoln: University of Nebraska Press.

Saarni, C. (1990). Emotional competence: How emotions and relationships become integrated. *Socio-emotional development. Nebraska Symposium on Motivation, 36*, 115–182.

Schumacher, R., Greenberg, M., & Mezey, J. (2003). *Head Start reauthorization: A preliminary analysis of HR2210, the "School Readiness Act of 2003."* Washington, DC: Center for Law and Social Policy.

Schweinhart, L. J., Barnes, H. V., & Weikart, D. P. (1993). *Significant benefits: The High/Scope Perry Preschool study through age 27.* Monographs of the High/Scope Educational Research Foundation (No. 10). Ypsilanti, MI: High/Scope Press.

Seitz, V., Abelson, W. D., Levine, E., & Zigler, E. (1975). Effects of place testing on the Peabody Picture Vocabulary Test scores of disadvantaged Head Start and non–Head Start children. *Child Development, 46*, 481–486.

Shonkoff, J. P. (2004). *Science, policy, and the young developing child.* Chicago: Ounce of Prevention Fund.

Shonkoff, J. P., & Phillips, D. A. (2000). *From neurons to neighborhoods: The science of early childhood development.* Washington, DC: National Academy Press.

Sroufe, L. A. (1979). The coherence of individual development: Early care, attachment and subsequent developmental issues. *American Psychologist, 34*, 194–210.

Stipek, D. (2004). Head Start: Can't we have our cake and eat it too? *Education Week, 23*(34), 43–52.

U.S. Office of Special Education Programs. (2004). *IDEA Part B trend data.* Table B5A. Washington, DC: Author. http://www.ideadata.org/docs%5CPartBTrendData%5CB5A.html. Accessed January 2005.

Wentzel, K. R. (2002). Are effective teachers like good parents? Teaching styles and student adjustment in early adolescence. *Child Development, 73*, 287–301.

Yoshikawa, H. (1995). Long-term effects of early childhood programs on social outcomes and delinquency. *Future of Children, 5*(3), 51–75.

Yoshikawa, H., & Knitzer, J. (1997). *Lessons from the field: Head Start mental health strategies to meet changing needs*. New York: National Center for Children in Poverty.

Zeanah, C. H., Boris, N. W., & Larrieu, J. A. (1997). Infant development and developmental risk: A review of the past 10 years. *Journal of the American Academy of Child and Adolescent Psychiatry, 36*, 165–178.

Zigler, E. (1970). The environmental mystique: Training the intellect versus the development of the child. *Childhood Education, 46*, 402–412.

Zigler, E., & Bishop-Josef, S. (2004). Play under siege: A historical overview. In E. Zigler, D. Singer, & S. Bishop-Josef (Eds.), *Children's play: The roots of reading* (pp. 1–14). Washington, DC: Zero to Three Press.

Zigler, E., & Butterfield, E. C. (1968). Motivational aspects of changes in IQ test performance of culturally deprived nursery school children. *Child Development, 39*, 1–14.

Zigler, E., Finn-Stevenson, M., & Hall, N. W. (2002). *The first three years and beyond*. New Haven, CT: Yale University Press.

Zigler, E., & Styfco, S. J. (2004). Head Start's National Reporting System: A work in progress. *Pediatrics, 114*, 858–859.

Zigler, E., & Trickett, P. (1978). IQ, social competence, and the evaluation of early childhood intervention programs. *American Psychologist, 33*, 789–798.

8

Parent Involvement in Preschool

Christopher C. Henrich and Ramona Blackman-Jones

The benefits of parent involvement in children's schooling are widely recognized by educators. Policy makers agree, encouraging practices to involve parents in schools by codifying them in federal law: parent involvement was the eighth goal of the 1994 Educate America Act (U.S. Department of Education, 1996), has been periodically required of school programs funded under Title I of the Elementary and Secondary Education Act (now called the No Child Left Behind Act; Arroyo & Zigler, 1993), and has been part of Head Start's national performance standards since they became law in 1975. As more states fund universally accessible preschool programs, planners would be wise to consider policies for involving parents in their children's preschool education. In this chapter we describe the most effective parent participation model to date, Head Start, and discuss how state programs can build on Head Start's success, using it as a template for practices that invite parents into schools.

We begin by summarizing the research on parent involvement in school and discuss the ramifications of the findings for universal preschool programs. We explain the mechanisms through which parent involvement is thought to be associated with children's academic achievement. We identify common barriers to parent involvement and ways of overcoming them. In addition to addressing the policy implications for state-funded preschool that can be gleaned from the research, we highlight opportunities that state preschool initiatives afford for a partnership between policy and research. This partnership can lead to better understanding of the dynamics of parent involvement and can further the development of effective strategies for including parents in their children's preschool education.

REVIEW OF THE RESEARCH

Parent involvement is a broad term that encompasses a number of ways in which parents can support their children's education. Epstein (1995) posited a framework of various types of parent involvement that contribute to student success. This framework, which has been almost universally adopted in the scholarly literature (Baker, 1996), includes six areas:

- Basic parenting obligations, such as providing a supportive home atmosphere for children
- School-to-home communications, such as newsletters, phone calls, and parent-teacher conferences
- Parent participation in school functions, such as attending special events and volunteering in the classroom
- Parent engagement in learning at home, as in creating a home environment conducive to learning and helping children with their schoolwork
- Parent involvement in school decision making, which might include activities such as attending school board meetings and joining parent-teacher organizations (PTO)
- Community connections, such as the PTO reaching out to local businesses to solicit support for the school

Although Epstein's framework has been heuristically adopted by many researchers, not all six of her types of involvement have been equally investigated. One meta-analysis identified four domains of parent involvement that have received consistent empirical attention: (1) parent-child communication about school and homework, which includes talking with children about their school day, showing an interest in school activities, and helping them with their schoolwork; (2) parental supervision, which includes television restrictions, setting aside time for homework, and home surroundings conducive to studying; (3) parents' educational aspirations for their children and whether they convey the message that they value academics; and (4) school contact and participation in school functions (Fan & Chen, 2001).

Most research on parent involvement has focused on school-age children. This work consistently shows that parent involvement, both at home and at school, is associated with higher academic achievement (e.g., Christenson, 1999; Fantuzzo, Davis, & Ginsberg, 1995; Grolnick & Slowiaczek, 1994; Henrich, 2001; Muller, 1993; Reynolds, Mavrogenes, Bezruczko, & Hagemann, 1996; Steinberg, Lamborn, Dornbusch, & Darling, 1992; Stevenson & Baker, 1987; Sui-Chu & Willms, 1996; U.S. Department of Education, 2001). In their meta-analysis of 25 studies, Fan and Chen (2001) found that parents' educational aspirations for their children and school participation had moderate associations with academic achievement, whereas parent-child communication and supervision had smaller effects. Although many of the studies included in the meta-analysis were cross-sectional (comparing similar groups of children of different ages), longitudinal and experimental research that followed the same groups over time also suggests that parent involvement in elementary school leads to increases in academic success (e.g., Jimmerson, Egeland, & Teo, 1999; Tizard, Shoefield, & Hewison, 1982).

Much less empirical attention has been focused on the effects of parent involvement in preschool. For example, Fan and Chen's meta-analysis included only one study with a preschool sample. Even though Epstein's framework was developed with school-age children in mind, her various types of parent involvement are applicable to preschool families. In Head Start, for example, parents are encouraged to be involved at home and at school in a number of ways spanning Epstein's six categories. Home involvement can entail receiving home visitors from the school, reading to children, and teaching them letters and numbers. Home involvement also includes many activities that are not necessarily academic but provide rich opportunities for learning. Examples are playing games and music with children and taking them on trips to places such as the store, playground, or park. Parents also support learning at home indirectly through their child-rearing practices; for example, nurturing children psychologically through sensitive parenting and physically by providing good nutrition and health care.

In Head Start, parent involvement at school is a program goal supported by a variety of activities designed to draw parents into the program. These go far beyond the typical parent-teacher conferences and volunteering in the classroom. There are parent education workshops and social events, times to observe in the classroom, and even opportunities to become employees at the Head Start center. Parents can also participate in program development and governance through the Policy Council, the governing body of local Head Start programs. By law, more than half of council members must be parents.

Research to date on the effects of parent involvement in preschool has focused predominantly on low-income, ethnic minority families enrolled in Head Start or similar programs. The findings in general show that parent involvement at home and at school boosts program effectiveness and promotes all aspects of school readiness. The most extensive data about parent involvement in Head Start come from the Head Start Family and Child Experiences Survey (FACES; O'Brien et al., 2002; U.S. Department of Health and Human Services, 1998), a comprehensive assessment of children and their families from 40 randomly selected Head Start programs across the nation. The FACES assessment asked parents about their participation in a number of activities both at home and at Head Start. Activities were summed into two constructs, representing home involvement and involvement at school. The types of activities comprising these two constructs are presented in Table 8.1.

The FACES results showed that parents who were involved in more Head Start activities also increased their home involvement over the course of the school year (O'Brien et al., 2002). Further, parents who became more involved in home activities reported that their children's emergent literacy and positive social behaviors increased and that problem behaviors decreased. Thus, the FACES findings indicate that higher parent involvement in Head Start is associated with increased involvement at home, both of which improve school readiness.

A couple of limitations to the FACES findings are that the measures used were parent-report and that the effect sizes, although statistically significant, were small. The FACES results, however, are consistent with other research findings on parent involvement in Head Start. For example, in the 1985 report of the Head Start Evaluation, Synthesis, and Utilization Project, McKey and colleagues conducted a meta-analysis on 20 sets of parent involvement data from five Head Start studies. They concluded that the overall effect size of parent involvement in Head Start activities on children's academic outcomes had what the researchers call "a medium-small effect" (McKey et al., 1985).

In a comprehensive study of New York City Head Start mothers, Parker and colleagues also found that high levels of preschool involvement, as assessed from program records, were associated with greater school readiness in kindergarten, as rated by teachers (Parker et al., 1997). Additionally, higher levels of parent involvement in Head Start forecasted higher levels of parent involvement one year later in kindergarten. Involvement in preschool was also associated with more nurturing parenting and more emphasis on learning at home. Positive

TABLE 8.1. *FACES Measures of Parent Involvement*

Home Activities	Head Start Involvement
Reading to child	Receiving a home visitor
Telling a story	Observing child's classroom
Teaching letters, words, or numbers	Attending parent-teacher conference
Teaching songs or music	Volunteering in classroom
Working on arts and crafts	Preparing food or materials for special events
Playing games, sports, with toys or exercising together	Participating in fund-raising activities
Going on errands with child	Attending parent education meetings/workshops
Involving child in household chores	Attending Head Start social events
Visiting a library	Helping with field trips or other special events
Going to a play, concert, or other live show	Attending Head Start event with other adult
Visiting a museum or historical site	Attending Head Start event with spouse/partner
Visiting a zoo or aquarium	Calling/visiting other Head Start parents
Talking with child about family history or heritage	Participating in Policy Council or other planning groups
Attending a community or ethnic/religious group activity	Preparing/distributing newsletters, fliers, or other Head Start materials.
Attending a sports event (child not a player)	

Source: U.S. Department of Health and Human Services, 1998.

changes in these aspects of the home learning environment over the course of the year were related to children's academic and behavioral progress by the end of Head Start (Parker, Boak, Griffin, Ripple, & Peay, 1999).

Other studies have also documented a positive association of Head Start parents' involvement at school and at home with school readiness. In a sample of Head Start and public preschool families in Washington, D.C., Marcon (1999) found that parent involvement in program activities, as assessed from school records, was linked to children's increased academic achievement in preschool and more adaptive and socially competent behaviors along all dimensions of the Vineland Adaptive Behavior Scales. Further, active parent involvement, such as volunteering at school, had stronger effects on children's performance than did more passive involvement, such as receiving home visitors or attending routine parent-teacher conferences. Interestingly, Marcon also found that boys were at higher risk than girls for poor educational and behavioral performance, and that parent involvement had a larger effect for boys.

As for the home involvement of Head Start parents, Payne, Whitehurst, and Angell (1994) found that the quality of the home literacy environment (i.e., amount of reading, number of books in the home, and visits to the library) was associated with children's expressive language ability. Whitehurst and colleagues conducted interventions in Head Start centers and other programs where parents and teachers were trained in shared reading techniques (Lonigan & Whitehurst, 1998; Whitehurst et al., 1994). This parent intervention produced increases in some child language abilities. Home involvement activities focused more broadly than just on reading have also been found to benefit children's reading and language skills (Jong & Leseman, 2001).

The studies reviewed here show that parent involvement in the child's activities both at home and in preschool boosts school readiness and that parent participation in Head Start leads to more involvement at home. However, the studies were predominantly correlational in nature, meaning that the findings only show two variables are related, not that one caused the other. Most of the studies were also relatively short-term. Stronger evidence about the long-term effects of parent involvement in preschool comes from a rigorous quasi-experimental intervention study, the Chicago Longitudinal Study. The CLS is an evaluation of a Head Start–like preschool program called the Child-Parent Centers (CPC), described by Reynolds and Temple in Chapter 3. Like Head Start, the CPC targets low-income families and provides extensive parental outreach and support. The evaluation showed that the CPC had positive effects on children's achievement and behavior, including less special education, grade retention, school dropout, and juvenile delinquency. These benefits persisted through adolescence and resulted in substantial economic returns on the investment in the program (Reynolds, Temple, Robertson, & Mann, 2001; Temple, Reynolds, Robertson, & Mann, 2002).

Parent involvement at school is one of the mechanisms through which the CPC preschool program achieved these lasting effects. Parents' reports of their involvement in preschool and kindergarten were associated with greater reading achievement and less grade retention through at least eighth grade (Miedel & Reynolds, 1999). Additionally, parents who participated in the preschool program were more likely to be involved in elementary school, as rated by teachers, and the more years that parents were involved in elementary school, the smaller the chances were of their children being referred for special education or being retained a grade (Chicago Longitudinal Study, 2000). In fact, parent involvement in elementary school partially mediated the long-term academic and behavioral effects of the preschool intervention, and parent involvement was just as important for children's long-term success as were the intervention's effects on cognitive ability (Reynolds et al., 1996; Reynolds, Ou, & Topitzes, 2002).

PARENT INVOLVEMENT: A MODEL OF MULTIPLE PATHWAYS

The literature reviewed here supports a model in which parent involvement during preschool influences children's academic success through four interrelated pathways:

1. Parent involvement in preschool is linked to involvement in supportive activities at home.
2. Parent involvement in preschool and at home has direct effects on children's concurrent academic performance.
3. Parent involvement in preschool and at home has effects on children's social behavior and motivation, which should in turn affect their school performance.
4. Parents who are involved in preschool are more likely to continue to be involved in elementary school, and this continued participation is associated with better academic achievement and behavioral adjustment.

This fourth pathway appears to be a key explanatory mechanism for how preschool interventions with children from low-income families can have long-lasting effects. The Chicago CPC clearly demonstrated this pathway by providing multiple opportunities for parent involvement not just through two years of preschool but all the way through third grade. Most preschool programs are brief, lasting only one academic year prior to kindergarten entry. If during this time parents learn to support educational goals actively, they will continue to do so if encouraged and given the chance. The Chicago Longitudinal Study demonstrates that, by investing in ways to involve low-income parents, programs can reap long-term economic benefits that outweigh the initial costs. These findings raise the prospect of states saving money in the long run by promoting parent involvement in publicly funded preschool programs.

OVERCOMING BARRIERS TO INVOLVEMENT

Parents from across the socioeconomic spectrum encounter a number of barriers to involvement in their children's preschool education (Henrich & Herk, 2003). Much of our understanding of these barriers comes from research generated by Head Start. In FACES, 50 percent of Head Start parents reported work schedules as an impediment to participation, and working parents were in fact less involved in the program (U.S. Department of Health and Human Services, 1998). Single parents were also less likely to be involved. Additionally, 35 percent of Head Start parents reported child care needs as a barrier, 19 percent cited lack of transportation, and 18 percent cited their own school or training schedules. Parker and colleagues' New York sample of Head Start mothers reported similar obstacles to their program involvement (Parker et al., 2001).

Despite these substantial roadblocks, Head Start maintains impressive levels of parent involvement. In the FACES survey, more than three-quarters of parents indicated that they received a home visit, observed their child's class, and attended a parent-teacher conference, each at least once in the past year. More than half of the parents reported doing each at least three times. More than 70 percent of parents reported they had volunteered in the classroom. Head Start parents also reported being very involved with their children at home. More than 90 percent indicated that they talked about school, played with their children, and took them on errands at least once a week; more than three-quarters of parents said they told their child a story and played counting games in the past week; and two-thirds reported reading to their child three or more times a week (U.S. Department of Health and Human Services, 1998).

Head Start's success is due in large part to an emphasis on "maximum feasible participation," the exact words used in the Economic Opportunity Act of 1964 (the legislation under which Head Start and other antipoverty programs were created). Maximum feasible parent participation has been defined in Head Start as a full partnership role for parents. Parents are not just given a list of activities in which they may choose to participate, but they are encouraged to grow their abilities and interests so they become empowered to affect their children's and their own future. Thus they not only have the opportunity to participate in educational activities at home and school, but they have a role in determining program operations and policies. (For more information on parent involvement requirements, see Head Start Performance

Standards, subpart C, section 1304.40.) Maximum feasible participation has enabled parents to advocate for policy changes at the federal level and educational and human resources at the local level. According to Zigler, maximum feasible parent participation is one of the policies that has made Head Start so successful and helped it survive numerous threats to its existence over the past four decades (Zigler & Muenchow, 1992).

Qualitative data from the national evaluation of the School of the 21st Century (Henrich & Herk, 2003) indicate that middle-income parents face many of the same barriers to involvement as do low-income parents. Head Start's success at overcoming these barriers might reasonably be expected to be replicable in universal preschool programs. Indeed, several state programs have directly adopted the Head Start performance standards pertaining to parent involvement (Ripple, Gilliam, Chanana, & Zigler, 1999).

POLICY AND RESEARCH IMPLICATIONS

This review of the research reveals some clear findings and policy implications. First, parent involvement in preschool is linked to children's academic achievement through multiple pathways, thereby boosting the power of well-designed preschool programs to foster the school readiness of children from low-income families. Second, there are substantial barriers to parents' involvement in preschool. Third, Head Start provides a model of how an emphasis on maximum feasible participation can successfully breach these barriers by coupling a philosophical commitment to reaching out to parents with precise program standards for how to do so. Finally, the Chicago Longitudinal Study demonstrates that encouraging involvement by low-income parents can be a good economic investment. The take-home message from the current body of research on preschool programs is that a commitment to involving parents is a crucial component of quality preschool education for children from low-income families and that it is an investment likely to pay off in the long-term.

Even though there is enough evidence to conclude that parent involvement in preschool is linked to children's school readiness in low-income families, questions remain about how parent involvement works during the preschool years. In the current political climate, there is rich opportunity for state preschool programs to serve as laboratories for investigation of the dynamics of parent involvement, which in turn can inform advances in programs and policy. We have identified four sets of interrelated questions that studies of state preschool programs are in a unique position to help answer:

- Do the effects of parent involvement in preschool vary as a function of socioeconomic status, ethnic minority status, and cultural background?
- Is there a minimum threshold of parent involvement needed to have an effect on school readiness; conversely, is there a point of diminishing return after which more involvement does not produce additional benefits?
- Is there a minimum amount of outreach needed to involve parents?
- Do levels of outreach to parents vary as a function of different state policies?

Do the Effects of Parent Involvement in Preschool Vary Across Groups?

In research with elementary and middle school samples, there is some evidence that the effects of various types of parent involvement at home and at school may differ as a function of socioeconomic status and ethnicity. For example, Desimone (1999) found that involvement at home was a significant predictor of achievement only for middle-income and white middle school students. She also found that parent involvement at school was a stronger, more consistent predictor of achievement for white and middle-income students than for African American, Hispanic, Asian American, and low-income students. On the other hand, Keith and colleagues (1998) looked at the same sample when the children were two years older and in high school. They found no differences in the effectiveness of parent involvement across ethnic lines at that time. There is also evidence that parenting styles may take on different meanings for adolescents from different cultures and, as a result, have differential patterns of association with academic achievement for different cultural groups (Chao, 1994; Henrich, 2001; Steinberg et al., 1992). These differences may be particularly strong for first-generation immigrants (Chao, 2001; Pham, Henrich, & Schwab-Stone, 2003).

Although enough parenting research on middle and high school students has been conducted with large and diverse samples to make ethnic, cultural, and socioeconomic comparisons, most of the preschool research has been conducted with low-income, ethnic minority families.

Ironically, the main limitation of this body of literature is that there is not enough diversity to determine whether the effects of parent involvement generalize to middle-income white families. In fact, there is some reason to believe that efforts to increase parent involvement may be less effective for middle-income families. Higher-income parents tend to be more involved in their children's education in the first place (Grolnick, Benjet, Kurowski, & Apostoleris, 1997; Kohl, Lengua, McMahon, & the Conduct Problems Prevention Research Group, 2000). Furthermore, children from higher-income families typically have fewer risk factors for academic failure – the very factors parent involvement is intended to counteract (Luster & McAdoo, 1996). Thus, with low-income families, there may be more room for improvement both in terms of parent involvement and children's school readiness. Marcon's (1999) finding that parent involvement was more effective for boys, who were also at higher risk for academic failure, suggests that parent involvement in preschool may work best for those who need it the most.

Research with kindergartners provides partial support for the supposition that parent involvement may be more effective for low-income children. Hill (2001) found that various types of parenting style and discipline were more strongly related to children's achievement for lower-income families. She also found ethnic differences. Parent involvement at school was more strongly linked to academic achievement for black families, whereas involvement in home activities was more strongly linked to math achievement for white families. However, to date there is insufficient research to conclude that parent involvement in preschool is less effective for middle-income families. Research with older children reviewed in the previous section suggests that parent involvement should be at least somewhat important regardless of socioeconomic status. The best way to determine whether parent involvement in preschool makes a difference across the socioeconomic spectrum is to evaluate the effects of parental involvement in programs that are universally accessible.

The growth of publicly funded universal preschool can provide researchers and program evaluators with the opportunity to examine possible socioeconomic and cultural differences in parent involvement. Three important questions need to be addressed: (1) Do low-income parents of preschoolers tend to be less involved at home and at school than their middle-income counterparts? (2) Do the benefits of parent involvement in preschool on school readiness come about mainly from bringing uninvolved low-income parents up to middle-income levels of participation, or is increased involvement better across the board, regardless of the initial level? (3) Do different aspects of parent involvement take on different meanings for various cultural groups? Research with older students suggests that they may, which would have implications for how program planners tailor parent outreach efforts to fit with the cultural values of the families being served. The potential for cultural differences also requires researchers and educators to treat parent involvement as a broad-based and flexible construct.

Are There Thresholds for the Effectiveness of Parent Involvement in Preschool?

Although most researchers and educators agree that parent involvement is beneficial, there is less consensus regarding the degree and level of involvement that is required. Marcon (1999) posed the questions of whether there is a minimum threshold of parent involvement needed to have an effect on school readiness and, conversely, whether there is a "point of diminishing return," after which more involvement ceases to have additional benefits. The literature to date cannot answer these questions because there is not enough consistency in how different investigators define and measure parent involvement. Some researchers treat parent involvement as a continuous variable, assuming that its relationship with school readiness is linear; others see it as a categorical variable, dividing it in into levels of low, medium, and high involvement. Studies also differ in whether they measure parent involvement by type of activities, frequency of an activity, or a combination of the two. With respect to parent participation in school, there is wide variation in the degree to which investigators rely upon self-report or use actual program records to determine levels of parent involvement. Compounding this issue are findings that the levels of agreement between multiple reporters of parent involvement tend to be low (Reynolds, 1992). Finally, there is little consistency across studies in the specific activities used to measure parent involvement.

We recommend greater standardization in measurement as the first step toward determining whether there is a minimum amount of parent involvement necessary to bolster school readiness. Measures should include the number, type, and frequency of activities to determine if one, two, or all three of these are important. Such measures have to be both specific in terms of their description of activities and broad in scope so they are useful in the variety of preschool settings and with the diversity of families they serve. The FACES measures are a good starting point because they include a variety of home and school activities that for the most part are applicable to all preschool centers, not just Head Start. Plus, many of the FACES school involvement measures could easily be adapted for a teacher's report (see Table 8.1). Researchers can of course add supplementary items. The FACES measures also assess frequency of involvement in each activity, so they provide flexibility in terms of how parent involvement is analyzed. These steps can provide preliminary answers to the question of whether the relation between parent involvement and academic achievement is linear (in that more is always better), or whether there is a minimum necessary threshold of involvement and/or a point of diminishing return.

Is a Minimum Amount of Parental Outreach Needed to Involve Parents?

The question of whether a certain amount of parent involvement is necessary to achieve school readiness has a parallel question on the school side. Is there a minimum amount of effort necessary to involve parents successfully? That is, is there a point where enough parents are involved enough of the time that more outreach to parents would not translate into more participation? This might seem like a ridiculous question, given the substantial barriers to involvement, including work schedules and child care needs, that face middle- as well as low-income parents. In fact, some have suggested that successfully involving parents probably requires designated full-time parental outreach staff (Melton, Limber, & Teauge 1999). Further, to achieve high levels of participation, it is likely that programs need to develop a comprehensive and well-planned strategy that includes more than just outreach. The extreme of this are program policies that *require* parents to maintain a certain amount of involvement (e.g., volunteering a certain number of hours in the classroom, reinforcing certain classroom activities at home; National PTA, n.d.). Despite such attempts to encourage or force participation, the existence of a minimal threshold of outreach is actually an empirical question, and one with ramifications for policy.

Research with older children highlights the complex interplay of various factors in predicting how involved parents are in their children's education, including school factors (Grolnick et al., 1997; Melton et al., 1999). There is not much empirical evidence about the effectiveness of various preschool practices for involving parents, although there is evidence that experienced teachers are more likely to have involved parents (Rimm-Kaufman & Pianta, 1999). This dearth of knowledge is not surprising, given that most of the relevant research stems from Head Start, a program whose philosophy and standards mandate a panoply of comprehensive services for parents. Investigators need to look at a wider array of practices used in preschools to explore the effects of various policies on parent involvement.

Do Levels of Parental Outreach Vary as a Function of State Policies?

Policies for involving parents in state-funded preschool programs are highly variable and almost always less stringent than those in Head Start. In 1998 the majority of the state programs had some form of policy regarding parent involvement (Gilliam & Ripple, 2004). Table 8.2 presents information on these policies, as compiled by Mitchell, Ripple, and Chanana (1998). The checklist in the table indicates five aspects of parent involvement in Head Start (home visitation, volunteering, parent education or other outreach through workshops or classes, parent-teacher conferences, opportunities for participating in program development), and whether each state program reported having similar policies. As can be seen in Table 8.2, parent involvement is taken quite seriously in some programs and nearly ignored in others. For example, some state policies contained no clear information about parent participation, and only a few had provisions for a full range of parent involvement activities.

It is not yet clear what impact these state policies have on program staff, parents, and children. In a review of all evaluations of state-funded preschools from 1977 to 1998, Gilliam and Zigler (2001) found only 3 states out of 10 that reported measuring program effects on parent involvement, and only 1 of the 3 (Texas) reported finding a statistically significant effect. Interestingly, the Texas program guidelines did not include any provisions for parent involvement. Thus, to date it is not known whether any of the state policies for involving parents are effective. What is needed is a comparison of how various state polices for reaching out to parents translate into program staff's practices, and how these in turn translate into degree of parent participation achieved. This type of research would inform state planners whether there are minimal provisions for parent involvement necessary to draw parents into school. This intervening step is key to understanding the link between written state policies and actual levels of parent involvement.

TABLE 8.2. *State Preschool Programs with Parent Involvement in Guidelines*

State	Home Visits	Volunteering	Parent Education/ Outreach	Parent-Teacher Conferences	Program Development
Alaska	√	√	√	√	√
Arizona	?	?	?	?	?
Arkansas	x	x	x	√	√
California	x	o	x	√	√
Colorado	?	?	?	?	?
Connecticut	?	?	?	?	?
Delaware	√	√	√	√	?
Florida	√	x	√	x	x
Georgia	x	√	x	√	x
Illinois	√	x	√	x	x
Iowa	x	o	o	o	√
Kentucky	√	√	√	√	x
Louisiana	x	x	x	√	x
Maryland	?	?	?	?	√
Massachusetts	x	o	√	o	√
Michigan	√	√	√	√	√
Minnesota	x	o	?	o	?
Nebraska	√	?	√	?	x
New Hampshire	√	√	√	√	√
New Jersey	?	?	?	?	?
New Mexico	?	?	√	?	?
New York	√	o	√	√	o
Oklahoma	?	?	?	?	?
Ohio	√	√	√	√	√
Oregon	√	√	√	√	√
Rhode Island	?	?	?	?	?
South Carolina	x	√	√	x	x
Tennessee	?	?	?	?	?
Vermont	√	x	x	x	√
Virginia	√	x	x	x	x
Washington	x	x	√	x	√
Wisconsin	x	x	√	x	x

Note: √= included in program guidelines; O = optional according to program guidelines; x = not included in program guidelines;? = not clear from information provided about program guidelines.
Source: Mitchell, Ripple, & Chanana, 1998.

CONCLUSION

In line with Campbell's (1969) vision of an "experimenting society" and the federal government's current emphasis on polices "based on advances in early childhood development" (School Readiness Act of 2003), we propose that more research be conducted within the context of state-funded preschool programs. These programs offer valuable opportunities for policy and research to advance synergistically the field of parent involvement in education. By addressing the questions posed in this chapter, researchers will build knowledge about the dynamics and effects of parent involvement in preschool, and state planners can begin to evaluate and hone their efforts to include parents.

Head Start has long been a pioneer in the partnering of policy and research (Henrich, 2004); nowhere is this more true than in the field of parent involvement. Guided by the concept of maximum feasible participation, Head Start originated the practice and proved the value of strong parent involvement in early education. Although Head Start's policies in this area have had a nationwide impact, they have been developed and applied exclusively with low-income parents. We conclude by posing the question of how the meaning of maximum feasible participation may differ for universal prekindergartens and the broader array of families they serve.

The research to date does not provide a clear answer to this question. The content of state policies to involve parents, the socioeconomic and cultural makeup of their local preschool populations, and the preferences of individual communities present too many variables to determine which practices work best at this time. Yet experience in Head Start has proved beyond a doubt that parent participation in young children's schooling is important, and it has created an effective model for involving parents in their children's learning both at school and at home. The questions posed in this chapter provide a framework for researchers and policy makers to work together in building on the Head Start model to develop equally effective ways of involving parents in publicly funded universal preschool programs.

References

Arroyo, C. G., & Zigler, E. (1993). America's Title I/Chapter 1 programs: Why the promise has not been met. In E. Zigler & S. J. Styfco (Eds.), *Head Start and beyond: A national plan for extended childhood intervention* (pp. 73–95). New Haven, CT: Yale University Press.

Baker, A. J. L. (1996). *Parents as school partners project: Final report.* New York: NCJW.

Campbell, D. T. (1969). Reforms as experiments. *American Psychologist, 24,* 409–429.

Chao, R. K. (1994). Beyond parental control and authoritarian parenting style: Understanding Chinese parenting through the cultural notion of training. *Child Development, 65,* 1111–1119.

Chao, R. K. (2001). Extending research on the consequences of parenting style for Chinese Americans and European Americans. *Child Development, 72,* 1832–1843.

Chicago Longitudinal Study. (2000). *Newsletter, Issue 1.* Madison, WI: Author.

Christenson, S. L. (1999). Families and schools: Rights, responsibilities, resources, and relationships. In R. C. Pianta & M. J. Cox (Eds.), *The transition to kindergarten* (pp. 143–178). Baltimore: Paul H. Brookes.

de Jong, P. F., & Leseman, P. M. (2001). Lasting effects of home literacy on reading achievement in school. *Journal of School Psychology, 39,* 389–414.

Desimone, L. (1999). Linking parent involvement with student achievement: Do race and income matter? *Journal of Educational Research, 93,* 11–30.

Epstein, J. L. (1995). School/family/community partnerships. *Phi Delta Kappan, May,* 701–712.

Fan, X., & Chen, M. (2001). Parental involvement and students' academic achievement: A meta-analysis. *Educational Psychology Review, 13,* 1–22.

Fantuzzo, J., Davis, G., & Ginsberg, M. (1995). Effects of parent involvement in isolation or in combination with peer tutoring on student self-concept and mathematics achievement. *Journal of Educational Psychology, 87,* 272–281.

Gilliam, W. S., & Ripple, C. H. (2004). What can be learned from state-funded prekindergarten initiatives? A data-based approach to the Head Start devolution debate. In E. Zigler & S. J. Styfco (Eds.), *The Head Start debates* (pp. 477–497). Baltimore: Paul H. Brookes.

Gilliam, W. S., & Zigler, E. F. (2001). A critical meta-analysis of all evaluations of state-funded preschool from 1977 to 1998: Implications for policy, service delivery, and program evaluation. *Early Childhood Research Quarterly, 15,* 441–473.

Grolnick, W. S., Benjet, C., Kurowski, C. O., & Apostoleris, N. H. (1997). Predictors of parent involvement in children's schooling. *Journal of Educational Psychology, 89,* 538–548.

Grolnick, W. S., & Slowiaczek, M. L. (1994). Parents' involvement in children's schooling: A multidimensional conceptualization and motivational model. *Child Development, 65,* 237–252.

Henrich, C. C. (2001). Parent involvement, motivation, and achievement over the transition to middle school (Doctoral dissertation, Yale University, 2001). *Dissertation Abstracts International, 62,* 1616.

Henrich, C. C. (2004). Head Start as a national laboratory. In E. Zigler & S. J. Styfco (Eds.), *The Head Start debates* (pp. 517–531). Baltimore: Paul H. Brookes.

Henrich, C., & Herk, M. (2003). *Parent involvement in prekindergarten.* Atlanta: Georgia State University Child Policy Initiative.

Hill, N. E. (2001). Parenting and academic socialization as they relate to school readiness: The roles of ethnicity and family income. *Journal of Educational Psychology, 93,* 686–697.

Jimerson, S., Egeland, B., & Teo, A. (1999). A longitudinal study of achievement trajectories: Factors associated with change. *Journal of Educational Psychology, 91,* 116–126.

Keith, T. Z., Keith, P. B., & Quirk, K J. (1998). Longitudinal effects of parent involvement on high school grades: Similarities and differences across gender and ethnic groups. *Journal of School Psycholoy, 36,* 335–363.

Kohl, G. O., Lengua, L. J., McMahon, R. J., & the Conduct Problems Prevention Research Group. (2000). Parent involvement in school: Conceptualizing multiple dimensions and their relations with family and demographic risk factors. *Journal of School Psychology, 38,* 501–523.

Lonigan, C. J., & Whitehurst, G. J. (1998). Relative efficacy of parent and teacher involvement in a shared-reading intervention for preschool children from low-income backgrounds. *Early Childhood Research Quarterly, 13,* 263–290.

Luster, T., & McAdoo, H. (1996). Family and child influences on educational attainment: A secondary analysis of the High/Scope Perry Preschool data. *Developmental Psychology, 32,* 26–39.

Marcon, R. A. (1999). Positive relationships between parent school involvement and public school inner-city preschoolers' development and academic performance. *School Psychology Review, 28,* 395–412.

McKey, R. H., Condelli, L. Ganson, H., Barrett, B., McConkey, C., & Plantz, M. (1985). *The impact of Head Start on children, families, and communities.* Final report of the Head Start Evaluation, Synthesis and Utilization Project. Washington, DC: U.S. Government Printing Office. (DHHS Pub. No. OHDS 85-31193)

Melton, G. B., Limber, S. P., & Teague, T. L. (1999). Changing schools for changing families. In. R. C. Pianta & M. J. Cox (Eds.), *The transition to kindergarten* (pp. 179–216). Baltimore: Paul H. Brookes.

Miedel, W. T., & Reynolds, A. J. (1999). Parent involvement in early intervention for disadvantaged children: Does it matter? *Journal of School Psychology, 37,* 379–402.

Mitchell, A., Ripple, C., & Chanana, N. (1998). *Prekindergarten programs funded by the states: Essential elements for policymakers.* New York: Families and Work Institute.

Muller, C. (1993). Parent involvement and academic achievement: An analysis of family resources available to the child. In B. Schneider & J. S. Coleman (Eds.), *Parents, their children, and schools* (pp. 77–113). Boulder: Westview Press.

National PTA's National Standards for Parent/Family Involvement. (n.d.). http://www.pta.org/parentinvolvement/standards/pfistand.asp. Accessed September 30, 2003.

O'Brien, R. W., et al. (2002). *A descriptive study of Head Start families: FACES technical report I.* Washington, DC: U.S. Department of Health and Human Services.

Parker, F. L., Boak, A., Griffin, K. W., Ripple, C., & Peay, L. (1999). Parent-child relationship, home learning environment, and school readiness. *School Psychology Review, 28*, 413–425.

Parker, F. L., Piotrkowski, C. S., Baker, A. J., Kessler-Sklar, S., Clark, B., & Peay, L. (2001). Understanding barriers to parent involvement in Head Start: A research-community partnership. *Early Childhood Research Quarterly, 16*, 35–51.

Parker, F. L., Piotrkowski, C. S., Kessler-Sklar, S., Baker, A. J., Peay, L., & Clark, B. (1997). *Parent involvement in Head Start.* New York: National Council of Jewish Women Center for the Child.

Payne, A. C., Whitehurst, G. J., & Angell, A. L. (1994). The role of home literacy environment in the development of language ability in preschool children from low-income families. *Early Childhood Research Quarterly, 9*, 427–440.

Pham, M., Henrich, C. C., & Schwab-Stone, M. (2003, April). *Roles of parents and teachers in Latino students' adjustment.* Poster presented at the Biennial Meeting of the Society for Research in Child Development, Tampa, FL.

Reynolds, A. J. (1992). Comparing measures of parental involvement and their effects on academic achievement. *Early Childhood Research Quarterly, 7*, 441–462.

Reynolds, A. J., Mavrogenes, N. A., Bezruczko, N., & Hagemann, M. (1996). Cognitive and family-support mediators of preschool effectiveness: A confirmatory analysis. *Child Development, 67*, 1119–1140.

Reynolds, A. J., Ou, S., & Topitzes, J. D. (2002, June). *Pathways of effects of early childhood intervention on educational attainment and delinquency.* Paper presented at Head Start's Sixth National Research Conference, Washington, DC.

Reynolds, A. J., Temple, J. A., Robertson, D. L., & Mann, E. A. (2001). Long-term effects of an early childhood intervention on educational achievement and juvenile arrest. *Journal of the American Medical Association, 285*, 2339–2346.

Rimm-Kaufman, S. E., & Pianta, R. C. (1999). Patterns of family-school contact in preschool and kindergarten. *School Psychology Review, 28*, 426–438.

Ripple, C. H., Gilliam, W. S., Chanana, N., & Zigler, E. (1999). Will 50 cooks spoil the broth? The debate over entrusting Head Start to the states. *American Psychologist, 54*, 327–343.

Steinberg, L., Lamborn, S. D., Dornbusch, S. M., & Darling, N. (1992). Impact of parenting practices on adolescent achievement: Authoritative parenting, school involvement, and encouragement to succeed. *Child Development, 63*, 1266–1281.

Stevenson, D. L., & Baker, D. P. (1987). The family-school relation and the child's school performance. *Child Development, 58*, 1348–1357.

Sui-Chu, E. H., & Willms, J. D. (1996). Effects of parental involvement on eighth-grade achievement. *Sociology of Education, 69*, 126–141.

Temple, J., Reynolds, A. J., Robertson, D., & Mann, E. (2002, June). *Age 21 cost-benefit analysis of the Chicago Child-Parent Centers.* Paper presented at Head Start's Sixth National Research Conference, Washington, DC.

Tizard, J., Shoefield, W., & Hewison, J. (1982). Collaboration between teachers and parents in assisting children's reading. *British Journal of Educational Psychology, 52*, 1–15.

U.S. Department of Education. (1996). *Goals 2000: Educate America Act, October 1996 update.* Washington, DC: Author.

U.S. Department of Education, National Center for Education Statistics. (2001). *Fathers' and mothers' involvement in their children's schools by family type and resident status.* Washington, DC: Author.

U.S. Department of Health and Human Services. (1998). *Head Start program performance measures: Second progress report.* Washington, DC: Author.

Whitehurst, G. J., Epstein, J. N., Angell, A. C., Payne, A. C., Crone, D. A., & Fischel, J. E. (1994). Outcomes of an emergent literacy intervention in Head Start. *Journal of Educational Psychology, 86*, 542–555.

Zigler, E., & Muenchow, S. (1992). *Head Start: The inside story of America's most successful educational experiment.* New York: Basic Books.

9

Professional Development Issues in Universal Prekindergarten

Kelly L. Maxwell and Richard M. Clifford

The term "prekindergarten" is used in this chapter to refer to the set of educational programs serving three- and four-year-old children that are part of a formal state initiative. The programs may be housed in public schools, Head Start classrooms, or community-based child care centers. Approximately 2.6 million, or 69 percent of four-year-olds in the United States receive care and education in a center-based program (West, Denton, & Germino-Hausken, 2000). Almost 1 million of them are in school-affiliated prekindergarten programs (Clifford, Early, & Hills, 1999).

Attention to the *quality* of these programs for young children has grown. Experts cite a growing consensus that children benefit from – and should receive – early education experiences in a caring environment (Bowman, Donovan, & Burns, 2001). Studies of intensive early intervention programs such as the Abecedarian Project (Campbell & Ramey, 1994; Ramey & Campbell, 1984), the Perry Preschool Project (Schweinhart, Barnes, Weikart, Barnett, & Epstein, 1993), and the

This chapter was partially supported by a grant from the Foundation for Child Development. The views expressed in this chapter are those of the authors and may not reflect those of the funding agency. Some sections of this chapter were developed based on the April 2002 working symposium, "Strategies for Preparing Highly Qualified Prekindergarten Teachers." The authors would like to acknowledge the contribution of the symposium participants: Leah Adams, Harriet Boone, Barbara Bowman, Marnie Campbell, Moncrieff Cochran, Renatta Cooper, Carol Brunson Day, Ellen Edmonds, Linda Espinosa, Stephanie Fanjul, Joelle-Jude Fontaine, Cindy Gallagher, Cristina Gillanders, Dan Haggard, Janet Hansen, Sheila Hoyle, Marilou Hyson, Bernie Laumann, M.-A. Lucas, Jeanette McCollum, Patricia Phipps, Stephanie Ridley, Sue Russell, Carolyn Trammell, Fasaha Traylor, and Pam Winton.

Chicago Child-Parent Centers (Reynolds, 1994; Reynolds, Temple, Robertson, & Mann, 2001) have shown the long-term positive effects of high-quality early care and education for children at risk for school failure. (See also Reynolds & Temple, Chapter 3.) Research also has shown that children who attend higher-quality community-based child care centers have better academic and social outcomes than do children who attend lower-quality programs (Burchinal et al., 2000; NICHD Early Child Care Research Network, 2000; Peisner-Feinberg & Burchinal, 1997; Peisner-Feinberg et al., 2001). This same research suggests that most center-based child care in the United States is of poor to mediocre quality that is not high enough to impact children's outcomes positively.

In response to a growing interest in school readiness and the accompanying need for high-quality early education, states have become more involved in providing educational services for children the year or two before kindergarten. Over the past decade, the public investment in these educational programs for three- and four-year-olds has soared. By 2002 state investments in prekindergarten programs reached almost $2 billion (Sandham, 2002). Estimates of the number of states funding these programs vary, but between 34 and 39 states plus the District of Columbia currently operate public prekindergartens in at least some school districts (Bryant et al., 2002; Olson, 2002). Preschool is available to all children in Georgia and Oklahoma, and Florida and New York have passed legislation to move in this direction (see Chapter 1).

With the early childhood education movement in the United States firmly underway, we believe state-sponsored prekindergarten will be available to all four-year-olds by the end of this decade. The major challenge is to offer *high-quality* prekindergarten programs for all children. As programs expand, maintaining quality will become increasingly difficult and must be addressed in long-term planning.

At the center of efforts to assure high quality is the issue of creating a pool of highly qualified teachers to staff these programs. In this chapter we focus on professional development issues in universal prekindergarten. We begin by briefly describing the relevant research on professional development. We then discuss the need for and supply of highly qualified teachers now and in the future. In the last section we highlight capacity issues in producing and maintaining a highly qualified work force, focusing on building a professional development system as part of the infrastructure of universal prekindergarten in this country.

DEFINING HIGHLY QUALIFIED PREKINDERGARTEN TEACHERS

The federal No Child Left Behind legislation calls for "highly qualified" teachers. What should the standard be for a highly qualified prekindergarten teacher? There are various perspectives on this issue.

The general consensus among early childhood professionals is that "highly qualified" is synonymous with a bachelor's (BA) degree in early childhood. In the *Eager to Learn* report, the National Science Foundation concluded from a review of the literature that every young child should have a teacher with a bachelor's degree in early care and education (Bowman et al., 2001). The American Federation of Teachers (2002) recommended that prekindergarten teachers in all settings, not just public schools, have a BA. Barnett (2003) also underscored the view of many leaders in the field that the bachelor's degree is the appropriate level of preparation that should be expected of pre-K teachers if children are to meet expected goals. There is also the issue of parity: most school-age children are taught by degreed, certified teachers, and many believe that preschoolers deserve the same level of quality.

An examination of state pre-K policies suggests that most states equate "highly qualified" with a bachelor's degree. In a survey of the 50 states plus the District of Columbia (Bryant et al., 2002), 65 percent (22) of the 34 states offering prekindergarten programs that responded to the survey required pre-K teachers to have a BA. Four of the responding states required a minimum of an associate's degree, and eight required a Child Development Associate (CDA) credential. These data should be interpreted cautiously, though, because they represent the stated standards and do not necessarily reflect the reality of program staffing. Because of a shortage of teachers who meet the minimum standard, many states have offered waivers to allow programs to hire teachers who are working toward the required education level but have not yet attained it.

The short supply of qualified teachers has not affected all states. A study of six states with well-established prekindergarten programs in diverse settings found that nearly 70 percent of their pre-K teachers have a bachelor's degree or higher, most in an early childhood-related field (Clifford et al., 2003). This estimate is much higher than the 50 percent or less generally cited in the literature (Saluja, Early, & Clifford, 2002) but is closer to the estimate of 86 percent for pre-K teachers in public schools who have BA degrees (U.S. Department of Education, 2003). About half of the pre-K programs in these six states were not housed in public school settings, which means that the high percentage of BA teachers is not due solely to public school requirements. Interestingly, only three of the six states in the study required a BA as the minimum teacher qualification. These data suggest that states are indeed moving toward the bachelor's degree as the standard for a "highly qualified" prekindergarten teacher, and that the more mature state prekindergarten programs have been relatively successful in matching supply with demand.

Research supports the view that teacher education is a critical component of quality. Children who attend higher-quality center-based programs have been found to show better academic and social outcomes than children who attend lower-quality programs (Burchinal et al., 2000; NICHD Early Child Care Research Network, 2000; Peisner-Feinberg & Burchinal, 1997; Peisner-Feinberg et al., 2001). Studies also suggest that early childhood teachers with more education are more likely to implement developmentally appropriate practices than their peers with less education (Cassidy, Buell, Pugh-Hoese, & Russell, 1995; Cost, Quality and Child Outcomes Study Team, 1995; Howes, 1997; Phillips & Howes, 1987; Whitebook, Howes, & Phillips, 1989). Some research suggests that teachers with bachelor's degrees in early childhood education appear to have the highest-quality classrooms and to be most capable of having a significant impact on the developmental progress of children considered at risk of later school failure (Cost, Quality and Child Outcomes Study Team, 1995; Henderson, Basile, & Henry, 1999; Whitebook et al., 1989).

We, like many other early childhood professionals, believe that the ideal standard is for teachers to have a bachelor's degree in early childhood education. Our interpretation of the research, however, is more cautious. In general, the early care and education literature suggests that "more is better" in terms of teacher education. However, we do not believe that the evidence to date definitively identifies the amount of teacher education required to provide a high-quality early childhood program. Thus the notion that level of education is important does not automatically imply that a BA degree in early childhood is necessary. In truth, we do not yet know the difference in quality provided by teachers with an associate's degree, for example, as compared with that provided by teachers with a bachelor's degree. Important policy-related research questions such as this need to be addressed rigorously before an unequivocal statement equating "highly qualified" with a bachelor's degree in early childhood education can be made.

Of course, research evidence is not the only factor to be considered in the debate about teacher qualifications. Many early childhood professionals want the standard for prekindergarten teachers to be the same as for public school teachers. They believe this strategy will raise the professionalism of the early care and education field and extinguish the perception that early childhood workers are "just babysitters." Others worry that setting the standard so high at the bachelor's level will exclude many experienced people now employed in the field and will reduce the ethnic diversity of the prekindergarten work force. Policy makers need to balance cost and practicality with quality considerations. They may look for the lowest possible level of education that is associated with quality care to assure a large enough work force to meet current demand and fit within budget constraints.

State policy makers and program administrators must weigh these factors and others when setting the hiring criteria for prekindergarten teachers. We do not believe that the research base is strong enough to definitively say that the bachelor's level is required to get high quality, but it is clear that formal education in the early childhood field is important. Thus, it seems prudent for states to establish the BA in early childhood education as the minimum standard at this time. With this standard in mind, we now consider how many BA-level teachers will be needed to provide universal prekindergarten in the United States.

THE NEED FOR HIGHLY QUALIFIED PREKINDERGARTEN TEACHERS

Of the approximately 19 million children between birth and age five in the United States, about 3.8 million fall into each age cohort (U.S. Census Bureau, 2000a). If a universal, voluntary prekindergarten program was available to all four-year-olds today, we would need 180,500 lead teachers (not counting assistant teachers or paraprofessionals). This number assumes that:

- 3,610,00 children, or 95 percent of the 3.8 million four-year-olds in the United States, are enrolled.
- Class sizes are capped at 20, as recommended by the National Association for the Education of Young Children (Bredekamp & Copple, 1997).
- There is one highly qualified teacher per class.

Based on census projections of a population of 4.4 million four-year-olds in 2020, we would need an additional 28,500 teachers to meet the 95 percent saturation point by that time (U.S. Census Bureau, 2000b).

If a bachelor's degree – in any field – was required, how much of the preschool work force currently meets that standard? This is a difficult question to answer. The existing studies do not employ uniform definitions of prekindergarten, and they often rely on samples selected more from convenience than from a commitment to empirical rigor, making cross-study comparisons problematic. In particular, it is difficult to know what percentage of the current work force is highly qualified, how long these teachers will remain in the pre-K work force, and the number of children who enroll in pre-K programs each year. Given the limitations in the data available to us, we offer our best estimates about the need and supply of qualified early childhood teachers. It is important to note that our estimates are national ones; the staffing patterns and extent of need will vary state by state.

The most recent counts indicate that there are approximately 96,000 teachers of preschoolers age three to five in center-based programs (Burton et al., 2002). The exact number who have a bachelor's degree is unknown, in part because there is no uniform requirement that they be certified or licensed like public school teachers. Also unlike the K–12 system, there is no mechanism in place for routinely collecting data across states on pre-K programs except for the Head Start Program Information Report data. Furthermore, there has been no national, comprehensive child care work force survey since 1990 (Willer et al., 1991).

Data from multiple studies suggest that between 31 percent (Whitebook et al., 1990) and 50 percent (Saluja et al., 2002; Willer et al., 1991) of preschool teachers have bachelor's degrees. We have chosen to base our estimates on the data provided by Saluja and colleagues. These investigators conducted a national survey of child care teachers across all sectors of center-based programs – public schools, Head Start, for-profit, church/synagogue-affiliated, and other public agencies or independent nonprofit programs. Although this study is limited by a low response rate and a likely overrepresentation of well-qualified staff, it is relatively recent and contains information on the specific education degrees of interest to us. Moreover, with respect to the questions at hand, optimistic estimates of the education of the current teacher work force are preferable to conservative estimates because they will yield the lowest prediction of how many qualified teachers are needed.

Using Saluja et al.'s optimistic estimate that 50 percent of preschool teachers currently have a bachelor's degree, we are about 132,000 shy of the 180,500 teachers needed for universal prekindergarten. The shortfall may be slightly less than this because some teacher assistants have bachelor's degrees as well. If the standards are defined at the higher level of having a bachelor's degree *in early childhood*, the Saluja survey indicates that only 31 percent of the current work force meets this qualification. Thus, we would need 152,000 additional teachers for universal prekindergarten.

What would the work force look like if "highly qualified" were defined at a lower level as teachers with an associate's degree? Saluja, Early, and Clifford estimate that 15 percent of preschool teachers have an associate's degree. Applying that percentage to the work force estimates suggests that, at most, 14,400 teachers currently have an associates degree. Thus, the current qualified work force of about 62,500 (48,000 BA + 14,400 AA) is still more than 118,000 short of the number of pre-K teachers needed to provide universal early care and education for all four-year-olds.

Clearly, even relying on the most optimistic estimates of teacher education, the United States does not have the qualified teacher work force needed to provide universal prekindergarten. What can be done to increase the supply of appropriately qualified teachers?

BUILDING A UNIVERSAL PREKINDERGARTEN PROFESSIONAL DEVELOPMENT SYSTEM

In the short term, the demand for early childhood teachers with bachelor's degrees will be high as states implement pre-K initiatives. We need creative strategies that can be mobilized quickly to meet this demand. We also must attend to long-term needs and build a self-sustaining professional development system that will continue to graduate highly qualified teachers to replace those who retire or move outside the pre-K system and to accommodate population growth in the pre-K age group.

System Principles

Professional development must be given the same attention in planning for universal prekindergarten as curricula, space, and other issues. In other words, strategies must not exist in isolation but instead

TABLE 9.1. *Guiding Principles for a Prekindergarten Professional Development System*

Quality	**Systems Approach**
Ensure that teachers are prepared to serve all children and families and to respect the diversity of children and families served.	Position professional standards, preparation, and development as key components of prekindergarten programs.
Accessibility	Promote continuity with the K–12 system.
Provide avenues for existing pre-k teachers to achieve higher standards of preparation and educational attainment.	Incorporate the cost of a well-prepared work force into the prekindergarten budget.
Support the development of a work force that reflects the diversity of children served.	Promote continuity with the early childhood care and education system for young children birth to 3.
Utilize proactive approaches to promote equity of access to professional development opportunities.	Offer teacher compensation comparable to public school personnel.
Evaluation and Accountability	Foster partnerships across constituencies (e.g., business leaders, advocacy groups, national organizations).
Use research and recommended practices to guide personnel development.	
Invest in monitoring and evaluating personnel preparation and performance.	Provide a continuum of professional development opportunities to pre-K teachers, administrators, and personnel preparation faculty.
Establish accountability for personnel preparation outcomes to families and the public.	

be coordinated within a systems framework. In 2002 the National Prekindergarten Center convened a meeting to discuss challenges and to make recommendations about how to address the enormous need for an expanded work force of highly qualified teachers in pre-K programs. The group prepared a broad set of principles to guide work in the area (see Table 9.1).

The principles fall into four broad categories: quality, accessibility, evaluation and accountability, and a systems approach. The *quality* of professional development is important to ensure that teachers are prepared to address the individual needs of children with a wide range of experiences and skills. This will require that personnel programs be evaluated in terms of the impact of their program on children, not just teachers.

Accessibility is evident in the principles that respect existing and potential pre-K teachers. Proactive approaches to promote equity of access to professional development opportunities for teachers, aides, and administrators are needed. The typical early childhood teacher is a low-income mother who works full-time. It is not enough to create non-traditional approaches to continuing education. We must also implement a variety of strategies to recruit and support these teachers to take advantage of interesting and relevant professional development opportunities.

Evaluation and accountability guidelines begin with the premise that professional development efforts should be guided by research about best practices. There must be strong monitoring and evaluation pieces for both personnel preparation and performance. Accountability cannot be limited to the professional development efforts themselves or to teachers. In the long run, accountability for professional development efforts – as with the other pre-K services and infrastructure components – must be defined as improved outcomes for children and families as well as benefits to the public.

Finally, professional development efforts should utilize a comprehensive *systems approach*. As states develop new prekindergarten programs, there is a danger of creating yet another "silo" in the early childhood system that is disconnected from services for younger children (birth to three) and from the public school system. Pre-K professional development efforts should promote continuity across these services for young children of various ages.

Most importantly, professional development efforts must be treated as an integral component of high-quality prekindergarten services. As states implement pre-K programs with limited funds, they may tend to focus on direct services. This short-term planning is necessary, of course, but so is long-term planning to build the foundation to support the system in the years ahead. Creating a professional development system as part of the prekindergarten infrastructure will not be quick or cheap. Kagan and Cohen (1997) recommend that 10 percent of early childhood program funds be invested in infrastructure, which includes professional development and other components.

One State's Approach

Implementation plans for North Carolina's More at Four prekindergarten program demonstrate that a focus on professional development should be a cornerstone of state preschool initiatives. The state plans to implement its preschool program across a seven-year period, expanding capacity each year until all of the projected 40,000 at-risk children can be enrolled. The state requires teachers to have a bachelor's degree and Birth–Kindergarten (B–K) teacher certification. Clifford and Maxwell (2002) studied expansion plans and projected the need for highly qualified pre-K teachers, the supply, and the cost of supporting new efforts to increase the number of teachers with the required education. As can be seen in Table 9.2, in the first year of the program 1,500 children were served. If one assumes a class size of 18 students, 83 pre-K teachers were needed. That year, 77 North Carolina college graduates held a B–K certification, representing 92 percent of the need met. In years 2 and 3, the existing personnel preparation programs would produce enough B–K teachers to meet 100 percent of the need to serve the projected number of children. By year 4, though, the existing B–K programs would produce only 65 percent of the needed pre-K work force. To expand at the planned rate, more efforts would be needed to increase the future supply of highly qualified teachers.

Early childhood leaders proposed that North Carolina rely on two types of scholarships already available to some residents. The first, scholarships through the T.E.A.C.H. Early Childhood® Project, supports early childhood teachers who are working toward a bachelor's degree. Given appropriate funding, we assumed that by year 3 of the implementation phase this scholarship would produce 100 certified pre-K teachers a year. The second type of scholarship, Pre-K Teaching Fellows, would expand the state's current Teaching Fellows program to support incoming college freshman who are interested in teaching. The scholarship would pay college expenses for these students if they receive a B–K certificate and teach prekindergarten for a specified time period. With appropriate funding to support both scholarship programs (an investment of approximately $19.9 million over the seven-year period), there would be enough well-qualified pre-K teachers to serve the 40,000 children projected to be eligible for the program.

This example demonstrates one state's efforts to align preschool planning with the teacher preparation system. Although a detailed analysis of capacity and costs like that for North Carolina is not available for the nation, we can discuss general issues related to the current capacity to produce the number of pre-K teachers needed for a universal system.

TABLE 9.2. *North Carolina as an Example of Current and Projected Need versus Supply of Highly Qualified Pre-K Teachers*[*]

	2001	2002	2003	2004	2005	2006	2007
Number of children served[a]	1,500	1,500	4,000	16,000	28,000	40,000	40,000
Number of teachers needed							
Total classes[b]	83	83	222	889	1,556	2,222	2,222
New classes[c]	83	0	139	667	667	667	333
Replacement teachers[d]	–	13	13	33	133	233	333
Total new teachers needed	83	13	151	700	800	900	333
Supply of new teachers							
Existing B–K institutions[e]	77	77	65	60	55	50	40
T.E.A.C.H. Early Childhood[f]	–	–	100	200	300	400	500
New teaching fellows[g]	–	–	–	–	50	100	150
Total yearly supply	77	77	165	260	405	550	690
Cumulative supply[h]	77	154	319	579	984	1,534	2,224
% of total need met[i]	92	185	144	65	63	69	100
Professional development proposed budget							
T.E.A.C.H. Early Childhood	$600,000	$600,000	$1,600,000	$2,000,000	$2,000,000	$2,000,000	$2,000,000
Teaching fellows	$650,000	$650,000	$1,300,000	$1,625,000	$1,625,000	$1,625,000	$1,625,000
TOTAL[j]	$1,250,000	$1,250,000	$2,900,000	$3,625,000	$3,625,000	$3,625,000	$3,625,000

Note: [*]The authors would like to thank Sue Russell for her advice and assistance with this example of teacher need versus supply.

[a] There are approximately 42,000 at-risk four-year-olds in North Carolina. At full implementation the penetration rates are expected to be 95%. Figures are approximated to the nearest 1000.

[b] Teachers are calculated at 18 children per class. Because some classes will be blended classes with both at-risk and nonrisk children, these estimates represent a lower bound of need.

[c] New classes equal total classes less previous year's classes.

[d] Replacement teachers are calculated at the turnover rate (for similar teachers) of 15% of the previous year's total number of pre-K teachers.

[e] The existing network of institutions of higher education in North Carolina produced 153 B–K graduates in the most recent school year (2000-2001). About 50% of these graduates will work in pre-K classes. After the T.E.A.C.H. Early Childhood and Teaching Fellows programs are up and running, we expect the number of traditional B–K students (without scholarships) to decrease.

[f] T.E.A.C.H. Early Childhood expects to have the stated number of B–K-trained graduates as shown.

[g] Teaching fellows take the full four years of undergraduate education to complete the BA/BS degree with the B–K certificate requirements.

[h] The cumulative supply is expected to reach the need by year 7. By that time either the programs will be scaled back or the pre-K program will expand to include children not at risk.

[i] Cumulative supply/total classes.

[j] To meet the need across the 7 years, North Carolina would need to invest $19.9 million in professional development.

Current Capacity

There are currently three general approaches to professional development for pre-K teachers: preservice, in-service, and lateral entry. Most education for pre-K teachers in the United States is preservice (i.e., prior to entering the work force). According to Early and Winton (2001), approximately 1,244 institutions of higher education (IHEs) in the United States have early childhood education programs, representing about 29 percent of IHEs that offer an associate's or bachelor's degree. Of these, less than half – approximately 300 – offer BA degrees in early childhood fields. Early and Winton and other researchers have also documented the difficulty with articulation agreements across two-year and four-year institutions, which enable students to move from an AA to a BA degree program (Cassidy, Hestenes, Teague, & Springs, 2001; Early & Winton, 2001).

Current IHEs are not prepared to meet the need for highly qualified pre-K teachers. For the 300 IHEs to produce almost 152,000 additional teachers with BA degrees in early childhood needed for universal prekindergarten, each IHE would have to graduate more than 500 teachers. Assuming that each program graduates 50 early childhood teachers a year, it would take 10 years to meet the *current* need for highly qualified pre-K teachers. Obviously, this will not work.

In-service training is another component of our current professional development efforts. Most in-service training for pre-K teachers is provided through workshops and does not lead to a degree. Although this type of training helps teachers enhance their skills, it will not increase the number of credentialed pre-K teachers.

Finally, lateral entry programs are sometimes used to prepare teachers who have a BA degree in an area other than early childhood or to enable public school teachers who currently teach older children to become certified in pre-K. Most of the current lateral entry, or alternative teacher certification, programs do not meet the professional standards outlined by the National Association for the Education of Young Children (Sluder & Irons, 1996). Of the three current professional development strategies, lateral entry is the least used avenue.

Barriers to Meeting the Need

An increase in capacity will not be enough to increase the supply of qualified prekindergarten teachers. There are a number of barriers that must be addressed in the system of professional development programs and policies. Here we highlight some of these barriers.

Defining the Profession

The defining characteristic of a profession is the existence of a common core of knowledge that is largely unique to members of the profession. Individuals must demonstrate a certain level of proficiency with respect to that knowledge before gaining entrance to the field (Mitchell, 1996). There is general agreement in the early childhood field on the common core of knowledge needed for good practice (NAEYC, 2001). However, these standards are not universally required in the existing hodgepodge of early childhood education settings (Mitchell, 1996). The current early childhood teacher work force ranges from those with less than a high school diploma to teachers with advanced professional degrees.

There is less consensus about the profession among the public. At some level, many adults who have reared their own children believe that no specialized education or training is required to teach preschool. This notion that parental knowledge and experience are sufficient to serve as a preschool teacher presents a major barrier to overcome. If early childhood education is viewed as something anyone can do, the public will not perceive a need for professional development programs or be willing to support them. Thus, although the content necessary for pre-K teachers is relatively well defined within the profession, the need for highly trained personnel in pre-K is not well accepted in the general population, making establishment of the profession still illusory.

Compensation

Teacher compensation has been linked to program quality (Cost, Quality and Child Outcomes Study Team, 1995; Whitebook et al., 1989). Compensation cannot be disentangled from professional development efforts to improve the qualifications of the pre-K work force. Many of those striving to professionalize the early childhood field have secondary goals of using the training and education programs to raise the standard of living of low-income women and to provide work opportunities so they can move off the welfare rolls. While these goals are laudatory, they place a particularly high burden on the professional development system because most of those living in poverty also have quite low education levels, meaning that considerable pretraining may be needed. Further, once workers attain higher levels of education, low pay often entices them out of the early childhood field into more lucrative positions. To end this common result, many early childhood advocates call for compensation of early childhood teachers to be equivalent to that of teachers in the K–12 public school system. If this is the goal, then even more substantial investments are needed to move the current work force out of poverty and up to the earnings level of K–12 teachers.

Diversity

The early childhood population in this country is becoming more ethnically and culturally diverse. Much of the recent population growth in the United States is attributable to immigration. The vast majority of these immigrants are non-Caucasian. These families tend to have higher birthrates and more young children than the general population. This increased diversity presents two challenges for the pre-K teacher work force.

First, early childhood personnel preparation must address individual and sociocultural diversity. Cross-cultural effectiveness has become a critical skill for early childhood professionals. They must be knowledgeable of and sensitive to different family beliefs about child rearing and developmental expectations (Lynch & Hanson, 1998). They must also have a range of skills and strategies to teach effectively children with varying skills, abilities, needs, and cultural backgrounds. A 1999 national survey of colleges and universities indicated that only 43 percent of programs offering BA degrees in early childhood required at least one course about working with children and families of different races and cultures (Early & Winton, 2001). Only 11 percent required a course in working with children who were bilingual or who had limited English proficiency. If teachers are to be competent in today's preschool classroom, then personnel programs must adapt quickly to provide the preparation needed to teach the increasingly diverse population of young children.

The teaching work force itself is the second challenge related to diversity. We must maintain a work force that is itself diverse and reflects the population of children served. The proportion of minority K–12 public school teachers is much lower than the proportion of minority children they teach (U.S. Department of Education, 1997). The diversity problem is not as acute among the current early childhood teacher work force. Findings from a national survey suggest that the ethnicity and culture of pre-K workers are much more reflective of their student populations (Saluja et al., 2002). For instance, 71 percent of preschool classrooms in the survey in which at least three-fourths of the children were African

American had teachers who were also African American, and 46 percent of classrooms in which at least three-fourths of children were Latino had Latino teachers. In the six-state study noted previously, 68 percent of the pre-K teachers were non-Latino white compared with 42 percent of the children (Clifford et al., 2003). Data from these two studies suggest that the early childhood work force is not as diverse as the children it serves, but comes closer than teachers in the K–12 system.

Maintaining a diverse work force also means that we need to develop a diverse cadre of leaders. In their survey of higher education preparation programs for early childhood teachers, Early and Winton (2001) found that more than 80 percent of faculty members were non-Latino white. We cannot expect such a homogeneous faculty to attract a diverse student population.

Uncertainty of the Need and Resources
Only a handful of states have a clear goal of making prekindergarten available to all families of young children. It is impossible to predict when this goal will be embraced across the 50 states. Gallagher, Clayton, and Heinemeier (2001) report that prekindergarten initiatives do not usually come through the education establishment but, to some degree, are forced on a reluctant education system. Given that universal *kindergarten* is not yet available in all states, there is no way of telling when the education system will adopt universal pre-K. Thus one can only guess at the future need for trained staff. Even when goals are set, such as in New York and Florida, actual implementation is constrained by the availability of funds and the continuing political will to allocate scarce resources to expansion of prekindergarten over other desired programs. The tendency, then, is to hold off on investing heavily in educating pre-K teachers until the programs are actually in place. Yet, by the time the doors open, the need for qualified teachers will be immediate and certainly greater than the supply.

Teachers Are Not the Complete Work Force
Finally, we have considered only preparation of teachers in this chapter. There is a pressing need to train other personnel critical to successful program implementation. The Cost, Quality and Child Outcomes Study Team (1995) provided evidence of the importance of effective program administrators in high-quality early childhood programs. For example, the team pointed out the value of active involvement of directors in working with teachers on curriculum issues. Yet we have virtually no

systematic effort to train such personnel. Second, the No Child Left Behind legislation calls for highly qualified teacher assistants in the K–12 system. Little attention has been given to preparing teacher assistants for pre-K programs. Finally, support staff, such as health consultants and speech-language therapists, also should be highly qualified.

Strategies for Promoting a Highly Qualified Prekindergarten Teacher Work Force

Credit-Bearing In-service Training

At least half of current preschool teachers do not have a BA degree. Even if current higher education programs could accommodate them all, few would be able to quit their jobs and go back to school. In-service training strategies that are credit bearing and lead to a degree may be a promising approach to increasing the needed number of qualified pre-K teachers. This will require collaborative efforts between community colleges, universities, and other training providers such as Child Care Resource and Referral agencies and state technical assistance centers.

We believe it is necessary to link training to the formal education system. Research on the effectiveness of in-service training on classroom quality and teacher behavior has been severely limited by the lack of consensus in defining and measuring the term "training." Current programs vary by type (e.g., on-site technical assistance, workshops), content (e.g., child development, behavior management), and auspices (e.g., in-house, public and private training services). There are simply not enough data on the results of various training options to warrant large increases in resources for these programs (Maxwell, Feild, & Clifford, 2005). The most promising strategy seems to be linking in-service training to the formal education system. Connecticut's Charts-A-Course is one example of such an effort (www.ctcharts-a-course.org). Teachers who complete 180 clock hours of in-service training are eligible to convert the hours into six college credits if they pass a competency exam.

Scholarships to Support Continued Education

Just as administrators in the early intervention field concluded several years ago when they struggled with job qualification issues, the work force with the most potential is the one we currently have (McCollum & Winton, 2002). Multiple strategies are needed to encourage and support current preschool teachers to work toward a BA degree. Scholarships can be used to help with the cost of tuition, books, and fees as well as to cover associated support costs such as travel, paid time away from work, and child care (Russell, 2002). Scholarships may also be necessary to cover practicum experiences that may require the teacher to work someplace other than her current work setting.

The T.E.A.C.H. Early Childhood® Project is one scholarship model that helps child care teachers to complete coursework in early childhood education and increase their compensation. Twenty states have implemented the T.E.A.C.H. Project (Child Care Services Association, 2003). Every T.E.A.C.H. scholarship program has four components: scholarship, education, compensation, and commitment. The scholarship typically covers partial costs for tuition and books. In return for receiving a scholarship, each recipient must complete a certain amount of education during a prescribed contract period. After completing their educational requirement, participants are eligible for increased compensation in the form of a bonus or raise. Finally, participants must commit to staying in their program or in the field for six months to a year, depending on the scholarship they receive. An evaluation of the first year of a T.E.A.C.H. cohort found that scholarship recipients who had taken, on average, four community college courses that year made larger gains in classroom quality than did a comparison group of teachers who did not participate (Cassidy et al., 1995). Evidence also indicates that turnover among T.E.A.C.H. recipients is much lower (less than 10 percent) than the general child care work force turnover rate of somewhere between 30 and 40 percent (Child Care Services Association, 2002). Although the long-term success of scholarship programs like T.E.A.C.H. has not yet been determined, the data available suggest that the T.E.A.C.H. Project is a promising model for building a highly qualified pre-K work force.

Recruitment

Strategies are needed to attract new people to the pre-K teacher work force. Teacher preparation programs must reach out to a full range of potential pre-K teachers – high school students, college students who have not yet selected a major, and teachers of older students, among others (Hyson, 2002). Federal grants, like those provided for early intervention, may be an effective tool for recruiting people into the early childhood teaching profession. Finally, recruitment should not focus solely on teachers but should also include teacher assistants, program directors, and teacher preparation faculty.

Link Compensation to Competency

As noted earlier, compensation cannot be separated from the issue of maintaining a qualified prekindergarten work force. The U.S. Army was very successful in improving the quality of its early care and education system, in part because it directly linked teacher competency to compensation (Campbell, Appelbaum, Martinson, & Martin, 2000). Teachers who completed certain training milestones were guaranteed a raise in salary.

If prekindergarten program administrators cannot find teachers who meet the qualifications established in their standards, then one option is for them to offer waivers to teachers who meet minimum criteria, specify a timeline for reaching a series of training or education goals, and provide salary increases for each goal attained. This approach is used in some state K–12 systems. It would enable pre-K programs to serve more children while encouraging teachers to attain higher qualifications. The Child Care WAGE$® Project is an example of such a strategy that provides salary supplements to child care teachers who move up the educational ladder. It is currently implemented in Florida, Kansas, North Carolina, and Oklahoma (Child Care Services Association, 2003).

Community College–University Partnerships

Four-year universities and two-year community colleges should forge strong partnerships to address the multitude of issues facing early childhood teachers in training (Hyson, 2002). For example, students who finish their associate's degree and try to move into a bachelor's program often lose credits for some of their courses that are not accepted by the new school. Articulation agreements between community colleges and universities would make it easier for students to transfer and continue their education without losing ground. New Mexico, for instance, has worked collaboratively to develop legislation and formal agreements to support articulation between early childhood programs in two- and four-year colleges (Turner, 2002).

Partnerships offer other advantages as well. Shared faculty, classrooms, and resources would help smooth the transition between colleges, make four-year programs more accessible to students, and foster professional development activities for both sets of faculty. The National Association for the Education of Young Children (2003) is working to create an approval system for associate degree early childhood professional preparation programs, similar to that for bachelor degree programs. Official recognition of AA programs will raise their reputation and may also help improve relationships between community colleges and universities.

Mentorship and Technical Assistance Programs

With the projected need for highly qualified pre-K teachers, we cannot afford to lose qualified teachers newly entering the work force. Providing new teachers with good, experienced teacher mentors is one strategy for supporting professional development and minimizing turnover. In the short term when states may not have enough highly qualified personnel to meet the need for classroom teaching, using well-educated specialists to supervise less-prepared teachers may be a particularly effective model for supporting quality. For example, the U.S. Army successfully employs training and curriculum specialists to provide on-site technical assistance and support to its teachers, placing a specialist in each child care center (Campbell et al., 2000). Depending on the size and organizational structure of the prekindergarten program, states may support specialists at the state, regional, county, district, or program level.

Accessibility

Because many current early childhood teachers work full-time and have families, the traditional college system may not work well for them. College administrators should develop creative ways to offer traditional courses. Examples include distance learning, offering courses in accessible locations in the community, or holding classes at nontraditional times. An evaluation of Project CONTACT, a distance learning project in North Carolina, suggests that providing high-quality courses via the Internet is more accessible and convenient for rural early childhood educators than traditional course offerings (Coleman & Torrence, 2002).

Faculty Training

The quality of pre-K teachers is only as good as the quality of their education, so efforts to support faculty in preservice training programs are also needed. Walking the Walk in North Carolina is one innovative project to support early childhood faculty as they prepare students to teach an increasingly diverse population of children. Walking the Walk is an outreach project funded by the U.S. Department of Education that is designed to prepare higher education faculty to recruit diverse students and to prepare them adequately to be culturally competent early childhood professionals (Winton, Catlett, & Thompson, 2002). The project uses a participatory approach with key stakeholders to produce changes in preservice personnel preparation. The model includes (a) identifying needs, priorities, and supports for addressing diversity issues; (b) providing models, materials, and experiences to community-based teams; (c) facilitating the development of action plans for addressing diversity issues; and (d) providing technical assistance and training to support the action plans. Innovative training models such as this are needed to ensure the professional development of the educators of preschool teachers.

CONCLUSION

Prekindergarten is not the first program to face daunting personnel problems. Historically, the early intervention field lacked qualified teachers and support staff. Over the years, though, a great deal of progress has been made in raising the qualifications of the work force. The U.S. Army has also worked diligently to improve the quality of early care and education, including improving the qualifications of its teachers. We have much to learn from these efforts.

The Federal Government's Role in Professional Development

The federal government traditionally has helped direct and financially support personnel preparation efforts in education and special education. Federal grants support both students and faculty and identify priorities in content (McCollum & Winton, 2002). Early intervention grants provided incentives for colleges and universities to expand and improve their education efforts in an area of need. The federal government also required states to develop a comprehensive system of personnel development for early intervention and to integrate it with other professional development systems (McCollum & Winton, 2002). Similar federal supports are needed in prekindergarten.

Quantity and Quality

Similar to prekindergarten now, the early intervention field faced a quantity-versus-quality conundrum in the 1980s (McCollum & Winton, 2002) and 1990s (Advisory Committee on Head Start Quality and Expansion, 1993). Should teacher education standards be lowered to meet the increasing numbers of children in prekindergarten? We believe the answer must be an adamant no. Quantity and quality must not be pitted against one another but instead conjoined so that a system is built to support growth in the number of well-qualified prekindergarten teachers.

Mandates to Produce Change

Congress has periodically legislated that an increasing percentage of Head Start teachers have at least an associate's degree in early childhood education. Without the necessary funding to meet this demand, Head Start has used its mandatory Performance Standards to encourage centers to hire more qualified teachers (Head Start Program Performance Standards, 1998). Policy makers did provide in successive reauthorization acts a quality set-aside to increase the salaries and benefits of the Head Start work force, among other program improvements. Similarly, the Individuals with Disabilities Education Act mandates the development of state personnel standards. Mandates do not have to be limited to program standards, though. The early intervention law also required and provided incentives for collaboration (McCollum & Winton, 2002). State administrators creating prekindergarten programs should consider mandating components and processes they believe are key to providing high-quality services.

Systematic Thinking

Building a high-quality prekindergarten system is complex, and professional development is only one of many system components. Solving a problem in one component of the system may create a problem in another. If program and staffing standards are set too low, for instance, the desired outcomes will not be realized and failure will be inevitable. Program administrators should think systematically about all components of prekindergarten – both program and infrastructure components – when planning, implementing, and running programs.

The need for highly qualified prekindergarten teachers is great, and the obstacles to providing a qualified work force are enormous. Yet the evidence is clear that the quality of pre-K teachers is central to the goal of ensuring that all children are prepared to succeed when they enter school. To date, there has been little systematic attempt to build a pre-K professional development system that meets the needs and overcomes the barriers. The current national and state interest in prekindergarten presents an opportunity for us to build the system we envision.

References

Advisory Committee on Head Start Quality and Expansion. (1993). *Creating a 21st century Head Start.* Washington, DC: U.S. Government Printing Office. (1994-517-593/80715)

American Federation of Teachers. (2002, December). *At the starting line: Early childhood education programs in the 50 states.* Washington, DC: Author. www.aft.org/edissues/downloads/EarlyChildhoodreport.pdf.

Barnett, W. S. (2003, March). Better teachers, better preschools: Student achievement linked to teacher qualifications. *Preschool Policy Matters, 2.* New Brunswick, NJ: NIEER.

Bowman, B. T., Donovan, M. S., & Burns, M. S. (2001). *Eager to learn: Educating our preschoolers.* Washington, DC: National Academy Press.

Bredekamp, S., & Copple, C. (1997). *Developmentally appropriate practice in early childhood programs* (Rev. ed.). Washington, DC: National Association for the Education of Young Children.

Bryant, D., Clifford, R. M., Saluja, G., Pianta, R., Early, D., Barbarin, O., Howes, C., & Burchinal, M. (2002). *Diversity and directions in state pre-kindergarten programs.* Chapel Hill: University of North Carolina, FPG Child Development Institute, NCDEL. http://www.fpg.unc.edu/~ncedl/PDFs/diversity_direct.pdf.

Burchinal, M. R., Roberts, J. E., Riggins, R., Zeisel, S. A., Neebe, E., & Bryant, D. (2000). Relating quality of center-based child care to early cognitive and language development longitudinally. *Child Development, 71,* 339–357.

Burton, A., Whitebook, M., Young, M., Bellm, D., Wayne, C., Brandon, R., & Maher, E. (2002). *Estimating the size and components of the U.S. child care workforce and caregiving population.* Washington, DC: Center for the Child Care Workforce and Human Services Policy Center.

Campbell, F. A., & Ramey, C. T. (1994). Effects of early intervention on intellectual and academic achievement: A follow-up study of children from low-income families. *Child Development, 65,* 684–698.

Campbell, N. D., Appelbaum, J. C., Martinson, K., & Martin, E. (2000). *Be all that we can be: Lessons from the military for improving our nation's child care system.* Washington, DC: National Women's Law Center.

Cassidy, D. J., Buell, M. J., Pugh-Hoese, S., & Russell, S. (1995). The effect of education on child care teachers' beliefs and classroom quality: Year one evaluation of the TEACH Early Childhood Associate Degree Scholarship Program. *Early Childhood Research Quarterly, 10,* 171–183.

Cassidy, D. J., Hestenes, L., Teague, P., & Springs, J. (2001). The facilitation of the transfer of credit between early childhood education/child development departments in 2- and 4-year institutions of higher education in North Carolina. *Journal of Early Childhood Teacher Education, 22,* 29–38.

Child Care Services Association. (2002). *T.E.A.C.H. Early Childhood® Project 2001–02 Annual Report.* Chapel Hill, NC: Author.

Child Care Services Association. (2003). *Child Care Services Association Annual Report: 2002–2003 Fiscal Year.* Chapel Hill, NC: Author. www.childcareservices.org.

Clifford, R. M., Barbarin, O., Chang, F., Early, D. M., Bryant, D., Howes, C., Burchinal, M., & Pianta, R. (2005). What is pre-kindergarten? Characteristics of public pre-kindergarten programs. *Applied Developmental Science, 9,* 126–143.

Clifford, R. M., Early, D. M., & Hills, T. W. (1999). Almost a million children in school before kindergarten: Who is responsible for early childhood services? *Young Children, 54,* 48–51.

Clifford, R. M., & Maxwell, K. L. (2002, April). *The need for highly qualified prekindergarten teachers.* Paper presented at the National Prekindergarten Center symposium, Preparing Highly Qualified Prekindergarten Teachers. http://www.fpg.unc.edu/~NPC/need.pdf.

Coleman, M. R., & Torrence, D. (2002). *Lessons learned: Project CONTACT (College Opportunity Networks and Technical Assistance for Child Care Teachers). Summary report.* Chapel Hill: FPG Child Development Institute, University of North Carolina.

Cost, Quality and Child Outcomes Study Team. (1995). *Cost, quality, and child outcomes in child care centers, technical report.* Denver: Department of Economics, Center for Research in Economic and Social Policy, University of Colorado at Denver.

Early, D. M., & Winton, P. J. (2001). Preparing the workforce: Early childhood teacher preparation at 2- and 4-year institutions of higher education, *Early Childhood Research Quarterly, 16,* 285–306.

Gallagher, J. J., Clayton, J. R., & Heinemeier, S. E. (2001). *Education for four-year-olds: State initiatives. Executive Summary.* Chapel Hill: University of North Carolina, FPG Child Development Center, National Center for Early Development and Learning.

Head Start Program Performance Standards. (1998). 45 CFR Part 1304.52. http://www.acf.hhs.gov/programs/hsb/performance/1304/1304_d3.htm.

Henderson, L. W., Basile, K. C., & Henry, G. T. (1999). *Prekindergarten longitudinal study: 1997–1998 school year annual report.* Atlanta: Georgia State University Applied Research Center. http://cspweb.gsu.edu/pre-k/report/prek9798Long.pdf.

Howes, C. (1997). Children's experiences in center-based child care as a function of teacher background and adult-child ratio. *Merrill-Palmer Quarterly, 43,* 404–425.

Hyson, M. (2002, April). *Field of dreams: Higher education and the preparation of early childhood teachers.* Paper presented at the National Prekindergarten Center symposium, Preparing Highly Qualified Prekindergarten Teachers. http://www.fpg.unc.edu/~NPC/preservice.pdf.

Kagan, S. L., & Cohen, N. (1997). *Not by chance.* New Haven, CT: Yale University Bush Center in Child Development and Social Policy.

Lynch, E. W., & Hanson, M. W. (1998). *Developing cross cultural competence: A guide for working with young children and families.* Baltimore: Paul H. Brookes.

Maxwell, K. L., Feild, C. C., & Clifford, R. M. (2005). Defining and measuring professional development in early childhood research. In M. Zaslow & I. Martinez-Beck (Eds.), *Critical issues in early childhood professional development* (pp. 21–48). Baltimore: Paul H. Brookes.

Mitchell, A. (1996). Licensing: Lessons from other occupations. In S. L. Kagan & N. E. Cohen (Eds.), *Reinventing early care and education: A vision for a quality system* (pp. 101–123). San Francisco, CA: Jossey-Bass.

McCollum, J., & Winton, P. (2002, April). *Lessons learned: Personnel for early intervention, birth to three.* Paper presented at the National Prekindergarten Center symposium, Preparing Highly Qualified Prekindergarten Teachers. http://www.fpg.unc.edu/~NPC/lessons.pdf.

National Association for the Education of Young Children. (2001). *NAEYC Standards for early childhood professional preparation at the initial license level.* Washington, DC: Author. http://www.naeyc.org/profdev/prep_review/2001.pdf.

National Association for the Education of Young Children. (2003). *NAEYC Standards for early childhood professional preparation: Associate degree programs.* Washington, DC: Author. http://www.naeyc.org/profdev/prep_review/2003.pdf.

NICHD Early Child Care Research Network. (2000). The relation of child care to cognitive and language development. *Child Development, 71,* 960–980.

Olson, L. (2002). Starting early. In Quality Counts 2000, *Education Week, 21*(17), 10–14.

Peisner-Feinberg, E. S., & Burchinal, M. R. (1997). Relations between preschool children's child-care experiences and concurrent development: The cost, quality, and outcomes study. *Merrill-Palmer Quarterly, 43,* 451–577.

Peisner-Feinberg, E. S., Burchinal, M. R., Clifford, R. M., Culkin, M. L., Howes, C., Kagan, S. L., & Yazejian, N. (2001). The relation of preschool child care quality to children's cognitive and social developmental trajectories through second grade. *Child Development, 72,* 1534–1553.

Phillips, D. A., & Howes, C. (1987). Indicators of quality in child care: Review of research. In D. A. Phillips (Ed.), *Quality in child care: What does research tell us?* (pp. 1–20). Washington, DC: National Association for the Education of Young Children.

Ramey, C. T., & Campbell, F. A. (1984). Preventive education for high-risk children: Cognitive consequences of the Carolina Abecedarian Project. *American Journal of Mental Deficiency, 88,* 515–523.

Reynolds, A. J. (1994). Effects of a preschool plus follow-up intervention for children at risk. *Developmental Psychology, 30,* 787–804.

Reynolds, A. J., Temple, J. A., Robertson, D. L., & Mann, E. A. (2001). Long-term effects of an early childhood intervention on educational achievement and juvenile arrest. *Journal of American Medical Association, 285,* 2339–2346.

Russell, S. (2002, April). *Inservice strategies for consideration.* Paper presented at the National Prekindergarten Center symposium, Preparing Highly Qualified Prekindergarten Teachers. http://www.fpg.unc.edu/~NPC/inservice.pdf.

Saluja, G., Early, D. M., & Clifford, R. M. (2002). Demographic characteristics of early childhood teachers and structural elements of early care and education in the United States. *Early Childhood Research and Practice, 4*(1). http://ecrp.uiuc.edu/v4n1/saluja.html.

Sandham, J. L. (2002). Adequate financing. In Quality Counts 2000, *Education Week, 21*(17), 43–45.

Schulman, K., Blank, H., & Ewen, D. (1999). *Seeds of success: State prekindergarten initiatives, 1998–1999.* Washington, DC: Children's Defense Fund.

Schweinhart, L. J., Barnes, H. V., Weikart, D. P., Barnett, W. S., & Epstein, A. S. (1993). *Significant benefits: The High/Scope Perry Preschool Study through age 27.* Ypsilanti, MI: High/Scope Press.

Sluder, L. C., & Irons, J. (1996). Investigating alternative certification for early childhood teachers. *Journal of Early Childhood Teacher Education, 17,* 82–87.

Turner, P. (2002). La Ristra: New Mexico's comprehensive professional development system in early care, education, and family support. Albuquerque: University of New Mexico. http://www.newmexicokids.org/Pro_dev/library/LaRistra.pdf.

U.S. Census Bureau. (2000a). *Projections of the total resident population by 5-year age groups, and sex with special age categories: Middle series, 2001 to 2005.* http://www.census.gov/population/projections/nation/summary/np-t3-b.pdf.

U.S. Census Bureau. (2000b). *Projections of the total resident population by 5-year age groups, and sex with special age categories: Middle series, 2016 to 2020.* http://www.census.gov/population/projections/nation/summary/np-t3-e.pdf.

U.S. Department of Education, National Center for Education Statistics. (1997). *America's teachers: Profile of a profession, 1993–1994.* NCES 97-460. Washington, DC: Author.

U.S. Department of Education, National Center for Educational Statistics. (2003). *Prekindergarten in U.S. Public Schools: 2000–2001,* by Timothy Smith, Anne Kleiner, Basmat Parsad, & Elizabeth Farris. Project Officer: Bernard Greene. NCES 2003-019. Washington, DC.

West, J., Denton, K., & Germino-Hausken, E. (2000). *America's kindergartners: Findings from the early childhood longitudinal study, kindergarten class of 1998–99, fall 1998.* Washington, DC: U.S. Department of Education, National Center for Education Statistics.

Whitebook, M., Howes, C., & Phillips, D. (1990). *Who cares? Child care teachers and the quality of care in America.* (Final report of the National Child Care Staffing Study). Oakland, CA: Child Care Employee Project.

Willer, B., Hofferth, S., Kisker, E. E., Divine-Hawkins, P., Farquahar, E., & Glantz, F. (1991). *The demand and supply of child care in 1990: Joint findings from the national child care survey 1990 and a profile of child care settings.* Washington, DC: National Association for the Education of Young Children.

Winton, P., Catlett, C. & Thompson, F. (2002, October). *Walking the Walk: A model for promoting diversity in early childhood teacher preparation programs.* Atlanta, GA: National Black Child Development Institute Conference.

10

What the School of the 21st Century Can Teach Us about Universal Preschool

With Matia Finn-Stevenson

A long-standing problem in the early childhood field is that there is no cohesive delivery system in place for preschool and child care services. Rather, we have a mix of fragmented services, some providing part-day preschool to four-year-olds, others providing all-day, year-round child care for children whose parents are working. Multiple funding streams support the programs, and a variety of institutional contexts exists – public schools, nonprofit and for-profit centers, churches, and community-based organizations – as well as licensed and unlicensed individual child care providers. Of significance is the general lack of quality that characterizes this nonsystem. Hence large numbers of preschool children attend programs that are of poor or mediocre quality, which has consequences for their healthy growth and development as well as their school readiness.

Universal preschool has the potential to create a better and more equitable early care and education system. Many issues have to be addressed about the governance, structure, and scope of a proposed system. In this chapter we discuss our experiences with the development and implementation of a universal school-based program known as the School of the 21st Century (21C). In some communities in Kentucky and Connecticut, the program is referred to as the Family Resource Center. 21C is a comprehensive program that includes, in addition to other components, universally accessible child care for preschoolers. The need for and rationale underlying 21C's development, and its implementation in more than 1,300 schools around the country, illuminate some of the key issues to be considered in formulating a policy for universal preschool. As Mintrom (2001) notes, documenting already established efforts provides compelling evidence for the workability of programs as well as lessons that can help form a desired policy.

What Is the School of the 21st Century?

The School of the 21st Century is often referred to as a program, but it is actually a comprehensive approach to the provision of several programs and services to families and children from birth to 12 years of age. It was established with the goal of creating a system for child care and early education. The need for such a system is critical. Brauner, Gordic, and Zigler (2004) note that the inadequate state of child care services is in part due to the fact that child care and early education are viewed as separate issues when in fact, they are synergistic. They further note that to address the child care problem, we need an infrastructure that combines care and education, placing educational components into child care and placing care into the educational system.

21C schools incorporate elements of both. These include:

1. All day, year-round care for children ages three and four. We refer here to developmentally appropriate care that ensures opportunities for play, social interactions, and learning. Although no specific curriculum is designated for the child care component, schools are given guidance to choose curricular activities that address all developmental domains: physical, social, emotional, and cognitive.

2. Before- and after-school and vacation care for children from kindergarten to age 12. This component addresses the need for child care during the hours when children are out of school and parents are at work. Although many school-age programs focus on academics, in 21C the emphasis is on providing children with the opportunity to choose among various types of activities, including but not limited to academic enrichment and homework. The rationale here is that children benefit the most when they attend programs that nurture multiple aspects of youth development and acknowledge the vital role of play (National Research Council, 2002).

Also included in 21C are several outreach services. One is home visitation to families with newborns and children up to age three, patterned after the Parents as Teachers (PAT) program. Parent educators visit the home to provide information to parents about child development as well as to screen children for potential developmental and learning problems. Also included in PAT are parent meetings held in the school building to welcome families, provide them with support, and make referrals to special services as needed. As new parents learn about their role in their children's development and education, a valuable outcome is enhanced parental involvement once children are in school (Pfannenstiel, Lambson, & Yarnell, 1996).

Among other 21C components is outreach to family and other child care providers in the community; information and referral for various services families may need; and health, mental health, and nutrition education and services. In some communities, schools also provide social services and infant care, based on local need as well as requests by parents. Additional components such as literacy training modules for preschool and school-age programs and support for schools with immigrant children are being added in response to new developments in the field, ensuring that the program continues to evolve and address current needs. All 21C components and services, although described separately, are part of the 21C "umbrella" and are coordinated as a whole.

Need and Rationale for the Program

Impact of Societal Changes on Children's Development
The need for a range of child and family support services in general and the School of the 21st Century is predicted by several developments, many of these related to societal changes that have occurred over the past several decades. A significant change is the huge increase in the number of working mothers and two-income families (U.S. Census Bureau, 2000). Other societal trends include a change in family structure caused by rising rates of divorce and never-married households, resulting in large numbers of children living in single-parent families; high mobility, especially in families with young children; and a lack of social capital, which refers to the dearth of adults in the lives of children and weak ties between families and their neighbors and kin (Putnam, 1995). The result has been increased isolation and alienation, with many parents raising children without any help and support.

These societal changes, as well as two other circumstances – the large number of young children who live in poverty (National Center for Children in Poverty, 2003) and the influx of children from low-income immigrant families (Fix & Passel, 2003) – create stressful conditions under which children are being reared. The harmful effects of environmental stress can be exacerbated during times of transition (e.g., from preschool to primary school) and can have profound developmental and educational consequences for children (Duncan & Brooks-Gunn, 1997; Shonkoff & Phillips, 2000; Vinson, Baldry, & Hargreaves, 1996).

The Need for Child Care

A major problem affecting families with young children is the lack of good-quality, affordable child care. The need for child care is evident in the statistics: 65 percent of mothers with children under age 6 and 78 percent of mothers with children ages 6 to 13 work outside the home; among mothers with infants under age 1, 59 percent are in the labor force or actively looking for work (U.S. Census Bureau, 2000). With their parents working, 13 million infants and preschool children – or 3 out of every 5 young children – are in child care. For school-age children, recent policy emphasis on before- and after-school programs has helped, but there remains a large unmet need: An estimated 7 million children are left home alone while their parents are working.

The need for child care was recognized in 1971 when federal policy makers were on the brink of establishing a national child care system. The structure of the system was contained in the Comprehensive Child Development Act, enthusiastically supported by Congress but surprisingly vetoed by President Nixon. Since that time, advocates have attempted in vain to create an interest at the federal level not only in establishing a formal child care system but also in ensuring quality care through federal guidelines. To date they have been unsuccessful, leaving the hodgepodge of child care services to proliferate and each state to develop its own regulations. Although the intent of state regulation is to address the needs of children and prevent them from harm, many states have failed to ensure even basic health and safety conditions in child care environments (Gallagher, Rooney, & Campbell, 1999; LeMoines, Morgan, & Azer, 2003; Marsland, Zigler, & Martinez, 2004; Young, Marsland, & Zigler, 1997).

The failure at the state level to assure a basic level of quality in child care has been noted in several national studies. The U.S. Consumer Product Safety Commission (1999) found pervasive health and safety violations in more than two-thirds of child care facilities, even though they were state-licensed. Other national studies have found that the average quality of care in child care centers (Helburn, 1995), in family child care homes, and in care provided by relatives (Galinsky, Howes, Kontos, & Shinn, 1994) is so low that it can compromise children's development. Children in poor-quality care have been found to have delayed language and reading skills and to display more aggression and behavior problems (Phillips, 1995). Children in high-quality care demonstrate greater academic skills and fewer behavior problems once they are in school (Cost, Quality and Child Outcomes Study Team, 1999), both of which contribute to the likelihood of continued school success.

Families can face numerous other problems related to child care. Examples include lack of available care for children whose parents work in nontraditional fields or have odd shifts (U.S. Census Bureau, 1997), lack of child care in poor neighborhoods (Queralt & Witte, 1998), and the fact that not much is known about appropriate care for children with disabilities (Shonkoff & Phillips, 2002). A major problem confronting most families is affording the child care they do find. These and other issues cannot be explored within the scope of this chapter, but are detailed in other of our publications (Finn-Stevenson & Zigler, 1999; Zigler, Finn-Stevenson, & Hall, 2002).

Schools of the 21st Century: A Response to the Child Care Crisis

The issues raised here underscore the continuing challenges of child care, which have been with us for several decades. Additional services and more money will not correct the problems because they are too pervasive and ingrained. What is needed is a coherent child care system, because the current nonsystem is difficult both to access and to improve. The School of the 21st Century is an effort to establish a child care system not by creating entirely new structures but by building on the existing educational system.

21C is based on six guiding principles, all established from research evidence about effective interventions (Zigler, 1987):

First, to meet the needs and promote optimal development of all children, a child care system must become a national priority. Instead of piecemeal services, the system must be part of the structure of our society, as is the case with public education. The purpose is to provide the stable, reliable, good-quality care that is vital to children's development and well-being as well as to their education. In using the term "good-quality care," we refer to care that is developmentally appropriate and provides children with opportunities for play, learning, and social interactions with peers and adult role models.

Second, good-quality care should be accessible to every child regardless of ethnic or socioeconomic group, instead of the present two-tier system in which some children receive good-quality care and others do not. Free public education is universally accessible because it is primarily a state-based system, and the same will be true for early care and education. The federal government's role is both to subsidize the care of the most needy children, as it currently does to some extent, as well as to support research, evaluation, and other efforts to enhance and upgrade the system. Although the use of the term "universal" in school-based programs brings up the notion of compulsory attendance, in 21C early childhood services are not mandatory. Rather, universality means equal access to care for those who need and want it.

Third, the overall goal of the child care system is the optimal development of the whole child. This means that equal weight must be placed on all developmental pathways: social, emotional, physical, and cognitive (Zigler, Singer, & Bishop-Josef, 2004). For purposes of research, social scientists often regard each developmental domain separately, and as a society we often pay more attention to cognitive development. However, all aspects of growth and development are interdependent and occur simultaneously, so it is counterproductive to nurture one and ignore the others. This third principle not only acknowledges that the child has a mind, body, and unique personality, it also reflects the fact that while child care may be regarded as a service for parents, it is first and foremost an environment where children spend a significant amount of time. Its quality affects all of their growth and development.

Fourth, parents and those who care for and educate children must work together to assure continuity in the child's experiences. Teachers certainly influence child development, but parents raise their children from the day they are born through young adulthood. The importance of parent involvement is noted not only for programs for preschool and younger children, but also as children progress through school (see Henrich & Blackman-Jones, Chapter 8).

The fifth principle is that child care providers are responsible for the quality of care children receive and have a significant influence on their developmental outcomes. Caregivers need recognition, support, and appropriate pay, including opportunities for ongoing training and career advancement.

Sixth, a national child care system must be flexible and adaptable. Because every family has unique child care needs, a universal system must provide a range of choices. Inherent in this principle is the recognition that there are differences not only among families but also among communities.

The guiding principles we have outlined represent 21C's theoretical framework. Principles to guide universal preschool policy are likewise important, a point made by Bailey (2002), among others. Bailey examined federal legislation for the education of children with disabilities, noting that the Individuals with Disabilities Education Act has a set of national regulatory guidelines to assure that certain principles shape the administration of the effort at the state level. He acknowledged that the regulations are in part controversial but concluded that without them, "we would see perhaps more cross-state variability than desired in the number and types of children served and in the nature, quantity and quality of services provided" (p. 10).

In 21C, the principles are used not only to provide a national context, but also to guide implementation at the local level. This enables each of the local schools to abide by a shared vision, but at the same time to have the flexibility to be responsive to each community's unique needs, a point we elaborate on later in the chapter. A universal preschool policy should also contain clear goal statements as well as theories of action, because the ultimate success of the effort will depend on how well programs are delivered in classrooms across the nation (Barnett, Finn-Stevenson, & Henrich, 2003).

Whether there will be national commitment to universal preschool policy remains to be seen, of course. If there is such commitment, many questions about how a national mandate for preschool for all children will be translated to practice will have to be answered. Some of these questions are addressed elsewhere in this book, but one in particular is relevant to this chapter: to what extent and in what ways will the public schools be involved?

The Role of Public Schools

The development of 21C is based on the notion that the most efficient way to implement an early care and education system is to tap into the existing institution of public education. Our country has a trillion-dollar investment in public school buildings, which are supported by tax dollars and used for only part of the day, nine months a year. By capitalizing on this investment and adding a child care component, we can increase the supply of child care as well as ensure affordable, good-quality care for all children (Zigler, 1987).

The idea of using the school for various nontraditional services is not new. It was evident in the community school movement that began several decades ago and has recently enjoyed a resurgence (Dryfoos, 1994; Martin, 2003). Placing preschool child care in the schools was considered in the 1970s, one argument being that schools are a resource that exists in every community. Reasons at the time included predictions that early childhood services would grow, and a single delivery system would prevent random development of programs (noted in Levine, 1978).

Opposition to the use of the school was extensive, however, and has continued over the years. Opponents cite lack of space; an overburdened educational system; perceived inability of some school personnel to relate to and work with low-income, ethnic minority children and families; and presumed parental dissatisfaction with schools. (For details on the debate, see Finn-Stevenson and Zigler, 1999.) Critics have also argued that if schools become involved in preschool services, there will be "a danger that there would be a drift toward a much more regimented, scholarly curriculum than [is] appropriate" and "that a transition to a totally different system is unlikely to offer improvements needed and might well cause some deterioration [of quality]" (Helburn & Bergmann, 2002).

Levine (1978) examined arguments on both sides of the debate and conducted a case study in five communities where schools provided child care. Although Levine ultimately opposed exclusive sponsorship by the schools, he saw the potential of their involvement in child care and regarded it as unwise for a national policy to exclude the schools. Since that time, increasing numbers of schools have opened their doors to very young children, and more educators and policy makers are considering ways public schools can expand programs for preschool children (e.g., Dwyer, Chait, & McKee, 2000; Hinkle, 2000). The National Center for Education Statistics found that in 2001–2002, 822,000 preschool children were enrolled in close to 20,000 schools – or 35 percent of all elementary schools in the United States (NCES, 2003).

Our position on the role of schools in universal preschool is evident: we think a system for the care and education of young children should be established within the existing structure of public education. Other organizations in the community will certainly work with the schools, perhaps by subcontracting some services or assuming care components for infants and toddlers. Of course, social and political realities are such that it is unlikely that a school-based system for early childhood efforts will evolve in the near future. However, it is clear that schools, even if they are not the prime sponsors of preschool, are becoming increasingly involved.

LESSONS LEARNED FROM 21C

The School of the 21st Century is one of the largest and most comprehensive school-based, universal child care programs. It is national in scope, with more than 1,300 schools in rural, urban, and suburban communities in more than 20 states. A strong asset is that the majority of 21C schools have been in operation for more than a decade. Their longevity establishes the feasibility of using the school for preschool and other nonacademic services and proves that such efforts are sustainable. Experiences with the 21C schools provide a rich source of information that has implications for universal preschool policies. Four main lessons are discussed here.

Within the Context of Preschool Education, Other Services May Be Provided

Although many families have the resources to meet their children's health and socioemotional needs, some families do not, and some children have high levels of need. These groups can often benefit from additional support services. Head Start has always provided additional services for children and families and is a model of a comprehensive service program for 21C schools and other successful early interventions. Further, the importance of the first years of life to later development and school success has long been recognized (Shonkoff & Phillips, 2000; Zigler et al., 2002). Nevertheless, some states' preschool initiatives are very narrowly focused. For example, they are not comprehensive but provide only educational services. In addition, most states just target the preschool years, some further limiting programs to children who are four years old (Porch, 2002; Raden, 1999). Support services must begin at an earlier age, from the prenatal period if possible, to prevent developmental problems and make school readiness more likely.

Equally important is continuity of services beyond the preschool period. As Reynolds (2000) points out, extending programs to the primary grades promotes successful transitions and may also help sustain the benefits of preschool intervention. In 21C, continuity of services is feasible in part because the school is the single delivery system for both early childhood and school-age programs. In addition, 21C schools offer not only preschool but also child care for preschoolers and older children outside of school hours. This service addresses the needs of working families and provides children with consistent environments conducive to healthy growth and development. In contrast, a part-day, part-year program would exclude participation of large numbers of children from working families, eroding continuity and perhaps the goodwill and support of these families for universal programs.

Financial Considerations

Costs for comprehensive, high-quality, extended day services are high, posing a strong argument against the formation of a universal child care system. However, in 21C a mix of funding streams and parental fees makes the program affordable and self-sustaining. We should note at the outset that although 21C schools benefit from the existing management structure and leadership in the school as well as the use of space, they do not depend on local tax dollars, nor do they draw from the school district's general operating budget. Rather, funding for 21C is based in part on parental fees, with a sliding scale system calibrated to family income. Federal and state subsidies support services to children from low-income households.

The financial design for 21C, and an illustration of how state funding for 21C may be conceptualized, are detailed elsewhere (Zigler & Finn-Stevenson, 1996). The design distinguishes between start-up and operational costs. After a start-up period of about one year, parent fees for child care provide core support for the operation of the program. In some 21C schools, these fees result in a surplus that is used to pay for other services for which fees cannot be assessed (e.g., home visitations) and for staff training and other activities. Where there is state support for part-day, part-year preschool, parents pay only for the wraparound child care. An advantage of blending various funding streams with parent fees is that separate services can be integrated without segregating the children. For example, children served by Even Start, state preschool funds for at-risk and special-needs populations, and Head Start are in the same classroom with fee-paying children.

Combining several public funding streams is not unique to 21C (Schilder, Kiron, & Elliott, 2003). However, the addition of parent fees enables 21C to provide services beyond preschool such as universal child care – features that may not have other sources of support. Further, public funds are vulnerable to cuts during periods of budgetary shortfalls, so fees provide a means to sustain operations. Of course, families who cannot afford to pay will still need public subsidies. Although a new funding source dedicated to universal preschool may become a reality, until then support can be drawn from current programs. For example, Greenberg and Schumacher (2003) examined the use of federal funding streams, including Child Care and Development Block Grants and Temporary Assistance to Needy Families, in universal preschool programs. They concluded that although states would need to make political and policy judgments to prioritize the use of these federal funds, the child care block grant in particular is a potential source of support for universal preschool initiatives.

Schools Can Provide Good-Quality Preschool

A common argument against providing services to young children in schools is that the education establishment is a rigid, centralized bureaucracy slow to adapt to the needs of increasingly diverse populations. Further, development in the early years is highly individual, so young children need a variety of curriculum approaches. Many fear they are unlikely to find them in schools, where standardized curricula are the norm and the focus is solely academic (Helburn & Bergmann, 2002). The concern that good-quality, developmentally appropriate care is beyond the ability of school-trained personnel is certainly a possibility. However, poor quality and an academic orientation are problems that currently exist regardless of the institutional context of the program (Mitchell, 1988).

Good-quality, school-based preschool is also possible. In a national study of 21C schools, funded by the U.S. Department of Education, we found relatively high-quality preschool programs as well as various practices that are related to good-quality care (Henrich, Finn-Stevenson, & Zigler, in progress). We conducted this three-year evaluation in school districts in five states. Our findings so far indicate:

- The preschool programs had a mean score of 5.70 on the Early Childhood Environment Rating Scale. The range of scores on this scale is 1 to 7, with 5 indicating good quality.
- The programs were child-centered; teachers reported spending an average of more than two hours a day on child-initiated activities.

- Teachers had spent a median of 8.5 years teaching preschool. About 80 percent of the teachers had a bachelors or masters degree in early childhood, and the rest had a Child Development Associate (CDA) credential.
- Staff turnover, another indicator of quality (Phillips, 1987), was much lower than the national average, with teachers reporting a median of seven years in the 21C preschool program.

Training for Implementation Makes a Difference

The high quality in 21C schools is due in part to the availability of training and guidance during the planning and implementation stages. The 21C national office, which is part of the Zigler Center in Child Development and Social Policy at Yale University, provides participating schools with assistance during start-up as well as with maintaining quality once programs are underway.

Technical Assistance and Training

To facilitate our support of individual school districts, the national office developed a training protocol and provides on-site and off-site technical assistance and training on program implementation. Members of the technical assistance staff, referred to as implementation associates, are based at Yale and have a designated number of schools in their region. They work with the leadership in each school intensely for about two years. As the schools become more proficient and implementation is underway, the associates assume an advisory role and consult less frequently.

Peer Training

The implementation staff is assisted by superintendents, principals, program coordinators, and others who have successfully established a School of the 21st Century and are willing to serve as peer trainers. We found that pairing these trainers with their counterparts in schools that are beginning implementation is an effective and efficient training approach. It not only enables educators to learn from one another but also provides an informal support system that can be an invaluable resource during the initial phases of getting the program up and running. This peer training approach is especially effective when we pair educators from similar districts (e.g., those in rural communities) who are likely to experience similar problems.

Training Events

Peer training opportunities also exist at the 21C National Academy, which is a national orientation and training conference held every summer, as well as at smaller training events held in several of the regions. The regional meetings focus on the specific needs of 21C schools in that area. They enable 21C educators to coalesce, network, and share lessons learned with others in their part of the country.

Although 21C does not include local training events, the national scope of a universal preschool policy may include them so classroom teachers can participate. In 21C, training for early childhood teachers occurs on an individual school basis. Workshops are given in the school, and child care providers and other early educators in the community are invited. In addition, some school districts have established partnerships with community colleges and other higher education institutions to provide teachers with access to in-service learning opportunities. Given the increased need for teachers that a universal preschool policy would bring about, linkages with higher education would be essential not only to address in-service needs but also to address existing shortages in professional preparation for early childhood careers (Bowman, 1997; Maxwell & Clifford, Chapter 9).

National Network

Our work also includes efforts to facilitate widespread implementation of the program. Toward this end we have created a School of the 21st Century National Network. Although informal relationships among 21C educators exist, the network enables us to formalize these as well as to keep up with growing numbers of 21C schools to ensure that services at the local level maintain a high level of quality and that we have the capacity to address the training needs of educators in mature 21C sites.

Within the 21C National Network, we are developing standardized professional materials and services and codifying procedures for working with schools that have varying levels of training needs and/or that are experiencing changes (e.g., an increase in the number of immigrant children). We have also implemented a tiered, fee-based network membership structure. This allows schools that have successfully completed implementation to continue to be affiliated formally with the program by becoming members. Various training opportunities on such topics as literacy and youth development are available to affiliated schools.

The National Network also offers a quality ladder, so schools can continually refine their efforts, eventually attaining status as demonstration sites and, later on, as schools of excellence. The demonstration site status is renewable every two years and entails an application process and review of the school to determine eligibility. Schools of excellence denote a school district's efforts to take 21C to higher service levels and extend their reach in the community. Both demonstration sites and schools of excellence serve as places to showcase effective 21C practices and the potential of the program.

Implications for Universal Preschool

The quality ladder serves two important functions. Obviously, it delineates goals of increasingly higher levels of quality so enthusiasm is maintained and local efforts do not become stagnant. Second, it allows us to maintain contact with the schools and share advances in the field as they develop. This and other efforts to support widespread implementation have enabled us to respond to the interest new schools have in starting the program as well as to keep up their interest once their program is operational. This national base is an essential ingredient of scale-up efforts and has been adopted by other successful initiatives, such as the reading program Success for All (Slavin, Dolan, & Madden, 1994). Mintrom (2001) also notes the importance of networking and sharing information, explaining that recognition of local achievements can be an important morale booster and can serve to accelerate program growth: "Advocates seeking to attain early childhood education for all in the United States could further their cause by consciously working to develop strong, informal ... networks ... that can provide rich opportunities for people from a variety of backgrounds and experiences to tap into each other's knowledge and know-how with the purposes of improving ... practice" (pp. 22, 23). Mintrom further notes that the time taken to develop such networks should be viewed as an investment that will "eventually speed the diffusion of desired policy" (p. 23).

Knowledge of Factors That Influence Implementation Is Important

Although regional and national networks are essential, they are not sufficient. Also important is an understanding of the local context and the practical information – what difficulties to expect, how to overcome these, and what specific steps to take – needed in the planning process (Fullan, 1992). This type of information can only be collected when program developers "immerse themselves into the local settings and contexts... and extend their ranks through participation... in implementation" (Elias, 1997, p. 261).

We have found in the course of working on 21C that effective implementation at the local level calls for more than simply hiring staff and finding space in the school building. The program has to become an integral part of the school (see Appendix A). To this end, a 21C coordinator is appointed. While early childhood teachers and other staff operate the programs, there are collaborations among the academic faculty and 21C staff as well as joint staff meetings.

Many changes take place once 21C is implemented. Younger children are in the building, the doors are open from as early as six in the morning until evening, and a year-round calendar and new transportation schedules are in effect. Beyond these observable changes, a transformation in philosophy occurs when schools take responsibility for addressing various nonacademic needs children and families may have.

These changes, and the comprehensive nature of 21C services, present challenges. Even less ambitious programs are not easy to integrate smoothly into established school routines (Fullan, 1992). Here we discuss some common factors that facilitate effective implementation (Kirby, Berends, & Naftel, 2001).

Commitment

Change is part of the definition of and, indeed, the goal of any school reform effort. In the School of the 21st Century and other programs (see, e.g., Education Commission of the States, 1999; Elmore, 2000), change is unlikely to occur unless there is commitment to the effort at all levels. One level of commitment is at the district level (Fullan, 2001; Slavin, 2003). The implementation of 21C occurs on a school-by-school basis, but the expectation is that all schools in the district will eventually adopt the program. The school district, headed by the school board and superintendent, is the primary organizational structure of the public school system and therefore involved in any reorganization that occurs when a new program is added. The support of district personnel is thus essential if reforms are to be implemented effectively, withstand leadership changes (which are bound to happen over time), and continue to be refined (Ucelli, 2001).

Equally important is commitment to the program at the building level. As the building administrators, principals provide essential leadership and must become actively involved in and facilitate the implementation process (Berends, Kirby, Naftel, & McKelvey, 2001; Fullan,

2001). Our studies have shown that 21C schools where principals report spending 10–20 percent of their time during the first year on the program are more successful in implementation and sustainability than schools where principals report spending 5 percent or less of their time (Finn-Stevenson, Linkins, & Beacom, 1992). A point person assumes daily coordination of 21C, but the principal sets the tone for the reform, encourages change, and initiates and maintains enthusiasm and high levels of effort.

Locally Driven Approach to Implementation

Meaningful change is most likely to occur if it is not imposed upon a school but is initiated from within. A locally driven approach to implementation is embedded in the design of 21C. The model does not mandate all the service components that make up the program or a uniform method for implementation. Rather, it provides a blueprint for action so schools can develop services on the basis of the needs and resources of the community. The result is considerable variation among 21C schools around the country. However, all 21C schools share a common goal – to promote children's optimal development by providing preschool, child care, and support services – and they adhere to the guiding principles described earlier. Although variations in scope of effort are noted, the majority of the schools grow to provide all of the program's core elements as well as additional services in response to community need and requests by parents.

Phase-in Approach

Implementation is phased in over a three- to five-year period, which we have found to be more manageable than attempting to begin all services at once. This "one step at a time" approach is essential given the numerous services that make up the initiative. It is also important for other school-based reform efforts because it allows a strong foundation to be built that can support future growth (Fullan, 2001). In 21C the decision about which services to begin with, and whether or when to add additional services, is made on the basis of a plan of action. The plan is developed during the initial planning process, which begins with: (1) an assessment of the needs of area families and an inventory of services available in the community; and (2) an organizational audit to determine what strengths and voids exist, and what financial and other resources and capabilities the school district and individual schools have.

This approach provides an individualized plan for the implementation of the program. It draws on the experiences of other 21C schools, so educators can learn how others have solved common problems such as lack of space (see Appendix B). The plan of action is periodically updated as various phases of the program become operational and the needs of the community change.

CONCLUSION

The current interest in universal preschool provides an opportunity to address the need for a national system for early care and education. The School of the 21st Century is a model of an efficient and effective system based in public schools. Although the role of schools in universal prekindergarten remains to be decided, there is no doubt that schools will be part of the picture. Many of the states and localities that have already implemented universal systems utilize public schools to some extent, which is why we believe their involvement is inevitable. While many of the state initiatives are relatively recent, longer experience with the School of the 21st Century proves that it is feasible for schools to provide preschool education. The model also shows that by using parent fees, schools can provide high-quality child care as well. The benefits to the school are considerable. Both preschool and child care experiences influence school readiness, so more children will enter kindergarten with the cognitive and social skills they need to succeed. Dovetailed child care services will help older students maintain developmental progress and do better in the classroom. Another significant benefit for a universal preschool policy that includes all-day, year-round child care is its appeal to working parents, who are likely the majority of the school's constituents. The 21C program provides a framework for a strong partnership among educators, child care providers, and parents to work together in the best interest of children. This partnership will influence if not determine the effectiveness of a universal preschool policy.

APPENDIX A: PRESCHOOL CAN BECOME AN INTEGRAL PART OF THE SCHOOL

When schools provide services such as child care, they must hire additional staff. Policy decisions must be made regarding staff qualifications, training, and pay. It is important that the child care staff be treated as part of the academic faculty. If they are considered a separate unit, the various child and family support services they provide can easily be viewed as add-ons rather than as essential to the school mission. This could result in a failure to realize the full potential of the program and its impact (Jehl & Kirst, 1992).

To facilitate integration, the entire staff should be involved early in the planning process. Regular whole-staff meetings can promote interactions among teaching and child care personnel and foster a shared vision that academic as well as the nonacademic support services are important functions of the school as a whole. Without this teamwork approach, there is the risk of resentments and infighting over space and materials (Fullan, 2001; Huberman, 1992).

We have learned in the course of implementing 21C that the support of classroom teachers is vital to the success of the initiative:

Teachers have a critical role in any school change initiative. By understanding the philosophy behind the School of the 21st Century, and working with full knowledge of the scope of its programs and services, teachers can help each student and each family to make the most out of the available services and programs. Teachers provide the machinery to make school reform a reality. No meaningful efforts to make schools better can succeed when imposed from the outside. It is only with the enthusiasm and involvement of teachers in each classroom that schools can be . . . made better. (Bush Center in Child Development and Social Policy, 1995, p. 11)

APPENDIX B: THE SPACE ISSUE

The addition of preschool classes in the school brings about many changes and adjustments, which can be a source of confusion, disruption, and negativity. Revisions in the school calendar, for example, necessitate maintenance and transportation changes as well as additional staff and costs. In our experience, the most disruptive change is the use of space. Lack of dedicated space for 21C services often means sharing classrooms, which can be a point of contention or an opportunity for collaboration, depending on how it is addressed.

The space issue often arises in arguments about whether it is feasible to provide support services in the school. Yet space availability is cyclical in nature and comes up whether or not support services are offered (Levine, 1978). Enrollments rise and fall depending on changes in birthrates and other factors (for example, housing changes in the community). At times these make some school buildings superfluous;

at other times they mean building new structures. The existence of so many 21C schools is testimony to the fact that the space issue can be overcome.

Dryfoos (1994) points out that how the space issue is addressed is often a reflection of the school's, district's, and community's commitment to the program. This has been our experience, reflected in three (of many) examples. Fifth-grade teachers in one school decided to move to a modular unit so the early childhood unit would feel welcome and part of the school. Several districts allocated funds for the purchase of modular units. One community supported a bond issue for new early childhood buildings to be built on the grounds of each of the district's 13 elementary schools. In a similar move, legislation passed in Ontario, Canada, requires all new school buildings to contain classrooms for before- and after-school child care.

Taking the long-term view, we believe that once universal preschool becomes more integral to the accepted goals of education, school buildings will be built with space for early childhood services. The same adjustment was made several decades ago to accommodate kindergartens, which are now part of nearly all school systems.

References

Bailey, D. (2002). *What can universal prekindergarten learn from special education?* New York: Foundation for Child Development.

Barnett, W. S., Finn-Stevenson, M., & Henrich, C. (2003, March). *From visions to systems of universal preschool.* Paper presented at the conference on child development and social policy: Knowledge to action festschrift in honor of Edward Zigler, Washington, DC.

Berends, M., Kirby, S., Naftel, S., & McKelvey, C. (2001). *Implementation and performance in new American schools: Three years into scale up.* Santa Monica, CA: Rand.

Bowman, B. (1997). New directions in higher education. In B. Bowman (Ed.), *Leadership in early care and education* (pp. 107–114). Washington, DC: National Association for the Education of Young Children.

Brauner, J., Gordic, B., & Zigler, E. (2004). Putting the child back into child care. *Social Policy Report, 18*(3).

Bush Center in Child Development and Social Policy. (1995). *The role of the teacher in the School of the 21st Century.* New Haven, CT: Author.

Cost, Quality and Child Outcomes Study Team. (1999). *The children of the cost, quality and outcomes study go to school.* Chapel Hill, NC: University of North Carolina, Frank Porter Graham Child Development Center.

Dryfoos, J. (1994). *Full service schools.* San Francisco: Jossey-Bass.

Duncan, G., & Brooks-Gunn, J. (1997). *Consequences of growing up poor.* New York: Russell Sage.

Dwyer, C. M., Chait, R., & McKee, P. (2000). *Building strong foundations for early learning: The U.S. Department of Education's guide to high quality early childhood programs*. Washington, DC: Education Publications Center.

Education Commission of the States. (1999). A promising approach for today's schools. *Comprehensive School Reform, 1*(3), 1–7.

Elias, M. (1997). Reinterpreting dissemination of prevention programs as widespread implementation with effectiveness and fidelity. In R. Weissberg, T. Gullotta, R. Hampton, B. Ryan, & G. Adams (Eds.), *Establishing preventive services* (pp. 283–289). Thousand Oaks, CA: Sage.

Elmore, R. (2000). *Building new structures for school leadership*. Washington, DC: Albert Shanker Institute.

Finn-Stevenson, M., Linkins, K., & Beacom, E. (1992). The School of the 21st Century: Creating opportunities for school-based child care. *Child and Youth Care Forum, 21*(5), 335–345.

Finn-Stevenson, M., & Zigler, E. F. (1999). *Schools of the 21st Century: Linking child care and education*. Boulder, CO: Westview Press.

Fix, M., & Passel. J. (2003, January 28–29). *U.S. immigration – trends and implications for schools*. Paper presented at the National Association for Bilingual Education NCLB Implementation Institute, New Orleans.

Fullan, M. G. (1992). *Successful school improvement. The implementation perspective and beyond*. Philadelphia: Open University Press.

Fullan, M. G. (2001). *The new meaning of educational change*. New York: Teachers College Press.

Galinsky, E., Howes, C., Kontos, S., & Shinn, M. B. (1994). *The study of children in family child care and relative care*. New York: Families and Work Institute.

Gallagher, J., Rooney, R., & Campbell, S. (1999). Child care licensing and regulations and child care quality in four states. *Early Childhood Research Quarterly, 14*, 313–333.

Greenberg, M., & Schumacher, R. (2003). *Financing universal pre-kindergarten: Possibilities and technical issues for states in using funds under the Child Care and Development Block Grant and Temporary Assistance for Needy Families Block Grant*. Paper commissioned by The Pew Charitable Trusts. Washington, DC: Center for Law and Policy.

Helburn, S. (Ed.). (1995). *Cost quality and child outcomes in child care centers: Technical report*. Denver, CO: Center for Research in Economic and Social Policy, University of Colorado.

Helburn, S., & Bergmann, B. (2002). *America's child care problems: The way out*. New York: Pelgrade.

Henrich, C., Finn-Stevenson, M., & Zigler, E. (in progress). *Quality in 21C schools*.

Hinkle, D. (2000). *Schools' involvement in early childhood*. Washington, DC: U.S. Department of Education.

Huberman, M. (1992). Critical introduction. In M. Fullan (Ed.), *Successful school improvement* (pp. 1–20). Philadelphia: Open University Press.

Jehl, J., & Kirst, M. (1992). Getting ready to provide school-liked services: What schools must do. *The Future of Children, 2*(1), 95–106.

Kirby, S., Berends, M., & Naftel, S. (2001). *Implementation in a longitudinal sample of new American schools*. Santa Monica, CA: Rand.

LeMoines, S., Morgan, G., & Azer, S. (2003). A snapshot of trends in child care licensing regulations. *Child Care Bulletin, 28,* 1–5.

Levine, J. (1978). *Day care and the public schools: Profiles of five communities.* Newton, MA: Education Development Center.

Marsland, K., Zigler, E., & Martinez, A. (2004). *Regulation of infant and toddler child care: Are state requirements for centers adequate?* Yale University, New Haven, CT. Unpublished manuscript.

Martin, M. (2003). *Making the difference: Research and practice in community schools.* Washington, DC: National Coalition of Community Schools.

Mintrom, M. (2001). *Achieving quality in early childhood education for all: Insights from the policy innovation diffusion research.* New York: Foundation for Child Development.

Mitchell, A. (1988). *The public schools early childhood studies: The district survey.* New York: Bank Street College of Education.

National Center for Children in Poverty. (2003). *Low income children in the United States.* New York: Author.

National Center for Education Statistics. (2003). *Pre-kindergarten in U.S. public schools, 2000–2001.* Washington, DC: Author.

National Research Council. (2002). *Community programs to promote youth development.* Washington, DC: Author.

Pfannenstiel, J., Lambson, T., & Yarnell, V. (1996). *The Parents as Teachers Program: Longitudinal follow-up to the second wave study.* Overland Park, KS: Research & Training Associates.

Phillips, D. (1987). *Predictors of quality in child care.* Written testimony, Committee on Education. Washington, DC: National Association for the Education of Young Children.

Porch, S. (2002, Spring). Early childhood education issues. *Educational Research Service Spectrum, 20,* 2, 4–11.

Putnam, R. D. (1995). Bowling alone: America's defining social capital. *Journal of Democracy, 6,* 65–78.

Queralt, M., & Witte, A. (1998). Influences on neighborhood supply of child care. *Social Service Review, 72*(1), 17–47.

Raden, A. (1999). *Universal pre-kindergarten in Georgia: A case study of Georgia's lottery-funded pre-K programs.* New York: Foundation for Child Development.

Reynolds, A. J. (2000). The added value of continuing early intervention into the primary grades. *CEIC Review, 9*(3), 16–18.

Schilder, D., Kiron, E., & Elliott, K. (2003). *Early care and education partnerships: State actions and local lessons.* Cambridge, MA: EDC.

Shonkoff, J., & Phillips, D. (2000). *From neurons to neighborhoods.* Washington, DC: National Academy Press.

Slavin, R. (2003, March 5). Converging reforms. Changing schools? Changing districts? How the two approaches can work together. *Education Week,* p. 64.

Slavin, R., Dolan, L., & Madden, N. (1994). *Scaling-up: Lessons learned in the dissemination of Success for All.* Baltimore: Johns Hopkins University, Center for Research on the Education of Students Placed at Risk.

Ucelli, M. (2001). *From school improvement to systems reforms*. New York: Rockefeller Foundation.

U.S. Census Bureau. (1997). *Who is minding preschoolers?* Washington, DC: U.S. Department of Commerce.

U.S. Census Bureau. (2000). *Families and living arrangements*. Washington, DC: U.S. Labor Department, Census Bureau.

U.S. Consumer Product Safety Commission. (1999). *Safety hazards in child care settings*. Washington, DC: Author.

Vinson, T., Baldry, E., & Hargreaves, J. (1996). Neighborhoods, networks and child abuse. *British Journal of Social Work, 26*, 523–543.

Young, K. T., Marsland, K. W., & Zigler, E. (1997). Regulatory status of center-based infant and toddler child care. *American Journal of Orthopsychiatry, 67*, 535–544.

Zigler, E. (1987, October). A solution to the nation's child care crisis: The School of the Twenty-first Century. In *Investing in the beginning* (pp. 27–33). Conference report. St. Louis: Parents as Teachers National Center.

Zigler, E., & Finn-Stevenson, M. (1996). Funding child care and public education. *The Future of Children, 6*(2), 104–121.

Zigler, E., Finn-Stevenson, M., & Hall, N. (2002). *The first three years and beyond: Brain development and social policy*. New Haven, CT: Yale University Press.

Zigler, E., Singer, D. G., & Bishop-Josef, S. (Eds.). (2004). *Children's play: The roots of reading*. Washington, DC: Zero to Three Press.

11

A Place for Head Start in a World of Universal Preschool

With Sally J. Styfco

When the idea for Head Start was developed in the mid-1960s, organized schooling for young children was uncommon. Some children from upper- and middle-income families attended "nursery school," as preschool was called, but the majority stayed home until they were old enough to begin elementary school. At the time, fewer than half the states offered kindergarten, although generally not in all districts nor was it compulsory. For many children formal education therefore began with first grade when they were six or seven years old. Head Start was thus a great national experiment to enroll children from poor families before they reached school age.

Forty years later, it is safe to say the experiment was successful. The Head Start model has been proved effective and has become the standard for comprehensive intervention services for at-risk children. Early childhood has become an active field of research, with voluminous results showing that quality preschool programs enhance school readiness and later academic performance and adjustment among children raised in poverty. Head Start's major contributions to this knowledge base established the program's worth and justified its expansion.

Serious expansion began in the late 1980s, when early education was rediscovered as the foundation for successful schooling. In what quickly became a "Head Start lovefest" (Chafel, 1992, p. 9), policy makers and office seekers of every political persuasion vowed to give the program "full funding." At the time, Head Start was serving less than 30 percent of eligible children (National Head Start Association, 1991). Although enrollment more than doubled between 1989 and 2003 (Administration on Children, Youth and Families, 2005), the program still serves only

50–60 percent of the target population. (Figures vary depending on the age range employed.) These numbers led John Merrow (2002) to write an article with the alarming title, "The Failure of Head Start." He did not mean the program was doing a poor job of preparing children for school. His thesis was that Head Start has failed to reach its potential because of limited access. After 40 years of operation, we believe it is reasonable to forecast that Head Start will never grow to sufficient size to seat all children who live below the poverty line.

The reasons go beyond the practical issues of resources and funding. For one, Head Start has always been politically vulnerable. Although it enjoys strong grass-roots support, over time policy makers have displayed the gamut of enthusiasm, indifference, and hostility toward the program's continued existence. Head Start historians are not surprised that the "full funding" rallying call heard as recently as President George H. Bush's campaign in the late 1980s became a call to disassemble Head Start's components and let the states try their hand at administering it during the early 2000s administration of President George W. Bush. Clearly, the debates between liberals and conservatives, advocates of big versus smaller government, and promoters of federal versus state powers will continue, and Head Start will always be caught in the middle. Its existence will always be perilous, and there is no guarantee it will survive the next threat, or the one after that.

Another damper prohibiting full expansion is that Head Start is not a perfect program. It was designed with structural flaws that are serious enough to trouble even its most ardent supporters. One is the limiting eligibility criteria. Children and families who are below the federal poverty line can attend. Those who make a little more, even a few dollars more, cannot. Yet not all children who live in poverty need the scope of services provided by Head Start, and certainly many from near-poor families would benefit greatly by attendance.

Beyond the arbitrariness of the income cutoff, the eligibility rules define Head Start as a segregated program. Poor children go to Head Start, while those from families with greater means go to other preschools. This practice bares Head Start to criticisms on moral, child development, and democratic grounds. Morally, it is just as wrong to segregate children by socioeconomic status as it is to segregate them by race. On the second point, developmentalists theorize that all children gain more academically and socially when they are in heterogeneous classrooms than when they are surrounded only by those with similar backgrounds (see Chapter 5). Finally, John Dewey taught that the ultimate goal of formal education is to prepare students to participate in democracy. American society is diverse, so government-forced segregation of preschool students seems a counterproductive way to begin the preparation process.

Head Start's early administrators were aware of the weaknesses posed by lack of socioeconomic integration. Early in Head Start's history, operating guidelines contained the provision that 90 percent of enrollment be reserved for families below the poverty line, thus permitting overincome children to occupy 10 percent of seats. When Edward Zigler served as the federal official responsible for Head Start, he attempted to integrate the program fully across economic groups by proposing a fee calibrated to family income for those above the poverty line who wanted to enroll their children. His effort was rebuked by Head Start's own constituents, who believed that their power would be usurped by socially and politically stronger middle-class parents. Even the 10 percent figure has proved elusive. Because Head Start has never been funded to serve all of its target population, there is rarely room for children from overincome families. And, judging from its political history, there never will be full funding to serve all children who live in poverty. Middle-class populations will continue to be excluded, and with them the hope for socioeconomic integration.

The solution to this problem is being crafted in the states. As we have been reading throughout this book, the majority of states are beginning to offer prekindergarten to at least some groups of children as part of their primary education systems. In the not-too-distant future, it is likely that all children in the nation will have access to public preschool. Head Start inspired and validated this movement and will remain a key player until that future arrives. But even as the program continues to provide and improve preschool services, there should be planning for eventual succession and for refocusing Head Start's mission on other unmet needs of young children.

In this chapter, we present three possible roles for Head Start in a world of universal prekindergarten. The first involves services for families and children before the age of three to prevent the accumulation of developmental risks. Another direction is to expand Head Start's child and family services. Public schools will provide preschool education to all children, while Head Start will provide the health and social support services that improve the chances that children who live in poverty will reach their academic potential. Finally, Head Start might focus on the growing number of preschoolers with special educational needs, evolving into a therapeutic preschool milieu. Each of these roles fills a vacancy in the early care and education landscape, and each builds on strengths and practical experience Head Start has developed over time.

HEAD START'S PAST AND PRESENT

Schooling for young children was not initially part of the plans for the War on Poverty when it was declared in 1964. The purpose of this massive national movement was to enable poor adults to achieve economic and political parity. Head Start became one of the programs of the war by happenstance, the brainchild of Sargent Shriver. As President Lyndon Johnson's chief strategist in the antipoverty effort, Shriver saw the lopsidedness in targeting programs to poor adults when nearly half of those living in poverty were children (Zigler & Valentine, 1997). He thought that the cycle of poverty could be broken by helping the children of the poor get better prepared for school so they would not start out already behind their more advantaged peers.

The idea of launching a nationwide preschool was unprecedented. In addition, the needs of young children who live in poverty and how best to meet them were not thoroughly understood at the time. Shriver sought to overcome these barriers by convening a group of experts to shape his idea into a deliverable program. The planning committee was chaired by the renowned pediatrician, Dr. Robert Cooke. The 13 members were professionals in the fields of public health, mental health, education, social work, and developmental psychology. (Edward Zigler was one of the three child psychologists in the group.) The members thus brought different perspectives to the problems that hamper poor children's readiness for school. Their unique viewpoints came together in a "whole child" approach to school readiness. They agreed that children need good physical and mental health, adequate nutrition, appropriate social and emotional skills, and good preacademic training when they begin school. They also need encouragement and support from home and their communities. From this consensus, the planners designed Head Start as a comprehensive services, two-generation intervention.

The parent involvement component was so novel to the education establishment at the time that it warrants further explanation. Head Start was originally meant to be a summer program, offered for a few weeks before children entered elementary school. The planners knew that in such a short time, no program could alleviate the ill effects of being reared in poverty. They hoped to enlist parents in the program so they could learn its educational goals and carry them on throughout their child's schooling. To ensure ownership of the mission, parents were invited to help plan and run their local centers. On another level, as part of the War on Poverty Head Start was based in the Community Action Program. The CAP was mandated to enable "maximum feasible participation" of low-income citizens in the war's antipoverty efforts. Involving parents at the level of governance thus was compatible with Head Start's goal to promote school readiness and the CAP's mandate to give power over programs created to serve disadvantaged groups to group members themselves. The compatibility soon weakened, however, when tensions developed between those who considered Head Start a child development program and the "poverty warriors" who saw it as a vehicle for community activism (cf. Greenberg, 2004; Harmon, 2004).

The doors to Head Start opened in the summer of 1965, soon after the planners completed their recommendations. Although many of the committee members would have preferred to start with a small pilot project, government officials were waging a war and wanted nothing less than a major offensive against poverty. A bulging war chest made it possible for Head Start to serve more than one-half million children in that first summer. Grants were written, reviewed, and funded at breakneck speed, leaving a bevy of program details unresolved. Some were eventually addressed, but some were not and haunt Head Start to this day. As we will explain, these shortcomings can finally be corrected when Head Start's service model is reconfigured as universal preschool becomes reality.

Current Structure

Head Start's basic features have remained close to the original design over the years. The main differences are that it is now generally an academic-year program, some services and operating protocols have been added, and enrollment and local presence have expanded. In Fiscal Year (FY) 2004, the program served almost 906,000 children and their families. (Statistics in this section are from the Administration on Children, Youth and Families, 2005.) Most are four years old, but three-year-olds constitute a significant minority (34 percent). Early in its history, Head Start was mandated to reserve at least 10 percent of seats for children with disabilities. In recent years, they have represented about

13 percent. Where there are waiting lists, Head Start staff are directed to give preference to children and families most in need of services. Thus, Head Start generally enrolls children who have the highest risks and may already be behind in developmental tasks.

FY2005 appropriations for Head Start were $6.8 billion, and the average cost per child was just over $7,200. The money flows from the U.S. Department of Health and Human Services directly to the community groups that run the local centers. These include public school systems, public agencies (including CAPs), nonprofit and (recently allowed) for-profit organizations, and groups serving migrant workers and Native American tribes. Each grantee is responsible for raising 20 percent of its budget locally, which may include the value of donated work and materials. Head Start is the payer of last resort for medical and some family support services. That is, staff attempts to link families to resources available in the community, but when families are not eligible or the services not accessible, costs are covered by the program.

The Program Performance Standards govern the services each Head Start center must provide. Communities may adapt the content to local needs, desires, and resources. Variation is assured because the policies and administration of each grantee and its delegate agencies are governed by a policy council and policy committee, respectively, as well as a parent committee. More than half the members of the policy groups must be parents, with the remainder drawn from the community. This built-in local governance underscores that within the parameters of the Performance Standards, Head Start is highly flexible and not a standardized program delivered uniformly across the nation.

Diversity in programming is further assured by Head Start's role as a national laboratory for the development of more effective services and delivery mechanisms. Notable experiments include home-based services, which are now an option for all grantees but are used most frequently in rural areas. Various means of providing all-day, full-year programs for children whose parents work have been launched, such as wraparound services and the Head Start–Child Care Partnerships. The national family support movement was given credibility by successful models developed in Head Start like the Child and Family Resource Program, to name just one. The search for ways to serve both older and younger children began early in Head Start's history. Experience with models to continue services into the early grades of elementary school (e.g., Project Follow Through, the Head Start/Elementary School Transition Project) has led to the incorporation of transition activities into the Performance Standards. As a final illustration, numerous trials over the years to reach children before the age of preschool have culminated in Early Head Start, which provides child development and support services to pregnant women and to families and children ages zero to three.

The experimental nature of Head Start, both in its origins and subsequent model development, dictated the need for research and assessment. Today, voluminous research has been conducted on the program and countless other early childhood interventions. The majority of this work has focused on results in the domain of cognitive development. The findings generally indicate immediate gains in IQ test scores that appear to dissipate within a few years. Such gains have been linked to better motivation, self-confidence, and more familiarity with the test content and testing situation (Zigler, Abelson, & Seitz, 1973; Zigler & Butterfield, 1968). Longer-term benefits have been found for academic achievement and adjustment, noticeably in reduced need for special education and less grade retention (Barnett, 2004). Longitudinal studies of a few programs have uncovered effects lasting into adulthood and beyond, including higher educational attainment, reduced delinquency and crime, and less welfare dependence (e.g., Campbell, Ramey, Pungello, Sparling, & Miller-Johnson, 2002; Reynolds & Temple, Chapter 3; Reynolds, Temple, Robertson, & Mann, 2001; Schweinhart, Barnes, & Weikart, 1993).

Note that not all of this research is specific to Head Start. Although the program and its participants have been featured in hundreds if not thousands of studies, the research has not resulted in a very organized knowledge base. This explains why reviews of the literature present the gamut of conclusions about Head Start's effects. For example, Barnett (1995, 2004) finds short- and likely long-term impacts, while the U.S. Department of Health and Human Services (2003) sees none. The Administration for Children and Families (2003b) reports positive effects lasting into grade school, while the same data set leads Whitehurst and Massetti (2004) to conclude there are no meaningful benefits. The General Accounting Office (1997) determined that there are not enough sound studies of recent vintage to conclude that Head Start has or does not have lasting benefits. As mentioned, most of the research has been limited to cognitive development, so Head Start's impact on other domains relevant to school readiness is even less clear. The scant evidence does suggest benefits to health, family well-being, socioemotional skills, and community development.

A comprehensive, methodologically rigorous evaluation is currently underway. The Head Start Impact Study employs a random assignment design to assess a range of potential effects of Head Start through first grade (Administration for Children and Families, 2003a). While the results are not yet compiled, we believe existing evidence is convincing that high-quality Head Start experiences do bolster school readiness and most likely later school adjustment. More tentatively, broader and longer-term results appear to be positive.

Changing Trends

Over time, social as well as political forces have prompted changes to Head Start's service model and course of direction. Social change is apparent in the demographics of the families and children who attend. The percentage from female-headed households has soared, as has the number who are homeless or in foster care. Cultural and ethnic diversity have expanded, with corresponding increases in the number of participants who speak languages other than English. A major shift from Head Start's early years is that the majority of parents are now in the work force or job training, a change dictated by single parenthood and overhauls to the welfare system. Poverty itself has become a more debilitating experience. Violence, gangs, firearms, AIDS, and drugs now affect daily life in too many poor neighborhoods. As one consequence, poor families today move more frequently, disconnecting them from social supports. All of these events have increased the level of stress among poor adults and children. As a result, behavioral and mental health problems have become more common in Head Start classrooms, and the program's family support services have been strained by the volume of parents with multiple problems and risk factors.

Head Start has responded to these new demographics by adjusting local programming. For example, to meet the needs of working parents, many centers are offering extended hours or partnering with neighborhood child care providers. Training and Technical Assistance and published guidance from the Head Start Bureau have focused on growing issues such as cultural sensitivity, English as a second language, enabling employed parents to remain involved in the program, and meeting the needs of children with disabilities or behavioral problems. Political changes over the years have both helped and hampered Head Start's efforts to achieve its mission in the face of new social realities.

It is certainly true that Head Start has received bipartisan support from generations of policy makers in Congress and the White House. There are some notable exceptions, including plans to phase out the program during the Nixon administration; President Carter's proposal to move it to the Education Department, where it undoubtedly would have been redefined solely as an academic program and block-granted to the states; and George W. Bush's desire to turn Head Start into a reading program and experiment with devolving it to the states. Yet, in general, lawmakers have progressively worked to strengthen and expand the program. Legislation to improve quality has had particularly beneficial effects.

Throughout the 1980s, not enough money and attention were devoted to the quality of services Head Start participants received. Not enough staff was available to monitor programs adequately, and Training and Technical Assistance was too underfunded to be of much help. Social service caseloads soared, poor pay and benefits made it difficult to attract qualified teachers, and facilities deteriorated (Chafel, 1992; Lombardi & Cubbage, 2004; Silver Ribbon Panel, 1990). Remediation was offered by the Human Services Reauthorization Act of 1990, which targeted funds to be set aside for quality improvements. Half of this money was reserved for improving salaries and benefits, with the rest marked for Training and Technical Assistance, facilities, and transportation. In 1993 President Clinton's Health and Human Services secretary, Donna Shalala, appointed the Advisory Committee on Head Start Quality and Expansion, a bipartisan group of policy makers, professionals, and laypeople. The committee's charge was to recommend ways to improve program quality and to plan expansion in a way that does not interfere with quality improvement efforts. Not since its birth had Head Start been granted such needed attention at this high level of government.

The Advisory Committee's report (1993) initiated a number of long-overdue corrections. For example, poorly performing centers were given special help to overcome deficiencies. Those that could not had their grants terminated and their programs taken over by other agencies. Never before had grantees been "fired." The Program Performance Standards were revised for the first time in more than 20 years to reflect new knowledge and to modernize services. Progress was soon visible in the areas of better salaries and benefits, reduced turnover, lower caseloads, and more training and education; programs also showed significant improvements on the majority of the performance standard indicators despite the fact that reviews became more stringent (Verzaro-O'Brien, Powell, & Sakamoto, 1996).

The quantity of attention and resources devoted to strengthening Head Start in the previous decade attest to the widespread belief in the program as a worthy (if imperfect) effort to improve the life chances of young children living in poverty. The Head Start experiment proved that school readiness is an achievable goal, a goal critical to children's further educational success. For a variety of reasons covered earlier in this book, in recent years Head Start's mission has been embraced by the educational establishment as a prerequisite to raising both academic standards and the likelihood of students meeting them. Yet as schools bring readiness programming into the mainstream, Head Start's mission is only partly accomplished. Universal access to preschool does not guarantee universal school readiness, nor can it alleviate the achievement gap between poor and wealthier children evident *before* entry into preschool. Some children and families face an array of disadvantages that impede preparation for school. Seeds for the interventions these groups may need have already been planted in the Head Start laboratory. They can be cultivated as Head Start's mission shifts from traditional preschool services to new approaches to support school readiness and academic success

AN EARLIER HEAD START

When the idea for Head Start was being developed, schooling for very young children was neither common nor socially accepted. The ideal was that mothers stayed home to care for and teach children until they were ready to leave the nest and begin elementary school. In fact, soon after Head Start began arguments were raised that the program services came too soon to offer academic benefits. Head Start providers, however, were wondering if their efforts were too late. Many of the three-, four-, and five-year-olds enrolled already showed effects of being reared in poverty. They began preschool with untreated health problems, speech and other developmental delays, attachment difficulties, and other issues that could put school readiness out of reach. Just two years after Head Start began, a demonstration program to reach infants, toddlers, and their families was launched. Called the Parent and Child Centers (PCCs), the aim was to provide health and social services; teach child development principles and life skills to parents; offer activities to stimulate children's cognitive, physical, and emotional growth; and to create links to supportive services in the community. The effort was small and received scant evaluation. Yet the concept was apparently compelling enough to persuade lawmakers to continue funding until 1994, when the program was folded into Early Head Start.

As long-lived as the PCCs were, they were not part of the impetus that created Early Head Start. Late in 1992, when William Clinton was preparing to assume the presidency, his transition team asked Edward Zigler and Sally Styfco (1993) to prepare a concept paper on offering Head Start intervention earlier in children's lives. The authors' thesis drew from accumulated knowledge on the importance of the early years to healthy child development and on well-grounded views then being circulated in the field. For example, the Silver Ribbon Panel (1990), a group convened on Head Start's 25th anniversary to study the challenges bearing on Head Start and its participants, recommended expanding the program's capacity to serve infants and toddlers. In 1992 Zero to Three published an authoritative report titled, *Heart Start: The Emotional Foundations of School Readiness*. This prominent group of experts argued that experiences during the earliest years begin the process of building confidence, curiosity, eagerness to learn, respect for limits, self-regulation, and other personality features that enter into successful schooling. The new President Clinton found these arguments convincing, and Congress took up the cause after Senator Edward Kennedy proposed legislation to create a younger version of Head Start.

Early Head Start was initiated in the 1994 reauthorization of the Head Start Act. A planning committee was convened to design the new program (Advisory Committee on Services for Families with Infants and Toddlers, 1994). To their credit, they were diligent about not repeating the mistakes made in the haste to launch the original Head Start program. Early Head Start began with a manageable 68 demonstration sites. Research and evaluation components were built into the program from the beginning. Unlike preschool Head Start that had no official quality standards for its first decade, Early Head Start was designed with attention to quality. The planners recommended ongoing monitoring, training and technical assistance, evaluation, and expansion of the Program Performance Standards to encompass services for infants and toddlers. (The standards were indeed revised and implemented in 1998.)

By FY 2004 there were more than 650 Early Head Start programs serving almost 62,000 families and children ages zero to three. An ongoing random assignment study of a national sample of programs has so far revealed generally positive results. Early Head Start was found to impact cognition, language acquisition, social and emotional development, parenting skills, and family outcomes (Love et al., 2002). The effects ranged in magnitude and were greater for some subgroups than others, but they were quite broad, suggesting "they might be important in the aggregate" (Barnett & Hustedt, 2003). Data continue to be collected and should indicate whether these early benefits translate into improved school readiness.

We must point out that Early Head Start's growth coincided with the renewed interest in early brain development that exploded in the media and halls of Congress. That movement was sparked by a report entitled *Starting Points*, by the Carnegie Task Force on Meeting the Needs of Young Children (1994). The group's purpose was to "provide a framework of scientific knowledge and offer an action agenda to ensure the healthy development of children from before birth to age three" (p. viii). Among the scientific works the task force chose to highlight were studies on the developing brain. They concluded that brain development in the first year of life is "more rapid and extensive than we previously realized" and also much more vulnerable to environmental influence (p. 7). This interpretation of a highly technical body of research gained immediate attention after the report's release. True to American entrepreneurial spirit, books, programs, and CDs appeared offering new parents ways to maximize cognitive stimulation to better "wire" their babies' brains, presumably creating permanent increases in intellectual capacity. Capitalizing on the renewed attention to cognition, many Head Start supporters embraced the early brain development studies as scientific justification for enlarging Early Head Start.

History should have guided them away from selling the new program with promises of intellectual gains. In the 1960s when Head Start was created, American psychologists were beginning to emphasize the force of the environment to impact intelligence and thus the value of early interventions to boost cognitive development. This "environmental mystique," as Zigler (1970) called it, created a widespread belief that intelligence was fluid and easily shaped by experience. Head Start rode this bandwagon for a time, with findings of 10-point increases in children's IQs after spending a few weeks in the program. When this advantage was found to be short-lived, the program came close to ending. As the national mood dropped from euphoria to hopelessness about poor children's chances of succeeding in school, Head Start operations languished due to policy makers' neglect and budgetary erosion.

Fortunately, unlike the original program, Early Head Start had clearly written goals showing its mission was not solely to raise intelligence. Rather, it was a multifaceted program designed to promote whole child and family development. Thus the program was not threatened when prominent scholars asserted that the early brain development work was misinterpreted and the conclusions it spawned premature (e.g., Bruer, 1999). Our position is that the early years are indeed critical to the physical maturation of the brain and hence to cognitive development. But the brain also controls the social and emotional traits that shape effort and motivation to learn. It would be ridiculous to try to promote cognitive development without simultaneously attending to physical health, nutrition, and social and emotional needs. They are inextricably related, something parents have known before cognitive science was invented.

Like the preschool version, Early Head Start today is a variable program tailored to the individuals enrolled. Services are delivered in the home, in centers, or both. Some models target parents more than children; others do the opposite. Services include access to prenatal and pediatric care, early diagnostic screening and treatment, teaching parents about child development, promoting family strengths and economic well-being, encouraging community responses to meeting family needs, and staff development. The ongoing evaluation has revealed some common problem areas that will hopefully receive attention at the programmatic level. For example, more must be done to involve fathers in their child's development and to meet parents' mental health needs; in many places staff are discovering that the lack of quality infant care poses threats to children's developmental progress and family efforts to raise their standard of living (Kisker, Paulsell, Love, & Raikes, 2002).

Early Head Start is structured as a preventive rather than remedial intervention. As has proved true for any number of topics, prevention is more effective, and typically more cost-effective, than treatment of problems after they become problems. Efforts to assure healthy child and family development deployed very early in life therefore hold more promise for a child's eventual success in school than do special education classes or court-ordered family services once a child has failed. Initial evaluation of Early Head Start is showing that benefits are indeed accruing to children and families in areas relevant to school readiness (Love et al., 2002). This ongoing research is addressing not only outcomes but implementation issues, so it will be useful in guiding service enhancements that further desired results. The program is growing slowly enough to incorporate indicated changes through updated training.

The need for Early Head Start becomes more critical as universal preschool education becomes a reality. Children from high-risk backgrounds once eligible for Head Start will be enrolling in local school systems. They will bring with them the same challenges to learning and school readiness that they now bring to Head Start. The public schools should be expected to provide high-quality early education, but it is unlikely they will all be designed to offer the comprehensive, two-generation services these children need to prepare for school. And although development from ages zero to three is very important for learning in preschool and beyond (e.g., Zero to Three, 1992; Zigler, Finn-Stevenson, & Hall, 2002), cost, logistics, and public mandate suggest that most schools will never serve children in this age range. (Exceptions include the School of the 21st Century [Finn-Stevenson & Zigler, 1999] and Missouri's Parents as Teachers program that brings home visitors to new parents in every school district.) Early Head Start can serve this population to mitigate risks and build supports within the family so when these children reach preschool age, they will be in a better position to benefit from preacademic training.

HEAD START AS A FAMILY SUPPORT PROGRAM

Head Start's planners and early administrators were aware that a brief summer program, or a year or even two of preschool, would not erase the ill effects of growing up in poverty or inoculate children against future developmental risks. They knew that intervention had to begin earlier and last longer for poor children to have a better chance of school success. In 1973 Head Start launched the Child and Family Resource Program (CFRP), which enrolled children and families from birth through age eight. A variety of services was offered, and parents could choose those they wanted. Caseworkers assessed each participating family's needs and helped create a specific service plan. Examples of benefits were medical and dental screenings, housing assistance, crisis intervention, adult education, child care, Head Start, transition to school programs, and social events. Many of these services were not provided by the CFRP staff but through referrals to community resources. Direct services were offered to fill gaps in what was available.

An evaluation by the Comptroller General (1979) found positive changes in the home environments of families a year after their participation ended. The study concluded that the types of changes produced were very likely to benefit children's school performance. The agency gave specific praise to the CFRP's inclusion of children under the age of four, a group it found to be extremely underserved by typical early childhood offerings. Despite the program's potential, and the high marks it received from the notoriously hardheaded Comptroller General, it was eventually defunded. The model lives on in various forms like community schools, family support service organizations, and a few state initiatives.

The support services offered through the CFRP were similar to those Head Start provides its participants. A key difference is that most families do not enroll in Head Start until their children are three or four years old, and they leave when children enter kindergarten. Once in the public schools, the focus is on the child's education and not on ancillary services the child or family may need. Rare exceptions are adult education such as English as a second language (ESL) and general educational development (GED) classes and, in some places, before- and after-school child care. When preschool becomes universal, the Head Start comprehensive services step will be missing, so children and parents who could benefit from a variety of services may never receive them. This is why we suggest that when Head Start programs phase out their preschool education duties, they could become general family support centers.

Head Start has a long history of helping to meet broad child and family needs. In fact, Head Start's service model initiated the national family support movement. There are now nearly 3,000 family support groups that have networked under the umbrella Family Support America, and surely many times that number exist. Head Start's experience in family support positions it well for operating service centers geared to its target population. It has developed needs assessment instruments and training for caseworkers and home visitors. Personnel are familiar with the service agencies in communities where Head Start operates. They are also versed in the eligibility criteria of various programs and in the referral process. Their role is to identify and link families with services available in the neighborhood, although Head Start is the "payer of last resort" when access cannot otherwise be gained. These procedures are readily transferable from current Head Start centers to new family support centers.

With deep community roots and a long track record of experimenting with service delivery models, Head Start has had some success in enhancing local services. For example, in some areas clinical services have become more available through partnerships with area universities and hospitals. Trial efforts to work with local child care providers have improved the quality of care in centers and family child care homes, improvements that benefit all children in attendance (e.g., Administration for Children and Families, 2003b). In Georgia, collaboration between the state prekindergarten program and Head Start enables some children to receive health and social services from Head Start (Raden, 2003), not unlike what we are suggesting here.

Splitting duties between Head Start family support centers and the public schools has many advantages. It is safe to conclude that public schools, with their experienced and well-paid teaching professionals, will never assume a great deal of responsibility for family needs, even though the home environment has a decisive impact on children's academic performance. It is also a fair assumption that elementary schools will provide better preschool education than Head Start generally offers. Although the education component has improved greatly in recent years, it has never been Head Start's strong point (Omwake, 1997). Salaries have been too low to attract highly qualified teachers, who can often earn twice as much and receive better benefits by working in public schools. Written curricula were not even required until relatively recently, and the language environment has been criticized as poor (e.g., Snow & Páez, 2004). A comparison of quality in state prekindergartens and Head Start confirms that the former generally have higher-quality educational services but are far behind Head Start in comprehensive services and parental involvement (Gilliam & Ripple, 2004).

Another advantage of the family support model over current practice in Head Start is that it does not homogenize low-income families as having the same problems requiring the same solutions. Some Head Start participants enjoy strong social support networks of friends and extended family; others are homeless. Some are college graduates temporarily experiencing a period of reduced income; others are high school dropouts who have never worked. And many families not eligible for Head Start could benefit greatly from some program services. Caseworkers at Head Start family support centers could refer them to local programs, many of which have higher income-eligibility standards than Head Start. Finally, staff will be able to more quickly address new needs and problems they see affecting participants because that will be their only job.

Stronger families are better able to support their children's learning, so family services will ultimately further the mission of the schools.

The public schools and Head Start will thus have complementary roles, one to educate children in a manner that smoothly interfaces with their preschool experience and one to address broader child and family issues so children are better able to learn what is being taught.

A THERAPEUTIC PRESCHOOL

Behavioral and emotional problems have become a serious concern in the public schools and, as more children attend preschool, at earlier levels of schooling as well. In a review of prevalence data, Raver and Knitzer (2002) describe a survey of child care providers that found 32 percent of children had behavioral problems; studies of Head Start participants found that between 5 and 33 percent exhibited problem behavior. The authors also report that 4 to 10 percent of young children have serious emotional disorders (meeting clinically significant criteria). The reporting of more precise rates of behavioral problems is complicated by differing definitions. It is clear, however, that the rates are not trivial and that nearly all classrooms of 16 to 20 students will have at least 1 student, if not several, who present significant behavioral challenges to teachers.

There is some consensus that incremental risk factors raise the likelihood of behavioral and psychological problems, and that such problems lower the likelihood of academic success (Durlak, 1998). Risks include living in a low-income household, being raised by a single parent, child abuse or neglect, exposure to violence, caregiver depression, poor health or nutrition, and numerous other experiences that are not conducive to optimal development. Preventive and early intervention services are undoubtedly most effective if delivered as soon as children start to display problem behaviors or emotional instability. Unfortunately, most children do not receive treatment until they are older and their issues have intensified to the point where they impede learning and become more difficult to alleviate.

Public schools are mandated under the Individuals with Disabilities Education Act (IDEA) to provide education to children as young as three who have disabilities. For children without identified disabilities, however, the provision of educational services is not required until age five to seven, depending on the state. School administrators can therefore legally dismiss children with problem behaviors from preschool. Parents might be told the child isn't mature enough for school yet, and to wait another year before enrolling again. In one study, children in a state prekindergarten system were 34 times more likely to be expelled than students in grades K to 12 combined (Gilliam & Shahar, in press). It is fair to assume that many were dismissed because of behavioral and safety issues. Increasing numbers of these public school rejects are finding their way to Head Start centers.

Head Start has long been required to serve children with disabilities, so personnel have developed expertise in this area. Further, Head Start administrators have also been witnessing increased mental health difficulties among their students and have responded with more staff training. Reflecting the new reality, the revised Performance Standards dictate a stronger emphasis on mental health. Of significant promise is the amount of professional expertise devoted to strengthening Head Start's mental health component (Yoshikawa & Knitzer, 1997), although many of the recommendations have yet to be acted upon. In coming years, Head Start could evolve into a therapeutic preschool treating children of all income levels whose educational or behavioral needs are beyond those addressed or safely contained in the typical prekindergarten classroom.

In addition to experience, other features of Head Start make it a good setting for delivering mental health services. Children with serious problems need, and often command, a great deal of individual attention. Although many states meet the high staff-to-child ratios mandated for Head Start, others do not, and some do not impose ratios at all (Gilliam & Ripple, 2004). (Of course, if Head Start becomes a therapeutic preschool, ratios will have to be raised further.) Another significant feature is parental involvement, which is a key part of Head Start and a critical part of therapeutic treatment. For example, children with behavioral problems can learn more appropriate behaviors through a system of consistent rewards and consequences. The system must be in place throughout the child's total environment, not just for the few hours a day spent in school. Parents must be enlisted to continue the treatment at home and to provide feedback about the child's progress. The amount of effort required is considerable, particularly when a parent's emotional resources are depleted when a child is out of control. Resources at the Head Start center can support them, including partnerships with staff, crisis intervention, respite care, and family support groups where ideas and feelings can be shared.

Of course, a legitimate argument can be made that children who have mental health needs should be served in mainstream settings, where they can learn more appropriate behavior and emotional responses from nonafflicted peers. It is certainly true that some treatments can be delivered in regular classrooms, which have the advantage of presenting more varied environmental stimuli and challenges disturbed children must learn to handle. And obviously not all children displaying behavioral or emotional problems need the intensive level of services suggested here. Activities that teach children to recognize and verbalize emotions or that discourage aggression can benefit everyone in the class. Yet the fact is that children evidencing severe behavioral or emotional difficulties are being turned away from prekindergarten and child care settings. Those with disruptive behaviors can create such turmoil in the classroom that the other students are affected and their learning interrupted. Safety issues, both for the child in crisis and anyone nearby, are paramount. And while children who are extremely withdrawn may not agitate peers, they may not learn much themselves.

It is also true that the interventions children with emotional and behavioral difficulties need cannot always be delivered most effectively in inclusive settings (Kauffman & Hallahan, 1995; Styfco, 2000). The IDEA mandates that children with special needs be served in the "least restrictive environment." A setting that is too restrictive for one child may not be supportive enough for another, so the law dictates that a range of treatment options be available. Head Start can be reserved for children from all income levels who need an intensive treatment regime before they can benefit from more inclusive schooling.

There will be many hurdles to overcome if Head Start is restructured as a therapeutic preschool. Therapy is expensive. Some of the cost might be covered by medical insurance (including Medicaid's Early and Periodic Screening, Diagnosis and Treatment services) and special education funds. Yet not all children referred will have clinically diagnosed disorders that might open up these funding streams. Not only is there a reluctance of mental health professionals to label young children, but it is difficult to match children's expressive symptoms (that change with developmental level) with official special education or psychiatric categories. Head Start's budget can cover some of the funding gap because the program will serve fewer children, albeit with more intensive intervention.

Another hurdle is that there is a nationwide shortage of child psychologists and psychiatrists, and the clinical social work profession has not been attracted to work in Head Start (Frankel, 2004). Yoshikawa and Knitzer (1997) suggest ways to address the staffing shortage, including using and building the ranks of mental health consultants, providing internships for college students whose work is overseen by trained clinicians, and partnering with a variety of community resources. They also encourage more research attention devoted to gathering better prevalence data on mental health problems and needs and the effectiveness of various treatment modalities. Such information is vital to the design of a therapeutic preschool model. Models exist, of course, but they are generally small, private efforts with selective enrollment, although some have been developed within Head Start (e.g., Murphy, Bishop-Josef, Nowlin, Pagano, & Jellinek, 2004; Murphy & Pagano, 2000; Shahmoon-Shanok et al., 2005).

These and other barriers not only can but must be overcome. The fact is that increasing numbers of young children of all socioeconomic levels are displaying symptoms of behavioral and emotional difficulties. Public prekindergartens and child care centers are struggling to address their needs but often not succeeding. Head Start's bailiwick is young, at-risk children. Within Head Start, significant attention has been devoted to children's mental health, appropriate services, and staff training. While the mental health component is still the weakest arm of Head Start (Yoshikawa & Knitzer, 1997), and many challenges remain (Knitzer, 2004), the program is far ahead of other early childhood services in addressing emotional health. As an early childhood laboratory, Head Start presents a compelling stage on which to build, evaluate, and refine effective mental health strategies.

CONTINUITY AND CHANGE

This chapter presents a visionary outlook on the form Head Start may take in a world of universal preschool. That world has not yet arrived. Momentum is surely building in the universal pre-K movement, and more children are attending preschool than were just a few years ago. Mirroring the history of universal kindergarten, each state will decide its commitment and rate of progress. Preschool may not be truly universal for 15, 20, or more years. Free public kindergarten, for example, took more than 100 years to spread nationwide (Muenchow & Marsland, in press), and the majority of states still do not make kindergarten compulsory (Graue, 2003). It appears safe to assume that Head Start will continue to operate in its current form for many years to come.

With universal preschool on the horizon, Head Start must not be an entity unto itself. It has a vital role in the transition years leading to the time when all children have access to preschool. It is the leading provider of early childhood services and has much knowledge to share. We would hope that as the states build their pre-K systems, they will have access to the methods that have been proved effective through trial and error in the Head Start laboratory. Head Start has shown the importance of quality, parent involvement, and comprehensive child and family services. All of these together promote school readiness, and the absence of one or more elements makes readiness less likely. Public preschools will not achieve their goals unless they apply this lesson. Head Start agencies in every state should become involved in state preschool planning.

With an eye to the future, Head Start must work to develop and hone the tools it needs now and will eventually need in greater quantities. For example, Early Head Start depends on home visitors, and it is becoming clear that more training in this specialty must be developed. More children and families appear to be affected by more risk factors than the single problem of poverty, and these factors cannot be effectively addressed in Head Start's standard nine-month program. Head Start must continue efforts to identify these families and offer intervention sooner and for a longer period of time. Ways to prevent, identify, and treat mental health problems should be a top priority. Educational services in Head Start are getting better, but improvement efforts cannot slacken. Accountability is another pressing issue that administrators must undertake. Obviously, Head Start still has work to do, both to benefit the children who will attend in coming years and to strengthen the settings where preschool will be delivered in the future.

We conclude by emphasizing that the three roles we have proposed for Head Start are not mutually exclusive. Serving infants and toddlers, addressing comprehensive child and family needs, and providing special educational services can be overlapping practices that may target overlapping populations. Each function builds on strengths Head Start has developed over time to meet the variety of needs of children at risk for school failure. Public schools can be expected to create strong educational programs but have little experience supporting child development beyond the classroom. In the coming world of universal preschool, public schools and Head Start can undertake complementary callings that together allow all children to achieve school readiness.

References

Administration for Children and Families. (2003a). *Building futures: The Head Start Impact Study interim report*. Washington, DC: Author.

Administration for Children and Families. (2003b). *Head Start FACES 2000: A whole-child perspective on program performance.* Fourth progress report. Washington, DC: Author.

Administration on Children, Youth and Families. (2005). *Head Start program fact sheet. FY 2004.* Washington, DC: Author.

Advisory Committee on Head Start Quality and Expansion. (1993). *Creating a 21st century Head Start.* Washington, DC: U.S. Government Printing Office. (1995-615-032/03069)

Advisory Committee on Services for Families with Infants and Toddlers. (1994). *Statement of the Advisory Committee on Services for Families with Infants and Toddlers.* Washington, DC: U.S. Department of Health and Human Services.

Barnett, W. S. (1995). Long-term effects of early childhood programs on cognitive and school outcomes. *The Future of Children, 5*(3), 25–50.

Barnett, W. S. (2004). Does Head Start have lasting cognitive effects? The myth of fade-out. In E. Zigler & S. J. Styfco (Eds.), *The Head Start debates* (pp. 221–249). Baltimore: Paul H. Brookes.

Barnett, W. S., & Hustedt, J. T. (2003). Preschool: The most important grade. *Educational Leadership, 60,* 54–57.

Bruer, J. T. (1999). *The myth of the first three years.* New York: Williams & Wilkins.

Campbell, E. A., Ramey, C. T., Pungello, E., Sparling, J., & Miller-Johnson, S. (2002). Early childhood education: Outcomes as a function of different treatments. *Applied Developmental Science, 6,* 42–57.

Carnegie Task Force on Meeting the Needs of Young Children. (1994). *Starting points: Meeting the needs of our youngest children.* New York: Carnegie Corporation.

Chafel, J. A. (1992). Funding Head Start: What are the issues? *American Journal of Orthopsychiatry, 62,* 9–21.

Comptroller General. (1979, February 6). *Early childhood and family development programs improve the quality of life for low-income families.* Report to Congress (HRD-79-49). Washington, DC: United States General Accounting Office.

Durlak, J. A. (1998). Common risk and protective factors in successful prevention programs. *American Journal of Orthopsychiatry, 68,* 512–520.

Finn-Stevenson, M., & Zigler, E. (1999). *Schools of the 21st Century: Linking child care and education.* Boulder, CO: Westview Press.

Frankel, A. J. (2004). Professional social work involvement in Head Start. In E. Zigler & S. J. Styfco (Eds.), *The Head Start debates* (pp. 329–338). Baltimore: Paul H. Brookes.

General Accounting Office. (1997, April). *Head Start: Research provides little information on impact of current program.* Washington, DC: Author. (Report No. GAO/HEHS-97-59)

Gilliam, W. S., & Ripple, C. H. (2004). What can be learned from state-funded prekindergarten initiatives? A data-based approach to the Head Start devolution debate. In E. Zigler & S. J. Styfco (Eds.), *The Head Start debates* (pp. 477–497). Baltimore: Paul H. Brookes.

Gilliam, W. S., & Shahar, G. (in press). Prekindergarten expulsion and suspension: Rates and predictors in one state. *Infants and Young Children.*

Graue, E. M. (2003). Kindergarten in the 21st century. In A. J. Reynolds, M. Wang, & H. Walberg (Eds.), *Early childhood programs for a new century* (pp. 143–162). Washington, DC: CWLA Press.

Greenberg, P. (2004). Three core concepts in the War on Poverty: Their origins and significance in Head Start. In E. Zigler & S. J. Styfco (Eds.), *The Head Start debates* (pp. 61–83). Baltimore: Paul H. Brookes.

Harmon, C. (2004). Was Head Start a Community Action Program? Another look at an old debate. In E. Zigler & S. J. Styfco (Eds.), *The Head Start debates* (pp. 85–101). Baltimore: Paul H. Brookes.

Kauffman, M., & Hallahan, D. P. (Eds.). (1995). *The illusion of full inclusion.* Austin, TX: Pro-Ed.

Kisker, E., Paulsell, D., Love, J., & Raikes, H. (2002). *Pathways to quality and full implementation in Early Head Start programs.* Washington, DC: Administration for Children and Families.

Knitzer, J. (2004). The challenge of mental health in Head Start: Making the vision real. In E. Zigler & S. J. Styfco (Eds.), *The Head Start debates* (pp. 179–192). Baltimore: Paul H. Brookes.

Lombardi, J., & Cubbage, A. S. (2004). Head Start in the 1990s: Striving for quality through a decade of improvement. In E. Zigler & S. J. Styfco (Eds.), *The Head Start debates* (pp. 283–295). Baltimore: Paul H. Brookes.

Love, J. M., et al. (2002). *Making a difference in the lives of infants and toddlers and their families: The impacts of Early Head Start.* Washington, DC: U.S. Department of Health and Human Services.

Merrow, J. (2002, September 25). The "failure" of Head Start. *Education Week,* p. 52.

Muenchow, S., & Marsland, K. W. (in press). Beyond baby steps: Promoting the growth and development of U.S. child care policy. In *Child development and social policy: Knowledge for action.* Washington, DC: American Psychological Association.

Murphy, J. M., Bishop-Josef, S. J., Nowlin, C., Pagano, M. E., & Jellinek, M. S. (2004). Testing a model mental health program in Head Start. Yale University, manuscript under review.

Murphy, J. M., & Pagano, M. (2000). *Enhanced mental health services in Head Start California Endowment Grant. Progress report, fourth quarter.* Boston: Massachusetts General Hospital.

National Head Start Association. (1991). *Head Start income guidelines are out of touch with poverty.* Alexandria, VA: Author.

Omwake, E. B. (1997). Assessment of the Head Start preschool education component. In E. Zigler & J. Valentine, *Project Head Start: A legacy of the War on Poverty* (2nd ed., pp. 221–228). Alexandria, VA: National Head Start Association.

Raden, A. (2003). Universal access to prekindergarten: A Georgia case study. In A. J. Reynolds, M. Wang, & H. Walberg (Eds.), *Early childhood programs for a new century* (pp. 71–113). Washington, DC: CWLA Press.

Raver, C. C., & Knitzer, J. (2002). *Ready to enter. What research tells policymakers about strategies to promote social and emotional school readiness among three- and four-year-old children.* New York: National Center for Children in Poverty.

Reynolds, A. J., Temple, J. A., Robertson, D. L., & Mann, E. A. (2001). Long-term effects of an early childhood intervention on educational achievement and juvenile arrest: A 15-year follow-up of low-income children in public schools. *Journal of the American Medical Association, 285,* 2339–2346.

Schweinhart, L. J., Barnes, H. V., & Weikart, D. P. (1993). *Significant benefits: The High/Scope Perry Preschool study through age 27.* Ypsilanti, MI: High/Scope Press.

Shahmoon-Shanok, R., Lamb-Parker, F., Halpern, E., Grant, M., Lapidus, C., & Seagle, C. (2005). Relationship for Growth Project: A transformational collaboration between Head Start, mental health, and university systems. In K. Finello (Ed.), *Handbook of training and practice in infant and preschool mental health* (pp. 402–424). San Francisco: Jossey-Bass.

Silver Ribbon Panel. (1990). *Head Start: The nation's pride, a nation's challenge.* Alexandria, VA: National Head Start Association.

Snow, C. E., & Páez, M. M. (2004). The Head Start classroom as an oral language environment: What should the Performance Standards be? In E. Zigler & S. J. Styfco (Eds.), *The Head Start debates* (pp. 113–128). Baltimore: Paul H. Brookes.

Styfco, S. J. (2000). Children with special educational needs: A case study of advocacy vs. policy vs. research. In E. Zigler & N. W. Hall, *Child development and social policy* (pp. 251–281). New York: McGraw-Hill.

U.S. Department of Health and Human Services. (2003). *Strengthening Head Start: What the evidence shows.* Washington, DC: Author.

Verzaro-O'Brien, M., Powell, G., & Sakamoto, L. (1996). *Investing in quality revisited: The impact of the Head Start Expansion and Improvement Act of 1990 after five years of investment.* Alexandria, VA: National Head Start Association.

Whitehurst, G. J., & Massetti, G. M. (2004). How well does Head Start prepare children to learn to read? In E. Zigler & S. J. Styfco (Eds.), *The Head Start debates* (pp. 251–262). Baltimore: Paul H. Brookes.

Yoshikawa, H., & Knitzer, J. (1997). *Lessons form the field: Head Start mental health strategies to meet changing needs.* New York: National Center for Children in Poverty.

Zero to Three. (1992). *Heart start: The emotional foundations of school readiness.* Arlington, VA: Author.

Zigler, E. (1970). The environmental mystique: Training the intellect versus development of the child. *Childhood Education, 46,* 402–412.

Zigler, E., Abelson, W. D., & Seitz, V. (1973). Motivational factors in the performance of economically disadvantaged children on the PPVT. *Child Development, 44,* 294–303.

Zigler, E., & Butterfield, E. C. (1968). Motivational aspects of changes in IQ test performance of culturally deprived nursery school children. *Child Development, 39,* 1–14.

Zigler, E., Finn-Stevenson, M., & Hall, N. W. (2002). *The first three years and beyond.* New Haven, CT: Yale University Press.

Zigler, E., & Styfco, S. J. (1993). An earlier Head Start: Planning an intervention program for economically disadvantaged families and children ages zero to three. *Zero to Three, 14*(2), 25–28.

Zigler, E., & Valentine, J. (Eds.). (1997). *Project Head Start: A legacy of the War on Poverty* (2nd ed.). Alexandria, VA: National Head Start Association.

12

A Model Universal Prekindergarten Program

The movement to establish public prekindergarten for all young children in the United States has steadily accelerated. Forty states now provide some form of classroom-based preschool services to at least some groups of children, whereas in the 1960s half the states did not even have universal kindergarten and just seven had limited programs for preschoolers (Gilliam & Marchesseault, 2005; Mitchell, 2001). Today there are throngs of advocates for universal preschool, including many outside the ranks of expected supporters like parents and early childhood educators. Surveys and public opinion polls repeatedly show that the majority of the public approves of state funding for prekindergarten programs and believes these should be available to everyone. As described in Chapter 1, private philanthropic foundations have mounted a national mission to promote universal preschool. Economists and members of the business community, whose opinions generally carry great weight among policy makers, have identified preschool as necessary to building a skilled and productive work force in coming generations. The time is right to capitalize on this momentum, to put our accumulated research on the benefits and cost-effectiveness of early education to use, and to urge all states to adopt or expand prekindergarten services. But this is also the critical time to guide the construction of these programs so they are of high enough quality to achieve the expectations being placed in them.

As this volume underscores, we are certainly not the first to take on this task. Many of the elements of an effective prekindergarten system recommended here appear in other descriptions of standards for preschool programs (e.g., Schweinhart, 2002), constitute part of

241

well-known and well-regarded accreditation guidelines (e.g., NAEYC, 2005), form the primary components of some state plans (e.g., California Department of Education, 2000), and exist in early childhood programming in several other industrialized nations (Bergmann, 1996; Kamerman, 2000; Olmsted & Montie, 2001). As social scientists, our perspective derives from what years of research in the developmental and prevention sciences have identified as the optimal ingredients of successful early childhood programming. We also consider what is politically and practically feasible, offering a model that can be attained as opposed to the perfect program that is only wishful thinking.

We begin by discussing some theoretical issues being debated by groups advancing different versions of universal prekindergarten. We then describe the components of our model program that support children's school readiness, which we define broadly to encompass cognitive, social, and emotional readiness, as well as good physical and mental health. Because the only place to begin a journey is where one is standing right now, we offer suggestions on how to get from here to there – from what is to what can be.

FRAMING THE ISSUES

Cognitive versus Whole Child Approaches

Arguments in favor of expanding access to preschool are generally premised on educational benefits. In many people's minds, the purpose of early education is to expose children to academic content such as letters, words, numbers, colors, shapes, and other information they will need later in school. Some "trendy" preschools go beyond these basic skills and offer training in reading, foreign languages, and classical music. Experts have been embroiled in a long-standing debate about what type of teaching is appropriate for three- and four-year-olds. David Elkind, for example, has warned about "the hurried child," while Grover Whitehurst has argued that earlier exposure to academics greatly increases children's chances of success in school (cf. Elkind, 2001; Whitehurst, 2001).

This issue is far from resolution. Our point in bringing it up is to emphasize that educational attributes are commonly associated with preschool. When survey participants say they support universal prekindergarten, they are probably thinking about classrooms, books, teachers, and report cards – not about having a vision screening, learning to empathize with a classmate in distress, or attending a parent-teacher conference. We have no qualms with the belief that education should begin early. Research on the developing brain shows that infants and very young children are capable of learning considerably more than scientists until recently thought possible. Yet much of this learning is not of the traditional academic type. A two-year-old is better off being taught not to pull sister's hair or run into traffic than being taught to read.

We espouse framing the issue of universal preschool from a developmental perspective in contrast to a purely academic perspective. We believe that preschool *should* provide a strong educational component, but it must also address the rest of the child. No one would argue against the statement that good physical and mental health are necessary for good school performance, so preschool must attend to these features. As we elaborated in Chapter 7, a variety of social and emotional skills must be acquired and practiced to ready children to tackle challenging academic content. Children who have good motivation and self-image, strong curiosity, and the abilities to regulate their emotions, listen to authority, and get along with others are the most likely to succeed in a classroom setting. Finally, children spend a lot more time at home than they do in school, so the involvement of their families in the educational process is crucial.

The whole child approach to early education is an ascendant position. Indeed, the nation's Head Start program has had health, preschool education, social and emotional development, parent and community involvement, and family support components since it began four decades ago. Many current advocates of universal preschool are likewise endorsing curricula that promote all aspects of development. Nobel Laureate in Economic Sciences, James Heckman, stated, "Although smarts matter, they're not the whole story. . . . Looking exclusively at cognitive skills ignores a much broader array of skills, which are actually very important for success in schooling as well as in many other aspects of life" (2004, pp. 8, 1). The reason they are important is that the cognitive and social-emotional domains are not isolated subsystems of development but rather are synergistic, each exerting a strong influence on the other.

The whole child approach is both sensible and proven, so why is preschool programming still framed as having primarily an educational or academic purpose? A harsh answer was provided by David Elkind, a past president of the National Association for the Education of Young

Children and author of *The Hurried Child* and *Miseducation: Preschoolers at Risk:*

> The short answer is that the movement toward academic training of the young is not about education. It is about parents anxious to give their children an edge in what they regard as an increasingly competitive and global economy. It is about the simplistic notion that giving disadvantaged young children academic training will provide them with the skills and motivation to continue their education and break the cycle of poverty. It is about politicians who push accountability, standards, and testing in order to win votes as much as or more than to improve the schools. (Elkind, 2001, p. 15)

Another reason for the educational focus is that academic progress is easier to measure than variables like social learning or parental involvement. Further, the nation's leadership has not consistently viewed preschool as more than traditional education classes. In the 1970s and early 1980s, a huge scientific effort was undertaken to devise an array of measures of cognitive, social-emotional, and other areas of developmental progress among Head Start students (see Raver & Zigler, 1991). The Reagan administration cut funding for the project, and as a result only cognitive measures were produced. In current times, the George W. Bush administration was adamant that preschool programs advance literacy and "numeracy." Accountability measures for Head Start implemented in 2003, called the National Reporting System, assess little more than these skills. This is despite the fact that scientific evidence – and common sense – make it clear that achievement in school and adult life depends on much, much more than IQ scores and related academic skills.

Many state leaders who are implementing or planning for universal preschool are wisely imposing program standards that address many areas of development. Oregon, for example, uses Head Start's broad Program Performance Standards for its preschool services. Some states, however, attend mainly to academic curricula and give little more than lip service to other areas of development that drive educational progress (Gilliam & Ripple, 2004). This narrow focus will only undermine the success of their programs and perhaps the public support that sustains them. Indeed, Aubrun and Grady (2004, p. 19) analyzed how issues concerning early childhood are being framed and concluded that the "Education frame currently favored by pre-K advocates supports a [narrow] set of policies," which are susceptible to public backlash and disappointing outcomes. These authors argue that "The developmental frame makes it easier for people to think about a number of different aspects of development, each of which can be helped or hindered by a child's circumstances" and allows people to see "how 'the rest of us' benefit . . . [that] there are benefits that accrue to a community and to a society when kids do better, such as stronger communities, better citizens around us" (pp. 8, 10).

We agree that discussions, plans, and promises surrounding universal prekindergarten must be couched in broad developmental terms. The purpose of preschool, after all, is school readiness. Children must be physically, psychologically, socially, *and* intellectually ready for school. Intellectual readiness simply is not enough. Framing the issue of universal preschool as a whole child service, as opposed to an educational service, is the approach underlying our model.

Targeted versus Universal Access

Throughout this book, we and our colleagues have used the term "universal preschool system" to mean voluntary preschool programming available to all children regardless of income, disability, risk status, where they live, or any other circumstance. However, even among strong proponents of expanded access to preschool, not everyone agrees that all children should be included. Some of the arguments against universality are that the cost would be prohibitive and that there are not enough facilities suitable to house young children or qualified teachers to staff them. Some argue that high-quality early education benefits children from poor families much more than those from wealthier homes, so targeted programs are a wiser use of taxpayer dollars and a better way to reduce the achievement gap between socioeconomic classes.

This debate was in evidence at a 2004 conference titled, "Building the Economic Case for Investments in Preschool," convened by the Committee for Economic Development and supported by The Pew Charitable Trusts and PNC Financial Services Group. As described in Chapter 1, the Pew Trusts are heading a consortium of private foundations that are combining energies to advance the cause of universal preschool. Speakers Art Rolnick of the Federal Reserve Bank of Minneapolis and economist James Heckman both endorsed early childhood programs for young children who live in poverty. W. Steven Barnett, also an economist, presented the competing case that all children benefit from high-quality early education. He noted that "school readiness is not just a problem of the poor" and that "universal programs are likely to be more effective at identifying and reaching all targeted children," who sometimes slip between the cracks because the targeted program is full, their caregivers fail to enroll them, or other reasons (Barnett, Brown, & Shore, 2004, p. 1). By offering preschool to everyone, those most in need of services will be more likely to receive them.

Our decision to support a prekindergarten system that is universal is based not only on developmental science but also on the realities of social policy construction. Our reading of the literature is that children who live in poverty or face other risks to their development or success in school do gain the most from high-quality early childhood programs. However, this does not mean that children from wealthier homes or better neighborhoods do not benefit from preschool, particularly those who spend much of their time in poor-quality child care settings. Our examination of this issue in Chapter 5 leads us to agree with Barnett et al. that "School readiness is not just a problem of the poor."

Another compelling reason to champion preschool for all children is that this may be the best way to attract the political will needed to mount and sustain these programs. The history of Head Start offers a sharp example of the susceptibility of a program reserved exclusively for poor children. After 40 years of operation, Head Start serves only about 60 percent of eligible children (fewer by some estimates). Promises for full funding made only a decade ago have given way to proposed cuts in the program's budget and actual cuts in enrollment. In our opinion, Head Start will never achieve full funding because of its confinement to lower-income families. If public education in America had begun as an entitlement only for the poor, it is doubtful the universal education system we have now would have evolved. Likewise, poor children will not have ready access to high-quality preschool services until they are available to all children.

Experience appears to support this assertion. The policy makers who brought Georgia's universal prekindergarten to reality understood "that programs that exclude middle-class populations are vulnerable to shifting political forces" (Raden, 2003, p. 99). Robert Lawrence, a Georgia Department of Education official, advised other states considering universal preschool, "you can't mount a sustainable program without support from the middle-class that votes" (quoted in Raden, 2003, p. 99). This lesson was followed by David Lawrence, who promoted the constitutional amendment approved by Florida voters to make preschool available to all four-year-old residents: "When we...focus on particular neighborhoods, then others tend to say: 'Oh, I see; it's about those children.' Building a real movement is about all children" ("Dave

Lawrence," 2004, p. 11). Framing experts Aubrun and Grady made a similar observation in their statement, "It is possible to generate a certain amount of good will and sacrifice on behalf of unfortunate 'Others,' but no more" than that. (2004, p. 15). As long as Head Start is "about *those* children," it will remain vulnerable and its target population will remain underserved. We believe the same will be true for prekindergarten programs that leave out the children of the majority of taxpayers.

Another benefit of constructing programs to accommodate all children is that quality is likely to be higher than in programs meant only for poor children. Again drawing from the history of Head Start, funding was never sufficient to provide uniformly high quality in the thousands of centers and classrooms across the country and U.S. territories. While many Head Start programs have managed to achieve excellence, services in some are mediocre or poor. During the 1990s Congress dedicated extra funds for quality improvements, resulting in measurable progress (Powell, 2004). Yet the budget fell short of supporting high quality in key areas, particularly staff qualifications and continuing education. Without the money to pay competitive wages and benefits, Head Start still struggles to attract and retain BA-level teachers and credentialed support staff. Now that the nation's budget deficit has soared and President George W. Bush has imposed a different vision for Head Start, the quality set-aside has dried up, training and technical assistance has narrowed its focus, and travel allowances for training events have been reduced. At the same time, additional expenses have been incurred for administering the National Reporting System, consuming funds from other program services.

We relate these events to underscore that programs for poor children are susceptible to the whimsical support of policy makers, changing national priorities, and political strategizing – events that middle-class parents would not stand for if they affected their children's care and education. Not only do wealthier parents have more choices in where they enroll their preschoolers, but they have a stronger political voice and are quick to use it in advocating for the best for their children. Few middle-class parents would choose a preschool where teachers do not have BA degrees or facilities are subpar. For quality in state prekindergartens to be high and stay high, a broad constituency is needed – one that includes the political clout of the middle class.

We find that the scientific arguments in favor of a developmental approach, the policy arguments in favor of universal access, and the value of including demographic groups likely to demand quality and wield the strong power of the vote are compelling enough to base our model prekindergarten system on these premises.

PROGRAM BASICS

The vision outlined here encompasses two broad dimensions of early childhood programs: *quality* and *comprehensiveness*, both of which are consistently linked to school readiness outcomes for young children. In brief, high-quality programs are those that, in addition to maintaining standards in basic structural features (e.g., staff-child ratios, teacher training), are developmentally appropriate, meaning they employ teaching techniques and promote outcomes appropriate to the child's stage of development and learning. Comprehensive programs are those that are of sufficient intensity to be effective, address all systems of child development, and involve individuals from the child's broader rearing environment.

The national Head Start program is the largest example of a comprehensive early childhood intervention, working with both parents and children and providing a variety of services that nurture physical, cognitive, and personality development. Portions of our model derive from Head Start's design as well as from elements of Parents as Teachers (PAT) and the School of the 21st Century (21C). PAT operates in every school district in Missouri and has been adopted in more than 3,000 sites throughout the nation and world (Parents as Teachers, 2004). More than 1,300 schools are in the 21C network (Chapter 10). All three programs bear witness to the workability of our model.

Our vision is anchored on the premise that child development is a continuous process. Children do not suddenly become ready for preschool, for kindergarten, or for third grade. They evolve to a particular stage of readiness by accomplishing the prior stage, building to each higher level through maturation and accumulated experience. This perspective suggests the need for ongoing programming, beginning with services for families and children from birth to age three, followed by preschool for three- and four-year-olds, transition services when children enter kindergarten, and follow-up programming as children move through the early grades. This comprehensive model of integrated services for children and their families from birth to approximately age eight actually existed for a time as the Child and Family Resource Program, a Head Start prototype (see Zigler & Seitz, 1982, for a description). A zero-to-five version, the Comprehensive Child Development Program, appeared to be less successful for quality and other structural reasons (cf. Abt Associates, 1997; Gilliam, Ripple, Zigler, & Leiter, 2000). The Chicago Child-Parent Centers, however, have proved to be highly effective when children are served from ages three to eight (Reynolds, 2000).

Because a universal prekindergarten system will serve children in the preschool years, here we explain the components targeted to this age group. Although dovetailed programming in the primary grades should be part of the planning, this task is the domain of elementary school administrators working in conjunction with early childhood personnel.

Infants and Toddlers

Our use of the term preschool-age encompasses all children from birth to kindergarten entry. Children ages zero to three are typically overlooked in preschool planning, but these years actually comprise half the time before a child enters school. As Florida's lieutenant governor put it, "In order to achieve [school readiness], we must start at the very beginning; that is not at age five, when they go to kindergarten, that is from the day they are born" (Jennings, 2003).

The zero-to-three phase of our plan is modeled on Missouri's Parents as Teachers program as well as Early Head Start and other successful home visiting projects (ACYF, 2002; Olds, 1997; Pfannenstiel, Seitz, & Zigler, 2002). Two-generation services (i.e., for parents and children) are delivered by trained home visitors. Ideally, parent education and support are provided from the early prenatal period; in reality, parents typically enroll after their baby is born. Children receive periodic developmental screenings, and parents learn what to expect at different stages of development, appropriate methods of discipline, and the importance of talking and reading to their child. When indicated, they are given assistance in locating and accessing community services. Parent education and support groups are regularly held to provide opportunities to network with other parents and to hear from guest speakers on various topics of child development.

In the 21C model, school personnel are also involved with community child care providers. They offer training, support networks, and other services to improve the quality of available care. The importance of this outreach effort should not be overlooked. The paucity of high-quality child care for infants and toddlers was noted by Early Head Start investigators, who worried that the benefits of the program could be undermined by less-than-optimal child care experiences. An effort was initiated to bring providers into compliance with Head Start's Program Performance Standards, resulting in some success in raising the quality of infant and toddler care in the neighborhoods where this was tried (Administration for Children and Families, 2002, 2004). In another study, Vandell and Wolfe estimated the value of quality improvements in care for one- to three-year-olds. They concluded "that a shift from the lowest rating to the highest rating for the caregiver would result in an improvement (relative to the mean) of about 50 percent in measures of children's school readiness, expressive language skill, and verbal comprehension. We also find that the cumulative impact of child care quality for 3-year-olds is significant" (2000, p. 3). An enemy of school readiness is poor-quality child care, and apparently the longer a child spends in poor care the greater the negative impact.

The effectiveness of the home visiting approach is not without controversy (Gomby, Culross, & Behrman, 1999). The PAT model, however, has documented both direct and indirect effects on school readiness, particularly for high-risk children who experience PAT followed by a quality preschool program (Pfannenstiel et al., 2002). What is not controversial is that poor-quality child care can hinder and even harm child development. The zero-to-three part of a universal preschool system must serve children and their caregivers where they are – at home and/or at child care.

Preschool for Ages Three and Four

Duration

Our vision of a universal preschool system recommends two years of prekindergarten for children ages three and four. (Of course, not all families will choose to send their children for two years, or choose to send them at all.) Our review of the evidence on program length (Chapter 6) reveals that longer programs can have a greater impact, particularly for children who face developmental risks. Yet even for children without obvious risks, preschool has clear benefits, and both groups reap advantages from attending school with one another instead of having only classmates whose backgrounds are similar to their own (Chapter 5). Further, whether rich or poor, many children today need child care because their parents work. A two-year program can alleviate this need and provide a partial solution to the tremendous heterogeneity of quality that currently exists in child care settings by maintaining uniformly high standards. Of course, for the program to be a truly viable option for working parents, the doors must be open all day, all year long. If necessary to support the program, families who use the extended day services should be charged fees on a sliding scale based on their income. For children who are not in out-of-home care, a year or two of developmentally appropriate, early education and socialization experiences can facilitate the transition between home activities and kindergarten.

Location

Like kindergarten, universal prekindergarten is logically administered by the public school system. Ideally, preschool classrooms will also be located in elementary schools. The use of public schools as a delivery mechanism for preschool services is already the practice in many states, and its value and feasibility are supported by research. For example, most of Oklahoma's prekindergarten programs are run by the public schools. An evaluation of the program led investigators to conclude that public schools are a "viable and effective vehicle for delivering educational services to young children" (Gormley & Phillips, 2003, p. 20). Similarly, the long-running Chicago Child-Parent Centers are located in and administered by the Chicago public school system. As noted by Reynolds, this organizational structure "strengthens continuity of service delivery in several ways, including providing centralized oversight by the school principal and having geographic proximity between preschool/kindergarten and school-age components" (2003, p. 176).

There are other reasons that the location of universal preschool in public school buildings makes practical and political sense. Elementary schools are already staffed by certified teachers, school psychologists, social workers, and other support personnel who are paid wages commensurate with their education. This is generally not true in other profit and nonprofit preschool and child care settings, where turnover is commonly higher and supportive services are often nonexistent. Public schools have also developed means of access to services needed by children with disabilities and/or chronic health problems. Finally, linking preschool to local schools achieves several important objectives: it makes school-based child care more physically accessible for families; children become familiar with the school environment at an earlier age, which should smooth their entry into kindergarten; it encourages meaningful transition services; it makes support services in the schools (e.g., special education, mental health, transportation, school nutrition programs) available to the prekindergarten children; and it allows the school facilities to be used more efficiently, thus making schools a more cost-effective community investment.

Of course, preschool programs can certainly be delivered in a variety of other community institutions and settings. A majority of Georgia's preschool classrooms, for example, is located outside of the public schools. The important point is to have a single entity be responsible for educational policies and practices, standards of quality, and oversight.

Class Size and Teacher-Child Ratios

Three- and four-year-olds are typically active and natural learners, but they are still very dependent on the adults around them to structure and support their learning. It is thus not surprising that smaller class sizes and higher teacher-child ratios, both of which allow teachers to interact more with each child, are correlated with greater benefits of early childhood programs (Chapter 6). The court-mandated Abbott centers in New Jersey are required to have classrooms staffed by a teacher certified in early education and an assistant, with a maximum of 15 children in each class. The resulting staff-child ratio of 2 to 15 was also found by Gilliam (2000) to be the ratio that best optimizes instructional opportunities in the Connecticut School Readiness Program. Head Start's Program Performance Standards and NAEYC's accreditation criteria require a minimum of two adults to a maximum of 20 four-year-olds. Beyond parameters such as these, academic and social-emotional learning may suffer. It is imperative that state prekindergarten planners resist the temptation to expand access to more children by enlarging classes and/or assigning more students to each teacher.

Teacher Qualifications

Given the importance of the teacher to a child's success in school, it is clear why higher levels of teacher education and training have been linked to enhanced classroom literacy activities and better child behavior and developmental outcomes (Chapter 9). Yet, while all 50 states require kindergarten teachers to have at least a bachelor's degree, only 20 states and the District of Columbia require similar credentials for teachers in state-financed prekindergarten programs (Doherty, 2002). In contrast, France, which provides universal public preschool for all three- and four-year-olds, requires that teachers have master's degrees.

The final report of the National Research Council's Committee on Early Childhood Pedagogy, *Eager to Learn: Educating Our Preschoolers*, calls for a substantial investment in the education and training of teachers (NRC, 2000). This recommendation was also made by Maxwell and Clifford in Chapter 9 of this book. These authors presented their reasoned assertion that there is not really enough good evidence to support the conventional wisdom that BA-level teachers are more effective than those with associate degrees. Erring on the side of caution, these experts chose to recommend the BA standard until the issue receives considerably more research. We agree. In our model system, prekindergarten teachers have a bachelor's degree and are certified in early childhood education. Assistant teachers should have as a minimum an AA or a CDA credential, with specific training in early child development.

Program Content

Ideally, preschool programs would all employ established, empirically supported, early childhood curricula that support both preacademic and social-emotional skills. Nearly every state universal prekindergarten plan or program calls for the use of such curricula. Federal policy makers have likewise been using the term "evidence-based curriculum" in the context of Head Start and elementary and secondary schooling. A number of excellent preschool curricula choices exist, although not all have been subjected to the rigorous scientific evaluation that would qualify them as "evidence-based." To further complicate the matter, children have individual learning styles, so the best curriculum for one student may not work as well for another. The National Research Council Committee on Early Childhood Pedagogy recommends that the federal and state governments "fund efforts to develop, design, field test, and evaluate curricula that incorporate what is known about learning and thinking in the early years" (2000, p. 13).

This needed work suggests a focus on the learning content of preschool programming, but plans must also be made to provide comprehensive services and to foster parental involvement with the school. Head Start's Program Performance Standards give specific recommendations for the types of activities that should be included in these components. For example, health screenings are arranged to identify children who have or who are at risk for developmental delays or disabilities, health or nutrition problems, and behavioral/social-emotional difficulties. Many schools already have venues to involve parents and should adapt these to the families of preschoolers. Family support services, such as links to adult education, job training, and medical or legal assistance, should also be planned. For both children and families, barriers to attendance such as transportation must be addressed.

Transition Services

The transition from preschool to kindergarten represents a challenge for most children (Ramey & Ramey, 1998). As noted by Pianta and Kraft-Sayre (2003, p. 2), "as children enter elementary school after preschool, they and their families experience a substantial shift in culture and expectations, including more formal academic standards, a more complex social environment, less family support and connection, and less time with teachers due to larger class size and more transitions during the day." Providing services to assist children and families in bridging the transition from preschool to kindergarten may help prevent the so-called "fade-out" of gains achieved in preschool as children progress through elementary school (ACYF, 2000; Pianta & Cox, 1999; Ramey, Campbell, & Ramey, 1999; Ramey, Ramey, & Lanzi, 2004). Based on a review of findings from four extended early childhood interventions, Reynolds concluded that programs that provide transition and follow-up services from preschool into kindergarten and the early grades, "can promote more successful transitions to school than preschool interventions alone" (2003, p. 188).

Transition services can take many forms and be tailored to the needs of a particular population and the structure of the local schools. As one example, the Foundation for Child Development has developed a "P–3" model that is designed "to align pre-kindergarten through third grade by reforming teacher preparation and certification and developing sequential learning experiences for children" as they move through the first five years of public schooling (Bogard, 2003, p. 3). An overriding principle is that transition programming should follow a developmental-contextual model. Practices that continue to provide connections between children's home and school environments, as well as curricular and pedagogical continuity between programs, are likely to be the most effective (Hodgkinson, 2003; Kagan & Neuman, 1998; Reynolds, 2003).

Assessment

Evaluation must be built into every aspect of preschool programming. This is the only way for teachers and planners to learn what is and is not working, and what refinements need to be made. Further, any program that consumes tax dollars must be held accountable. The public has a right to know that the services they are paying for are delivering the outcomes they were promised.

The first accountability question that must be asked is, Are our programs of high quality? The research clearly shows that high-quality programs are more likely to lead to good child outcomes than poor or mediocre programs. Implementation veracity must be scrutinized, because often a program that looks good on paper loses a lot in translation to the classroom. Research on Early Head Start, for example, revealed that as programs became established, those that were able to implement more quality standards sooner had better results than those that still bore less resemblance to the model (Administration on Children, Youth and Families, 2002). Only when we are sure that the adults are accountable for implementing high-quality programs should evaluation efforts shift to measuring child outcomes.

The best ways to measure young children's progress have become a matter of controversy. The No Child Left Behind Act demands large-scale, standardized tests targeted to basic cognitive skills that assess the degree to which children are meeting academic goals. This methodology was imposed on preschoolers in Head Start, who are tested twice a year on cognitive tasks measured by the National Reporting System. The developmental approach to school readiness, however, encompasses much more than academic achievement. Broader assessment techniques are recommended to gather richer and more useful outcome data.

What is needed is the use, and in some instances the development, of nationally normed, reliable, ecologically valid, and developmentally meaningful instruments that can be administered efficiently by trained classroom teachers and/or evaluators. Results from these periodic assessments should be employed by school personnel to reflect on and revise their practices to meet the needs of children in their care, by local and state governments to track the progress of their student population, and by researchers to understand further the developmental pathways by which children become school ready and the implications for later academic progress. Moreover, the careful and strategic use of assessment can support a larger experimental research agenda on program effectiveness, leading to better understanding of how different elements of programs alone and in combination influence short- and long-term outcomes for children with various backgrounds.

FROM VISION TO PRACTICE

In this chapter, we have drawn upon the wealth of knowledge and evidence presented throughout this book to make the case for the features of a model universal preschool system that we believe are essential to achieve school readiness for all young children. Our model is designed to offer comprehensive, linked programming for children from birth to age five and beyond. Services include home visiting for families of children ages zero to three, preschool for three- and four-year-olds, and transition services for children as they enter kindergarten. Dovetailed programming will be provided in elementary school as children move through the early grades. The preschool component of this integrated plan is a full-day, full-year program for two years, located in or administered by the public schools. Class sizes are small, and teachers are required to have bachelor's degrees and certificates in early education. The curriculum emphasizes the development of both cognitive and social-emotional skills, comprehensive services are offered, parent involvement and support services are part of the program, and valid periodic assessments are made to track children's progress and to inform program improvements. The common characteristic shared by all of these components is uniformly high quality.

We cannot overemphasize the importance of quality in early childhood programming. The evidence reviewed in this book proving the effectiveness of preschool services was derived largely from excellent programs. Policy makers are fond of citing the results of the Perry Preschool and Chicago Child-Parent Centers, both of which improved school performance, reduced crime and delinquency, and appeared to save a great deal of taxpayer money in the long run. These results are by no means guaranteed. Programs that provide fewer services, are less intense, or have lower quality are unlikely to achieve comparable outcomes. Educators and policy makers anxious to roll out preschool programs should restrain their enthusiasm and make sure they do it right.

The high-quality, comprehensive preschool system we recommend will take time to build. A workable plan is to construct the system piece by piece. The 21C model, for example, which is not a program per se but a constellation of services administered by public schools, is typically implemented in phases by adopting schools.

Barnett et al. (2004) suggest several ways school districts can move toward universal prekindergarten. At first, eligibility might be limited to targeted populations such as those with disabilities, children from poor families, and children learning English as a second language. This is what many states do now and is a good starting point. Enrollment criteria can gradually be raised until all four-year-olds have access. Three-year-olds can then be admitted in the same order. The zero-to-three phase of our system can be added as planning and resources permit.

Resources are of course the biggest impediment to implementing universal preschool. Facilities must be acquired and renovated to accommodate young children. In Ontario, there is a law that all new school construction contain early childhood classrooms. Maxwell and Clifford (Chapter 9) suggest several ways to build the size and skill level of the early childhood work force. Obviously, interim and long-term solutions to these practical problems are available.

The most imposing barrier to universal prekindergarten is undoubt-edly financial. High-quality programs, run by trained professionals, are not cheap. But trying to reduce costs by reducing quality is a waste of money because the desired outcomes will not be realized. An encour-aging fact is that 40 states have already found ways to fund preschool programs of various sizes. Some states have used creative solutions like lottery proceeds, tobacco taxes, beer taxes, and sales levies. Some states supplement their federally funded Head Start programs to expand access. The federal government currently supports a variety of programs targeted primarily to high-risk groups of young children, including Head Start, Early Head Start, and Title I of the No Child Left Behind Act (a small part of which is used for preschoolers). Federal moneys also augment state expenditures under the Child Care and Development Block Grant and, to a small extent, the Individuals with Disabilities Education Act. Finally, the majority of parents are already paying for some form of preschool or child care services.

We believe that a universal preschool system can be funded using a combination of these resources. Current funding streams should be maintained, with the federal government providing funds for children and families at highest risk and state and local governments supporting expanded access to the rest of the population. Parents should be charged fees calibrated on a sliding scale based on income and ability to pay.

The use of fees based on family income is not new. The Comprehen-sive Child Development Act of 1971, the first and last comprehensive child care legislation passed in the United States (but vetoed by President Nixon), included many elements similar to the model proposed here, including federal standards for quality, financing for staff training and facilities, and mechanisms for operating on a fee system (Cohen, 1996). The 21C model employs a sliding-scale fee with great success, as do the child care block grants, and many nations use it to support their early education programming (World Bank, 2005). Most parents of three- and four-year-old children already pay for some form of care, so it should not be too much of a stretch to ask them to pay the public schools in return for high-quality, developmentally appropriate early care and education. Even where schools absorb the costs of the prekindergarten session, parents should be expected to pay for the before- and after-school care as well as the care provided during school vacations.

Financial experts are beginning to explore new possibilities for methods to pay for universal prekindergarten. Rolnick and Grunewald (2003) suggested that the state of Minnesota fund the Foundation for Early Childhood Development, an endowment created to support the costs of early education, instead of sports stadiums and subsidies to businesses because the return on investment is greater. The national Foundation for Child Development issued a paper describing several innovative funding proposals, concluding with a recommendation for intricate changes in the federal income tax code (Scrivner & Wolfe, 2002). Where there is a will there is a way, and the interest in devising ways to finance universal preschool is an encouraging sign that solutions will be found.

CONCLUSION

We have presented a vision of a model program to inspire local, state, and federal officials to set goals and move forward on the issue of universal prekindergarten. Our vision may seem lofty, but we do not believe it is out of reach. Most states are already becoming involved in preschool programming, some on a larger scale than others. Head Start, Early Head Start, PAT, and 21C are operating throughout the country, proving that the various components of our model are amenable to large-scale implementation.

The political and public will for universal preschool is stronger now than ever before, and powerful advocates have joined the movement. Now is an opportune time to create a national model, one that states can use in their planning to ensure that their programs are of sufficient intensity, breadth, and quality to enable all children to achieve school readiness. Decades of scholarship have produced the knowledge needed to inform the design of such a system. All that is needed is the national will to construct it.

References

Abt Associates. (1997). *National impact evaluation of the Comprehensive Child Development Program. Final report.* Cambridge, MA: Author.

Administration for Children and Families. (2002, December). *Pathways to quality and full implementation in Early Head Start.* Washington, DC: U.S. Department of Health and Human Services. http://www.acf.hhs.gov/programs/opre/ehs/ehs_resrch/reports/pathways/pathways_title.html. Accessed May 2005.

Administration for Children and Families. (2004). *The role of Early Head Start programs in addressing the child care needs of low-income families with infants and toddlers: Influences and child care use and quality.* Washington, DC: U.S. DHHS.

Administration on Children, Youth and Families (ACYF). (2000). *Head Start children's entry into public school: A report on the National Head Start/Public School Early Childhood Transition Demonstration Study.* Washington, DC: U.S. DHHS.

Administration on Children, Youth and Families (ACYF). (2002). *Making a difference in the lives of infants and toddlers and their families: The impacts of Early Head Start.* Volume 1, Final Technical Report. Washington, DC: U.S. DHHS.

Aubrun, A., & Grady, J. (2004). Framing the birth to three agenda: Lessons learned from pre-K campaigns. Providence, RI: Cultural Logic LLC. http://www.zerotothree.org/policy/policybriefs.framing9-04.pdf. Accessed March 2005.

Barnett, W. S., Brown, K., & Shore, R. (2004, April). The universal vs. targeted debate: Should the United States have preschool for all? *Preschool Policy Matters*, Brief Issue 6. New Brunswick, NJ: National Institute for Early Education Research.

Bergmann, B. R. (1996). *Saving our children from poverty: What the United States can learn from France.* New York: Russell Sage.

Bogard, K. (2003). *Mapping a P–3 continuum (MAP): P–3 as the foundation of education reform.* New York: Foundation for Child Development. http://www.fcd-us.org/uploadDocs/4.30.04.bogard.MAPrelease.final.pdf. Accessed June 2005.

California Department of Education. (2000). *Prekindergarten learning development guidelines.* Sacramento: Author.

Cohen, A. J. (1996). A brief history of federal financing for childcare in the United States. *The Future of Children, 6*(2), 26–40.

"Dave Lawrence: Champion for Florida's kids." (2004). *Preschool Matters, 2*(1), 11.

Doherty, K. M. (2002, January 10). Early learning. *Education Week, 17*(21), 54–56.

Elkind, D. (2001, Summer). Much too early. *Education Matters*, pp. 9–15.

Gilliam, W. S. (2000). *The School Readiness Initiative in South-Central Connecticut: Classroom quality, teacher training, and service provision.* Yale University Child Study Center, New Haven, CT. Unpublished manuscript. nieer.org/resources/research/CSRI1999.pdf.

Gilliam, W. S., & Marchesseault, C. M. (2005, March 28). *From capitols to classrooms, policies to practice: State-funded prekindergarten at the classroom level.* National Prekindergarten Study, Technical Report #1. Yale University Child Study Center, New Haven, CT. Unpublished manuscript.

Gilliam, W. S., & Ripple, C. H. (2004). What can be learned from state-funded prekindergarten initiatives? A data-based approach to the Head Start devolution debate. In E. Zigler & S. J. Styfco (Eds.), *The Head Start debates* (pp. 477–497). Baltimore: Paul H. Brookes.

Gilliam, W. S., Ripple, C. H., Zigler, E., & Leiter, V. (2000). Evaluating child and family demonstration initiatives: Lessons from the Comprehensive Child Development program. *Early Childhood Research Quarterly, 15*(1), 41–59.

Gomby, D. S., Culross, P. L., & Behrman, R. E. (1999). Home visiting: Recent program evaluations – analysis and recommendations. *The Future of Children, 9*(1), 4–26.

Gormley, W., & Phillips, D. (2003). *The effects of universal pre-K in Oklahoma: Research highlights and policy implications.* Crocus Working Paper #2, Center for Research on Children in the United States, Georgetown Public Policy Institute & the Georgetown University Department of Psychology, Washington, DC.

Heckman, J. J. (2004, April 21). Lecture, City of Denver, CO.

Hodgkinson, H. L. (2003). *Leaving too many children behind: A demographer's view on the neglect of America's youngest children.* Washington, DC: Institute for Educational Leadership.

Jennings, T. (2003). Retrieved from Children's Campaign Inc. http://www.iamforkids.org/newsdata/view_ind/519.

Kagan, S. L., & Neuman, M. J. (1998). Lessons from three decades of transition research. *Elementary School Journal, 98,* 365–379.

Kamerman, S. (2000). Early childhood intervention policies: An international perspective. In J. P. Shonkoff & S. J. Meisels (Eds.), *Handbook of early childhood intervention* (2nd ed., pp. 613–629). Cambridge: Cambridge University Press.

Mitchell, A. W. (2001). *Education for all young children: The role of states and the federal government in promoting prekindergarten and kindergarten.* Working Paper Series. New York: Foundation for Child Development.

National Association for the Education of Young Children (NAEYC). (2005, Spring). *Accreditation Update, 6*(2). http://www.naeyc.org/accreditation/pdf/6.2AccUpdate. Accessed May 2005.

National Research Council. (2000). *Eager to learn: Educating our preschoolers.* Committee on Early Childhood Pedagogy. B. Bowman, M. S. Donovan, & M. S. Burns (Eds.), Commission on Behavioral and Social Sciences and Education. Washington, DC: National Academy Press.

Olds, D. L., Eckenrode, J., Henderson Jr., C. R., Kitzman, H., Powers, J., Cole, R., Sidora, K., Morris, P., Pettitt, L. M., & Luckey, D. (1997). Long-term effects of home visitation on maternal life course and child abuse and neglect. Fifteen-year follow-up of a randomized trial. *JAMA, 278,* 637–643.

Olmsted, P. P., & Montie, J. (Eds.). (2001). *Early childhood settings in 15 countries.* Ypsilanti, MI: High/Scope Press.

Parents as Teachers National Center. (2004). *2004 Annual report.* St. Louis: Author. http://www.parentsasteachers.org/site/pp.asp?c=ekIRLcMZJxE&b=308088. Accessed June 2005.

Pfannenstiel, J. C., Seitz, V., & Zigler, E. (2002). Promoting school readiness: The role of the Parents as Teachers program. *NHSA Dialog, 6,* 71–86.

Pianta, R. C., & Cox, M. J. (Eds.). (1999). *The transition to kindergarten.* Baltimore: Paul H. Brookes.

Pianta, R. C., & Kraft-Sayre, M. (2003). *Successful kindergarten transition: Your guide to connecting children, families, and schools.* Baltimore: Paul H. Brookes.

Powell, G. (2004). Quality in Head Start: A dream within reach. In E. Zigler & S. J. Styfco (Eds.), *The Head Start debates* (pp. 297–308). Baltimore: Paul H. Brookes.

Raden, A. (2003). Universal access to pre-kindergarten: A Georgia case study. In A. J. Reynolds, M. Wang, & H. Walberg (Eds.), *Early childhood programs for a new century* (pp. 71–113). Washington, DC: CWLA Press.

Ramey, C. T., Campbell, F. A., & Ramey, S. L. (1999). Early intervention: Successful pathways to improving intellectual development. *Developmental Neuropsychology, 16,* 385–392.

Ramey, C. T., & Ramey, S. L. (1998). Commentary. The transition to school: Opportunities and challenges for children, families, educators, and communities. *Elementary School Journal, 98,* 293–295.

Ramey, S. L., Ramey, C. T., & Lanzi, R. G. (2004). The transition to school: Building on preschool foundations and preparing for lifelong learning. In E. Zigler & S. J. Styfco (Eds.), *The Head Start debates* (pp. 397–413). Baltimore: Paul H. Brookes.

Raver, C. C., & Zigler, E. (1991). Three steps forward, two steps back: Head Start and the measurement of social competence. *Young Children, 46*(4), 3–8.

Reynolds, A. J. (2000). *Success in early intervention: The Chicago Child-Parent Centers.* Lincoln: University of Nebraska Press.

Reynolds, A. J. (2003). The added value of continuing early intervention into the primary grades. In A. J. Reynolds, M. C. Wang, & H. J. Walker (Eds.), *Early childhood programs for a new century* (pp. 163–196). Washington, DC: CWLA Press.

Rolnick, A., & Grunewald, R. (2003). Early childhood development: Economic development with a high public return. Federal Reserve Bank of Minneapolis, *The Region (Supplement), 17*(4), 6–12.

Schweinhart, L. J. (2002). *Making valid educational models central in preschool standards.* New Brunswick, NJ: National Institute for Early Education Research, Rutgers University.

Scrivner, S., & Wolfe, B. (2002, October). *Universal preschool: Much to gain but who will pay?* Working Paper Series, Foundation for Child Development. www.ffcd.org.

Vandell, D. L., & Wolfe, B. (2000). *Childcare quality: Does it matter and does it need to be improved?* Washington, DC: U.S. Department of Health and Human Services.

Whitehurst, G. J. (2001, Summer). Much too late. *Education Matters,* pp. 9, 16–19.

World Bank. (2005). *Financing options in early child development.* http://web.worldbank.org/WBSITE/EXTERNAL/TOPICS/EXTEDUCATION/EXTECD/0,contentMDK: 20259114~menuPK:527328~pagePK:148956~piPK:216618~theSitePK:344939,00.html. Accessed May 2005.

Zigler, E., & Seitz, V. (1982). Social policy and intelligence. In R. Sternberg (Ed.), *Handbook of human intelligence* (pp. 586–641). Cambridge: Cambridge University Press.

Summary and Recommendations

Because we want this book to be immediately useful to busy people – policy makers and their staffs, education administrators, and others trying to make universal preschool happen – here we provide a summary of the previous pages. We do hope everyone will make time to read the whole book, which describes the empirical and theoretical underpinnings of our recommendations for a universal preschool education system.

Early childhood education is considered by many to be a cornerstone for American education reform. The Goals 2000: Educate America Act, which guided education reform in the United States during the 1990s, specified school readiness as the very first goal: "By the year 2000, all children in America will start school ready to learn." The legislation articulated that the goal was to be achieved through universal access to "high-quality and developmentally appropriate preschool programs," parent involvement, and attention to children's physical and mental health. Five-plus years after our deadline, although progress has been made, we remain woefully short of this vision.

Significant research over the past 40 years has demonstrated the positive effects of high-quality preschool programs. Benefits include:

- Improved school readiness
- Reduced grade retention
- Reduced need for costly remedial and special education services
- Improved educational test scores
- Increased high school graduation rates and postsecondary education
- Increased employment rates and family income

262

- Reduced criminal activity and likelihood for incarceration
- Reduced dependence on welfare

These findings derived mainly from studies of model early intervention programs that maintained very high quality and were funded well enough to pay for it. They served only high-risk children from low-income families. A reasonable question is whether such positive results will also be found in more mainstream populations and programs. The answer appears to be yes. Emerging data are now demonstrating the potential value of preschool education for children of all economic groups who attend large-scale public programs.

Bolstered by these findings, there has been accelerating momentum to establish universal prekindergarten. Educators, child development experts, economists, business leaders, law enforcement officers, private foundations, child and family advocacy groups, and others have called for early education to provide all children with what they need to succeed in school. Better educational outcomes, it is hoped, will give them a better chance to become responsible, productive citizens. National foundations, such as The Pew Charitable Trusts and the Foundation for Child Development, as well as government agencies, are investing considerable resources to learn more about the conditions in which early education works best and how that information can be used to inform national, state, and local policies.

Currently, 40 states fund prekindergarten programs, but most of these are targeted to low-income families, and nationally less than 10 percent of preschoolers attend these programs. In 1995, Georgia became the first state to offer prekindergarten to all children regardless of family income, followed by Oklahoma in 1998. Both of these states mainly serve four-year-olds. New York and Florida have made substantial moves toward universal access, but funding issues have for now hampered implementation. Several other states have made measurable progress toward universality. Clearly, the movement toward universal access to preschool for all children is well underway.

Despite good intentions, not all state preschool programs have been designed to achieve their goals. A tabulation by the National Institute for Early Education Research showed that only one state program (Arkansas) contained all 10 benchmarks the institute used to define quality. Decision makers and advocates must understand that only high-quality programs will produce the outcomes we want for our children. The research clearly highlights the elements of quality that must be present to advance school readiness. The purpose of this book is to bring together the current data and expert thinking to help policy makers writing preschool legislation and education administrators planning what they hope will be effective programs. We offer a model of a universal preschool system as a goal they should strive toward, in incremental steps if need be, to deliver on the promise of school readiness for all young children.

Here we highlight the primary reasons why a universal system of high quality preschool services is needed now. We follow with a series of specific recommendations for designing, implementing, funding, and evaluating programs to assure quality.

THE RATIONALE FOR UNIVERSAL PRESCHOOL EDUCATION

The case for universal prekindergarten rests on three core findings from several decades of research:

Preschool programs enhance school readiness. As many as 30 to 40 percent of children enter kindergarten and first grade without the basic building blocks of school readiness. Mastery of early literacy and math skills – for example, recognizing letters of the alphabet and the sounds they represent, being familiar with numbers and counting, knowing colors and shapes, loving stories and picture books, and expanding vocabulary – puts children solidly on the road to educational success. School readiness, however, is about much more than these cognitive skills. Preschool also prepares children for the social and emotional demands of school. To succeed in the classroom, children must learn to share, take turns, listen to the teacher, ask for help, express frustration in appropriate ways, try hard, and cooperate with others. Prerequisites to the cognitive and social-emotional skills children need are good physical and mental health and abundant encouragement and support from their families. Obviously, while academic skills are important, they alone do not make a child ready for school or guarantee academic success.

Preschool programs fill a critical gap for working families. Access to high-quality preschool programs also meets the needs of families struggling to balance work and child rearing. Today, the majority of mothers of young children are in the paid labor force. Unfortunately, the child care system in the United States is in a state of crisis. Quality standards vary widely among states and, even where benchmarks are high, they are often not monitored or enforced. Thirty-three states set the bar so low they officially sanction child care rated "poor" or "very poor" on standardized measures. Some child care is so poor that children's health, safety, and development are jeopardized. High-quality, developmentally appropriate early educational experiences such as preschool have the potential to meet both child care and school readiness needs. To fill this mission, preschool programs must be open the length of the workday, year-round.

Preschool programs are cost-effective. Cost-benefit analyses demonstrate the far-reaching positive effects of high-quality preschool programs. Cost savings accrue both from short-term effects related to the decreased need for special education services and grade retention, and from long-term reductions in expenditures related to social services and criminality. Benefits also derive from higher earnings achieved through better educational outcomes. Conservative cost-benefit analyses indicate that for every dollar spent on preschool, 4 to more than 10 dollars are saved by the time children reach adulthood. Some estimates place the public savings even higher.

A VISION FOR UNIVERSAL PRESCHOOL EDUCATION

For too long, American children and families have relied on a patchwork of disparate early care and education programs tied to socioeconomic status. Middle-class and near-poor families struggle to afford preschool programs good enough to prepare their children for school. Poor families can enroll in Head Start, but the program has never been fully funded to have space for all eligible children. Child care subsidies are theoretically available, but there are not enough funds for everyone meeting the eligibility criteria, and subsidies do not guarantee parents will be able to find good care. Even with close to a million children enrolled in state-funded prekindergarten programs, and a similar number enrolled in the federally funded Head Start program, millions more are unserved or underserved. It is unfortunate but not surprising that the United States' school readiness statistics reflect the general lack of access to preschool and the pattern of inconsistent quality.

Based on a thorough consideration of four decades of research on early education, early intervention, child care, and parental involvement, we recommend a coordinated, two-part system of universal prekindergarten education. In this system, a broad array of components is available on a voluntary basis to all children and families across the United States, regardless of economic status or geography. The first part of this system is designed for children from birth to three years of age – a span that is more than half of the preschool period. (We should note that while the emphasis is on four-year-olds in most state preschool systems, and the consensus of early childhood experts is that preschool should target the ages three and four, our view is that preschool services should encompass children from birth to kindergarten entry.) Services for infants and toddlers include periodic developmental screenings to facilitate the early detection of developmental problems so intervention services can be offered immediately before problems compound and require more extensive treatment. Services for caregivers include information on child development and how to support children's learning, choosing a quality child care setting, and referrals to social services when needed.

The second part of this system is a voluntary preschool program for all three- and four-year-old children. Early education services are provided in a classroom environment and are appropriate for the developmental needs of young children. The curricula support children's school readiness, targeting language and academic skills as well as physical and mental health and social-emotional development. Classrooms are staffed by qualified teachers, have reasonably small class sizes, and provide adequate support services for children and adults. Parents are involved as partners in their children's education. Regular evaluations are conducted to assure and improve quality.

Universal preschool is being developed by the states, just like the public elementary, secondary, and higher education systems were built in America. State efforts need to be supported by federal agencies. For example, the federal government should continue funding early intervention for at-risk populations, and it should support and disseminate research on effective practices. To assist state planners, we offer the following recommendations as a road map for developing, implementing, and supporting universal preschool.

Recommendation 1: Defining School Readiness

A clear definition tells us where we want to go. With a good definition in hand, preschool planners will know what services should be offered and how to design accountability measures to track how well the program is meeting its goals. We embrace a whole child approach to preparing for school, assigning equal importance to all five domains of school readiness identified by the National Education Goals Panel:

- Physical well-being and motor development
- Social and emotional development

- Approaches to learning (motivation, curiosity, independence, etc.)
- Language use
- Cognition and general knowledge

Recommendation 2: Curriculum

The curriculum should address all areas of development that contribute to school readiness and be developmentally appropriate, meaning that it should accommodate the range of developmental progress of all young learners in the class. The curriculum should not be a downward extension of the kindergarten program, but should coordinate with and build the skills that will be needed at the kindergarten level.

Recommendation 3: Comprehensive Services

Comprehensive services should be available to meet the developmental needs of the whole child. These include health/mental health and nutrition services in addition to more traditional educational content. Access to family support services should be available to parents, such as connections to education, job training, help with housing and child care needs, and social supports.

Recommendation 4: Parent Involvement

Preschool programs should have clearly articulated plans for encouraging and facilitating parent involvement. Connections between the home and school environments can be made through periodic home visits and parent participation in a variety of school activities.

Recommendation 5: Duration and Intensity

Preschool programs should be offered for at least two years, meaning they should be open to three- and four-year-olds. Programs should operate all day, year-round, to meet the needs of working families. To offset the increased costs, parents will pay a fee calibrated to family income.

Recommendation 6: Settings and Collaboration

Where possible, preschool programs should be located in and administered by public school systems. This location gives young children access to existing support services like nutrition programs, special education supports, and speech and language specialists available to elementary school students. It also encourages curricular and pedagogical links between preschool and kindergarten (and preferably through grade three). This provides developmental continuity and facilitates smooth transitions. Preschool can also be delivered in the community, but to assure quality and consistency, services should be administered by a single entity. Whether administration is state or local, educational services must be sensitive to the cultural needs of individual communities.

Recommendation 7: Quality

A universal preschool education system must have clearly articulated standards of program quality that are linked to positive developmental outcomes. Good models are the Head Start Program Performance Standards and the accreditation criteria of the National Association for the Education of Young Children. Essential standards include:

- Teacher-child ratios of no more than 10 preschoolers per teacher or assistant teacher
- Requirements that teachers have a minimum of a bachelor's degree as well as specialized training in early childhood education, and assistant teachers have at least a CDA credential or associate's degree in early education
- Ongoing professional development through coursework and in-service training, similar to what is required of elementary school teachers
- Teacher, paraprofessional, and administrator compensation at a rate that is competitive with elementary school staff with the same level of training, experience, and work hours
- Classrooms, playgrounds, and materials that are safe and developmentally appropriate for preschool age children

Recommendation 8: Program Accountability and Monitoring

To assure compliance with quality standards, there should be a monitoring system that includes on-site observations of the education and care children receive, with results tied to tangible quality improvement plans. Appropriate assessments of children's developmental progress should be used to determine if the program's goals are being met and to inform program modifications.

Recommendation 9: Work Force Development

States should invest in supporting the training infrastructures needed to create and sustain a highly qualified preschool teacher work force. There are many successful work force development initiatives that can be modeled, including credit-bearing in-service training, scholarships, and differential compensation based on education.

Recommendation 10: Funding

Funds for the universal preschool system must be adequate to support high-quality programs, periodic monitoring, and quality enhancement efforts. The funding structures being developed in the states should be maintained until preschool eventually becomes part of the public education system just like kindergarten and high school. The federal government should continue to support services for children and families at highest risk. Parents should contribute, with their fees calibrated on a sliding scale based on income and ability to pay. Support for the federal Head Start program must be maintained to fill wide gaps in the early care and education landscape. Although Head Start's preschool education services will not be in demand when universal prekindergarten becomes available, the program can address other unmet needs that thwart school readiness. These include services for families and children ages zero to three, providing a therapeutic nursery school for the increasing number of children of all income levels with serious emotional or behavioral problems, and coordinating comprehensive services where schools are unable to do so.

Index